CONTEMPORARY FEMINIST THEORY AND ACTIVISM

CONTEMPORARY FEMINIST THEORY AND ACTIVISM: SIX GLOBAL ISSUES

Wendy Lynne Lee

CRITICAL ISSUES
IN PHILOSOPHY

broadview press

Library and Archives Canada Cataloguing in Publication

Lee, Wendy Lynne
  Contemporary feminist theory and activism : six global issues / Wendy Lynne Lee.

(Critical issues in philosophy)
Includes bibliographical references.
ISBN 978-1-55111-904-5

  1. Feminist theory. 2. Feminism. 3. Social action. I. Title. II. Series: Critical issues in philosophy

HQ1190.L44 2009   305.42   C2009-905832-4

Broadview Press is an independent, international publishing house, incorporated in 1985. Broadview believes in shared ownership, both with its employees and with the general public; since the year 2000 Broadview shares have traded publicly on the Toronto Venture Exchange under the symbol BDP.

We welcome comments and suggestions regarding any aspect of our publications — please feel free to contact us at the addresses below or at broadview@broadviewpress.com.

North America
PO Box 1243, Peterborough, Ontario, Canada K9J 7H5
2215 Kenmore Ave., Buffalo, New York, USA 14207
Tel: (705) 743-8990; Fax: (705) 743-8353
email: customerservice@broadviewpress.com

UK, Europe, Central Asia, Middle East, Africa, India, and Southeast Asia
Eurospan Group, 3 Henrietta St., London WC2E 8LU, United Kingdom
Tel: 44 (0) 1767 604972; Fax: 44 (0) 1767 601640
email: eurospan@turpin-distribution.com

Australia and New Zealand
NewSouth Books
c/o TL Distribution
15-23 Helles Avenue, Moorebank, NSW, Australia 2170
Tel: (02) 8778 9999; Fax: (02) 8778 9944
email: orders@tldistribution.com.au

www.broadviewpress.com

Edited by Martin Boyne

Designed by Chris Rowat Design, Daiva Villa

This book is printed on paper containing 100% post-consumer fibre.

PRINTED IN CANADA

Contents

Preface

Part of what informs the following pages is an abounding sense of celebration. As I began to write this book, I found myself rediscovering many of the wonderful feminist writers, theorists, and activists that have inspired me for the better part of 30 years. The opportunity to reintroduce thinkers such as Alison Jaggar or Donna Haraway to a new generation of students reminds me of how forward-looking our twentieth-century ideas of liberation and justice really were, and how hopeful we were about a more equitable future for women and girls. I also found myself reignited by newer and/or less well-known theorists such as Gwen Kirk or Saba Mahmood, whose interpretations and criticisms of the feminist movement's accomplishments and conflicts offer new perspectives and new strategies for articulating a meaningful activism.

Part of what also informs these pages, however, is a sense of urgency—even frustration. While we have certainly seen significant and progressive change with respect to the status of women, it has also become impossible to ignore the fact that many of the opportunities that Western women enjoy are "purchased," often literally, through the exploitation of developing-world women, children, and indigenous peoples. Take, for example, the women's marathon sponsored by Nike. As an opportunity for women to participate in both an endurance sport and an opportunity to support breast-cancer research, the Nike marathon exemplifies much of what's really good in the feminist movement. It's therefore all the more troubling to have to confront the darker fact that the marathon is made possible via the backbreaking labor of women and children in Vietnam, Indonesia, and China, who survive on little more than subsistence wages making shoes which, while they may cost the Western consumer $100, cost less than $5 to produce.[1] And Nike, of course, is not alone. As we'll see in the following pages, the price of emancipation turns out to be high, but it turns out to be very much higher for those less well-positioned in what we now call the "global community."

That the feminist, anti-racist, and social-justice movements have brought our attention to these facts has certainly not rendered our movements popular with big corporations like Nike; indeed, the use of derogatory epithets such as "femi-Nazi," "tree-hugger," and now "liberal" or "leftist" indicates the ferocity with which adherents to the corporate (and sometimes religious, or otherwise politically conservative) status quo resist change that might require higher wages, safer working conditions, more stringent environmental regulations, or greater freedom for workers. It's no surprise that backlash might attend the substantial progress of the various movements, but what is somewhat surprising is how much we—the activists and theorists who have made progressive change a feature of our lives—have conceded to the global community's widening disparities of access to fair wages, equal representation, or the real exercise of human rights. My aim, then, is first and foremost to encourage the reader not merely to think through some really tough issues, but to think through them in terms of what difference a deeper understanding might make to the way, both individually and collectively, that we *live*.

This urgent need for action doesn't end with economic injustice. With the rise of more and more misogynist versions of religious tradition, an increasingly shrill and bigoted rhetoric concerning sexual identity and orientation, and the accelerating deterioration of the environment, it is clear that no one set of issues—say, equal pay, reproductive freedom, or freedom from religious oppression—fully characterizes what it means to work for emancipation. As we grapple with issues that are at once more global—should I run that marathon?—and more local—is the contamination of my county's water table a feminist issue?—than ever, the quest to define what

---

[1] See <http://www.thirdworldtraveler.com/Boycotts/NikeThird_facts.html>.

counts as "feminist" takes on a new complexity both in theory and in action. In what ways are issues such as nonhuman animal welfare, torture, terrorism, and climate change feminist issues? To discover this, moreover, demands that we renew our commitment to join forces with other progressive activists and theorists, to communicate more effectively across differences and conflicts, to see that a truly vibrant feminism transcends borders, nationalities, and religions—not because any one-sized notion of emancipation fits all, but because the technologies of the global community afford us a greater opportunity than ever to listen to one another.

Part, then, of what informs and inspires these pages is deeply personal. I came to regard myself as a member of the feminist movement as a very young single mother on welfare. And I was among the extremely fortunate. One day in 1982 I was standing in a line at the Colorado Springs welfare office waiting to collect the month's $106 food-stamp allotment when another young woman (who happened to be African American) standing behind me tapped me on the shoulder to ask why an obviously middle-class white girl with nice jeans should get food stamps. I was indignant, and then humiliated, and while the opportunity to reflect on the possible meanings of this brief encounter may not have come until later—when I entered the University of Colorado—it nevertheless opened a door to thinking a great deal more about things like justice, equality—and suffering. The fact is, I have children for whom I *need* the world to be better. And as I have gotten older, I see with an almost painful clarity that my children are everyone's children, and that everyone's are mine. I don't mean this as some hokey metaphor. What I mean is that in a world where we are all connected through the technologies of the Internet, weapons of mass destruction, genetically enhanced food, black-market organ trading, sex trafficking, global warming, floating plastic islands, and global markets, we are *all* connected—right down to our DNA. There are no movements, no matter how progressive, just, well organized, or well funded that can go it alone if what we want is a world that offers a livable future to our kids. What I intend to show is that the pulse of this possible future remains essentially feminist, anti-racist, and environmentally driven in that, like its twentieth-century predecessor, it begins and ends in standing up for the vulnerable and the exploited—whether they be women, men, children, indigenous peoples, nonhuman animals, or the environment—and the last of these most of all, for without a livable environment, the conditions for justice are forlorn.

Acknowledgements

Books take a long time to compose, and a great deal of patience—mostly from others. Thanks, then, are in order to the people whose patience, diligence, criticism, and thoughtful suggestions made this particular writing possible. Thanks first to book editor Alex Sager at Broadview for seeing in a proposal the possibility of something worth reading, for making many and helpful suggestions, and for sticking it out through months of revisions. Thanks to Martin Boyne who is just the best copy editor ever. Thanks to the countless feminist writers over the years who have offered me support, criticism, and ideas—even across many miles of cyberspace while I stick it out in beautiful, conflicted, rural America. Thanks to my colleagues in the Philosophy Department at Bloomsburg, especially Kurt Smith who is consistently in my corner. And, lastly, a thousand thanks to my family, to my son Lindsay Lee-Lampshire, whose own journey through philosophy reminds me why I love this discipline so much, to my daughter Carley Lee-Lampshire, whose sense of the possible lights up every corner of my world, and to my mom, Gloria Lee, who, at nearly 80, reminds me that life is about what we think—but then it's about what we *do*.

Chapter I

Introduction: The Future(s) of Feminism

WHERE WE ARE

With the twenty-first century on the horizon, many feminist theorists and activists began to take stock of the successes, close calls, and work remaining to be done in a twentieth-century movement that brought women not only the right to vote, but also an exhilarating array of liberations and enfranchisements barely imagined by our mothers and grandmothers. From divorce and property law to (more) equal pay and the recognition of reproductive rights, feminist theory and practice—and sweat, risk, and labor—had achieved revolutionary progress for many women. Nevertheless, as the twenty-first century began its own course, a number of thorny questions and issues either emerged as relatively new to feminist thinking or—as was more likely—resurfaced as sobering opportunities for critical self-reflection on "our" revolution. Who had been liberated? What exactly has this meant? What and who had been sacrificed? Who had we failed? Who was included in this "we"? What work remained to be done? Some, of course, think the answer to this latter question is "nothing." Indeed, the number of young women I encounter in my courses who disparage "feminism" as an "F" word is a frustrating reminder of both how successful the movement has been and how much it has yet to accomplish, particularly with respect to getting those most benefited by it to take seriously what it has meant for them. And many of these students, male and female, are in fact among the most advantaged in the world: they are able to go to college, live in the affluent West, are unlikely ever to have gone without food, and are likely to have at least some access to the Internet.

When I query my students about their view of the feminist movement, I get a conflicting mix of answers. Some appear to think that it's been so successful that women can put away their burnable bras, take it for granted that they get an equal shake in public and private life, and assume that what's been good for Western women—taken as a single homogenous group—has equally well enfranchised "our" sisters in the developing world. This latter point, of course, perhaps like most of their assumptions, is just false. But the wonder of it is not its falsity *per se*, but rather that, for all the movement's success, it has not fully accomplished its single most important mission: passing on a brightly lit, forward-pointing torch to its daughters and sons, a "torch" capable of illuminating the problems confronting a globalized world. For all our sincere effort we have somehow left a sizable breach into which those of profoundly conservative economic, religious, and explicitly anti-feminist conviction have rushed. All one need do is tune into Fox News, or listen a moment to talk-radio shows such as Rush Limbaugh, to see that the success of any contemporary social movement—not only feminism, but also civil rights, gay rights, environmentalism, and animal welfare—is not something we can take for granted. Indeed, Limbaugh's is no lone voice calling out from the wilderness; he commands an army of self-proclaimed "dittoheads" committed to a deeply conservative, and arguably misogynist, ideology of the "right." Such a worldview is represented in the second kind of answer I sometimes hear when I query my students: women have gone "too far," want "too much," "fail to understand their place," are an "affront to God," and have "abandoned their natures."

What any of this means, of course, might be mitigated: it's not surprising that those men who feel that their unearned privileges are the most endangered by a movement to liberate women would be inclined to make such charges. But it's not just men who are making them. It's young white women mesmerized by what they see as "role models," such as the 2008 Republican vice-presidential candidate Sarah Palin, whose view of women's reproductive rights and of the status of lesbians, gay men, bisexuals, and transgendered/transsssexual persons represents a return to the restrictive sexual morality that feminists reject. It's also young black women, whose depiction in popular music video as "bootie" is demeaning, if not plainly misogynist. The issues we must now confront are not, in other words, "merely" about backlash against the movement, but also about women's return to servitude in the midst of real possibilities for greater equality and empowerment. The issues before us are philosophical in the sense that they're about what women and men believe about women and men; they're political, too, because what we believe count as "issues" are what motivate action and give meaning to the feminist slogan "The Personal is Political." And lastly, however we determine "the issues" for the future of the movement is a profoundly moral matter because—and although this is a cliché—our actions, both personal and political, have consequences. Indeed, it is precisely the contemplation of the consequences of feminist activism that provides the foundation and impetus for this book.

I am not claiming that the late-twentieth-century emergence of the anti-feminist "moral majority" or its more recent incarnation in the neo-conservatism of the Republican Party (as well as among many socially conservative Democrats) is the "fault" of the feminist movement (even if it is in part a backlash against it). What I am claiming is that there are issues beyond the twentieth-century's vision of reproductive rights, equal opportunity, sexual identity, and freedom from sexual violence and racism to which the feminist movement has not yet paid adequate attention. Issues once conceived as primarily national in scale can no longer be adequately understood without considering their global dimensions; what's good for American women, moreover, does not necessarily translate into what's good for women elsewhere—regardless of how emancipatory or liberating we regard our own feminist vision to be. As my students remind me, moreover, the extent to which the Internet affects the ways in which we conceive of ourselves as persons, citizens, and agents also affects the ways in which we conceive the world itself and our responsibilities to it. Can access to the Internet be defined in terms of traditional feminist analyses of class, race, and sex? Does access—or lack of access—contribute to the creation of a new underclass? Is this rightly conceived of as an economic underclass, or does membership in the global community alter the conditions of what counts as exploitable labor? Who is empowered by the Internet? Who is made more vulnerable? These are very difficult questions. Indeed, only one thing seems certain: addressing any one of them demands a level of analysis and activism that, while certainly attentive to the excellent work of the past, is acutely attuned to the economic, political, and cultural complexities that access to the Internet makes impossible to ignore.

Most of the issues the feminist movement now confronts are global in scale: international sex trafficking, terrorism, climate change, just to name a few. This fact, moreover, accentuates the importance of seeking out connections and allies in other movements whose goals are, if not necessarily identical, at least complementary to our own. Sex trafficking, for example, affects not only the welfare and status of girls, but also raises important questions about the vulnerability of poor, often developing-world, families. Climate change is an issue not merely for environmentalists, but for developing-world peoples who stand to lose the most to eroding shore lines, desertification, and tsunamis. To be clear, I am not suggesting that the feminist movement bears greater responsibility for confronting these issues than do other movements. My aim, however, is to encourage a renewed commitment to the communication necessary to work in concert with environmentalists, anti-racism activists, animal-welfare advocates, and social-justice activists. No easy task. But if we are to avoid the impression, as feminist theorist Kirstie McClure (1992: 342) puts it, that our relationships both within feminism and to our allies in other movements are more about "internecine conflict" than enduring liberation, economic justice, human rights, animal welfare, or environmental sustainability, we must seek to understand not only the differences among our commitments, but also their many points of intersection. It's time, I think, to risk a bit more by way of serious self-reflection within the feminist movement, reflection energized by the recognition that these points of intersection offer new opportunities to work toward greater justice on a global scale. Many feminist activists and others are already engaged in this project, of course, but we do not yet have a clear manifesto to unite us. I do not intend this book to be that manifesto, but rather one voice in the conversation moving toward its realization.

The Beautiful Places We Have Been
Adopting a reflective tone, McClure writes that

> [f]or feminist critical practice in these late days [of the twentieth century],
> the question of the character of 'the political' — and thus necessarily the
> allied questions of what constitutes political theory, political practice, and
> their mutual relation — raises the disconcerting dilemma of how to artic-
> ulate oppositional practices in this seeming hollow between a revolution
> always already not quite arrived and the uneasy fluidity, apparent frag-
> mentation, and internecine conflict, of disparate oppositional agencies.
> (1992: 342)

Her point is that perhaps the greatest challenge confronting feminism in the twenty-first century is that of redefining itself as a political movement in light not only of its own history and internal
conflicts, but also of what "political" itself may mean for the new
century. Her words capture the character, cadence, and discord of a
movement whose many aspects form a complex, conflicted, yet hopeful whole. Less identifiable as a single unified political movement
than it once was, feminist theory and activism now comprise a
matured but nonetheless fluid cacophony of ideas and practices, a
movement whose influence on the interpretation of history, the critique of capitalism, religion, science, medicine, and art, the theorizing of sexuality and race, and the revaluing of the environment and
of nonhuman animals is enormous.

Perhaps no single work could provide an adequate synopsis of
this history. But the work that may come closest is Alison Jaggar's
landmark 1983 *Feminist Politics and Human Nature*. Central to
twentieth-century feminist analyses of labor, family, politics, and sexuality, Jaggar's now standard distinctions among feminisms — liberal,
psychoanalytic, Marxist, radical/cultural, and socialist — offered twentieth-century theorists and activists ways of imagining a feminism
that was neither a monolith nor merely a conglomerate, dominated
neither by a single feminist perspective nor by conflicts among competing allegiances. *Feminist Politics and Human Nature* did not, however, put an end to conflicts within feminism; rather, it provided a
way of organizing ideas and points of view such that a deeper and

more genuinely emancipatory discourse could take place among women from many walks of life, each differing geographically, culturally, religiously, economically, and sexually. Indeed, if Jaggar's distinctions are not as useful to twenty-first-century feminists as they were to earlier advocates, it may be because her acute historical erudition and theoretical sophistication created an activism that could only point beyond itself. That is, while Jaggar lays much of the conceptual groundwork for feminist activists and thinkers, her work was also destined to inspire just that appropriation, critique, and alternative theorizing that propels a movement forward.

This is so, I think, for at least three reasons: one historical, one theoretical, and one political/practical. First, feminist historical scholarship has advanced academic light years since the appearance of *Feminist Politics and Human Nature*. Inspired by feminist thinkers like Jaggar, Shulamith Firestone, Marilyn Frye, Sarah Hoagland, Judith Butler, and many others, feminist historical critique has become emblematic of the phrase "the personal is political." That is, if the meaning of our personal lives includes historical and cultural location, they must be as politicized as the locations in which they take place — geographically, economically, and socially. Such locations are, moreover, always gendered, in the sense that gender plays a role at every level of expectation, action, and conflict. Equipped with these insights, feminist historians of the ideas of both traditional figures such as Aristotle or Immanuel Kant or, more recently, lesser-known figures, especially women such as Teresa of Avila or Charlotte Perkins Gilman, show that if gender influences the formation of ideas "all the way down" to our concepts of the real, the rational, the ethical, and the beautiful, then it cannot fail to be central to the ways in which those ideas have informed our present attitudes and values. The implications of feminist historical critique for the ways in which we understand institutions — military, scientific, economic, cultural, medical, familial, and so on — takes both our past and its omissions seriously, in the endeavor to imagine a future not beholden to the patriarchal past.

Shifting away from an androcentric or male-centered vision of history as a chronicle of military conquest, property acquisition, or empire building, feminist historians of specific periods and institutions have introduced alternative readings of "classic" texts, querying everything from how contributions are evaluated as "history-making" to why history is divided into periods that reflect some kind of reality. Many feminist scholars have also turned their attention to less commonly read texts that chronicle the lives, struggles, and accomplishments of women, children, gay men, lesbians, nonhuman animals, the enslaved, the disenfranchised, indigenous peoples, and the environment itself—in other words, subjects frequently ignored in the making of "real" history. Projects such as Luce Irigaray's (1985) Freudian/Lacanian interpretation of Plato, Charlene Haddock Seigfried's (1996) feminist reading of John Dewey's pragmatism, Gwyn Kirk's (1997) ecological reading of Marx and Engels, Sharyn Clough's (2003) reading of Donald Davidson, Judith Butler's (1993) queering of psychoanalysis, or my own Wittgensteinian analyses of the languages of racism/heterosexualism (Lee 1999a, 1999b, 2003) defy ready classification and suggest new organizing strategies that both include and transcend Jaggar's focus on notions like class and family structure.

Second, although Jaggar does take into account some measure of the influence of post-structuralist and postmodern theorists, the influence of thinkers such as Jacques Derrida, Jacques Lacan, Michel Foucault, Naomi Scheman, Judith Butler, Bruno Latour, Katherine Hayles, Alphonso Lingis, Donna Haraway, and countless others, had yet to be fully appreciated among feminists writing in 1983. Since that time, however, the influence of ideas identified with Continental philosophy, psychology, and political theory has come into its own among European and American feminist writers who have as fraught but fertile a relationship with the so-called "postmodern" as earlier feminists had with the American/British "analytic" tradition. As will become evident in the chapters that follow, I claim no particular allegiance to any tradition but rather have sought to articulate an open critical practice whose relevance to what I think to be a handful of key issues is, I'll argue, vitally important. I realize, too, that especially for a student encountering feminist ideas for the first time, such an approach might seem a bit without moorings. This is true, but my hope is that this will encourage just such a reader to be confronted first with the issues, and then with the theory that—regardless of its tradition—might demonstrate why such issues fall into the orbit of feminist concern, and what might ground a relevant praxis, or theory-grounded moral and political practice.

Third, while Jaggar's recommendations for a socialist feminist praxis—a practice informed by theory—made good sense in light of the issues faced by late-twentieth-century women, the twenty-first-century's technological advances, political changes, economic shifts, and environmental dilemmas demand an even greater awareness of the countless ways the feminist quest for liberation applies to other disadvantaged groups and social movements. There simply is no turning back the clock on globalization. As resources like the Internet have opened up new avenues to the world beyond our national borders, the complexity of our ecological, political, economic, technological, and social interdependence has come more clearly into view. What "liberation" means in this global context itself stands in need of considerable reflection, given, for example, the rise of religious fundamentalism, the possible inclusion of nonhuman animals in the moral community, and the ever-growing economic disparities between wealthier Western nations and the developing world. Indeed, the price of denying the interdependence of the human condition, is not only the continuation of the maladies we inflict (or at least condone) on the most vulnerable among us, but could also be the eventual extinction of ourselves and our fellow beings. Whatever the meaning of freedom was in the last century, the current century's definition must recommit to values such as conservation, critical self-reflection, and an intimate sense of the worth of both human and nonhuman beings, institutions, and ecological systems. It is this sense of freedom—one securely tethered to its attendant responsibilities—that informs the following chapters.

WHERE I AM GOING WITH THIS BOOK

My mission, then, is neither to reproduce the history of the feminist movement—this has been done amply well by others—nor to provide abbreviated and therefore inadequate accounts of its primary figures. Instead, I have chosen a sampling of fairly narrow subjects, each intended to embody an aspect of a contemporary feminist theory, critique, and practice. Each chapter is intended to be read as a thread included in a complex weave of ideas and thinkers, as a complementary, mutually reinforcing part of an evolving project. My primary aims are threefold. First, I will demonstrate the relevance of feminist theorizing to issues that may seem less directly about the status and emancipation of women—for example, terrorism, species extinction, or climate change—but which, especially in a globalized economy, are more relevant now than ever. Second, I will show how feminist thinking can usefully illuminate the conceptual, political, economic, and morally relevant links between a range of pressing contemporary issues: for example, the connection between ongoing environmental deterioration and the role of human beings with respect to nonhuman nature, or our attitudes toward reproductive technologies such as in vitro fertilization with respect to who has access to them or what role sexual identity, economic class, and geographic location play in determining this access.

Lastly, I will argue that a feminist theorizing that is adequately equipped to confront the issues of a young but rapidly changing century offers real hope to a future that is challenging, but by no means hopeless. These are familiar issues, of course, but I plan to show how a feminist approach can elucidate some of the key relationships among seemingly disparate issues that are likely to define the twenty-first century, and to demonstrate that such an approach has the power to unite its sister movements into a coherent, ethically defensible, emancipatory "not-quite-whole" (McClure 1992: 342). The point of philosophy, Karl Marx argued, is not merely to understand the world, but to change it—for the better. Yet, while I still think this is true, I also know that the world imagined by Marx is very different from the world in which we live; and I know that what is absent, elided, distorted via what it means to have access to the Internet is itself an essential part of what we must come to understand if this change is really to be possible. What I'm after is no less the continuing revolution imagined by my foremothers, yet one that includes many a subject matter beyond what my foremothers could have imagined.

Sexual identity and politics, reproductive technology, economic inequality, the culture industry, religious fundamentalism, and the status of nonhuman others—why these six issues? The ways in which each issue has an impact upon human and nonhuman life has undergone significant transformation, particularly with respect to technology. The technologies, for example, of sex reassignment have changed immensely over the last quarter-century and have become fully commodified in a globalized market largely devoted to the reproduction of Western conceptions of sexual identity, attraction, beauty, and culture. Similarly, the technologies through which religious fundamentalism has become an exportable good—including communications technology on the one hand, and weapons of mass destruction on the other—have changed the very ways in which we think about religion and the implications of religious conviction. How we define what counts as "fanaticism," for instance, intersects with questions central to the feminist and anti-racist movements, particularly in terms of the conditions that may help to create soldiers for God, foster the misogyny of the Taliban, or engender backlash against what is perceived to be unrestrained Western materialism. Much the same, of course, might be said for other issues—say the continuing exploitation of women, girls, and some men, in pornography. But while pornography has certainly seen an incalculable expansion of its range via the Internet and other forms of communications technology, it has not, I suggest, undergone as revolutionary a transformation as, say, our thinking about climate change in virtue of our access to information about melting ice caps or vanishing polar bears. Access to pornography has become easier, and the amount of pornography has grown —this is nothing to be underestimated, and there are some serious social consequences. However, the amount of information on climate change isn't just greater, or access to it easier; rather, we start to think about the world in ways we may have never considered before, especially with respect to how our vision of the "good life" intersects and affects the environment and its dependents on a global scale.

As Max Horkheimer and Theodor Adorno argue in the *Dialectic of Enlightenment* (1972), the real revolution of the twentieth century was not so much about the "good life" and its ideals of equality or opportunity as it was about how such ideals could be translated into products manufactured on a mass scale and marketed as emblematic of these ideals. The trouble, they argue, is that just as "equality" has come to be defined as equality of consumption, "opportunity" as the opportunity to compete on the "open" market, and "freedom" as the freedom to choose from among an endless array of products and services, so too has "culture" become identified with the exhibition of wealth—at least for those in a position to compete. Furthermore, such wealth is not valued in terms of, say, ideas, or art, or music, or health, or democratic institutions for their own sake, but rather for its "commodifiability": what people are willing to pay, or in other words, its exchange value. Multinational corporations and their brand names institutionalize the production of this culture of consumption, and with it its essential characteristics: the never-ending demand for the "new" and the summary disposal of the "old." Such a culture, on this view, is essentially the product of an industry, a worldview within which consumption is valued for its own sake, and whose aim is its own reproduction in the form of producer/consumers conceived of as the "free agents" of the "global community." But, as I will soon discuss, not all producer/consumers are well positioned with respect to either equality or opportunity, and many of these are women, children, racial minorities, indigenous persons, or the differently abled. The emergence of the culture industry thus raises key questions about who constitute its real beneficiaries and who might remain largely invisible to its quest to reproduce itself.

Consider, for example, an economically destitute woman from India who contracts her womb through an Indian agency for surrogacy service to an affluent American couple. Is she a free agent? What about a transsexual woman or man who seeks sex reassignment through an agency in Thailand advertising start-to-finish procedure packages on the Internet? How about the teenage anorexic who diets herself into kidney failure in order to fit a Western ideal of beauty? Such agents might be rightly considered to be "free" in the sense that each could choose otherwise—the Indian woman can continue in destitution or turn, say, to prostitution or factory labor instead of contract surrogacy; the transsexual can forego her or his transition or, if it is economically feasible, opt for more expensive American medicine; the anorexic can just eat. As feminist theorists and others have shown us, however, none of these cases is this simple. And, as I will argue, the story of the culture industry does not divide neatly into what people "just" can and cannot do, are empowered or disempowered to do, are in a position to do or not do. For just as each of these very differently located individuals occupies a place in the global economy at least partly defined by sex, ethnicity, and economic class, each is vulnerable to an array of factors that limit— if not eradicate—the extent to which they can meaningfully be called "free." Following Karen Warren's (2002 [1990]) argument that social status is largely defined in terms of a binary logic of domination, I argue that however well concealed they might be by the lofty rhetoric of equality, opportunity, and freedom, each of these cases illustrates the extent to which being defined as the inferior "half" of a binary pair determines the cash value, metaphorically and literally, of these ideals. In other words, however much technologies like the Internet, IVF, novel surgical procedures, and so on seem to make possible, this "possible" remains very much the turf of those whose prerogative to dominate, exploit, and commodify determines the practicable freedom of others.

That this turf is predominantly male, white, and heterosexual is unsurprising; what is surprising is the extent to which our appeal to notions like "free market," "information highway," and now "global community" is actually complicit in the continuing oppression of those whose labor makes the commodities of this community possible. We now, for example, define an important aspect of our freedom in terms of membership in the global Internet community, which has become a virtual precondition for securing basic goods such as credit, job interviews, and the like. But this fact is responsible for the newest division of haves and have-nots, namely, those who have access to the Internet and those who don't. We cannot miss, and it does matter, that these are many of the same people—particularly women, indigenous peoples, and children—who work at what Jaggar and others have called the "McJobs" of outsourced global labor, or who are most vulnerable to sex trafficking, or who end up living next to trash incinerators, or who are stigmatized for being "different," and hence defined by the logic of domination as inferior. At one level, then, the "global community" appears to reiterate and reinforce age-old distinctions of class and prerogative; at another, however, it creates a new class composed of those whose lack of access to the Internet locates them as the new unskilled, undereducated, and hence exploitable labor. Does the Indian contract surrogate have access to the Internet? Perhaps—if she can afford the hourly fee, walk some distance to the nearest Internet café, leave her children, and if she knows how to use the technology. Is the aspiring transsexual free to contract for sex reassignment online? Definitely—if he or she has access to the Internet in a location free from harassment, can afford the procedure, and occupies a social status stable enough to weather the post-operative transition. Is the Internet useful to the anorexic?

Sure—"How to become a better anorexic"[1] offers advice on how to be more successful at self-starvation and denial, and although it's intended as a satire, it no doubt attracts young women committed to the contemporary culture industry's promotion of thinness as beauty.

In this light, it's not all that surprising that the appearance of what seems to be a denunciation of the "global community" manifests itself in religiously motivated acts of terrorism aimed at the centers of global trade. The September 11th suicide bombers exemplify the rejection of the culture industry in that their targets included two of its most unmistakable trade and military institutions—the World Trade Center and the Pentagon—and in virtue of the attackers' willingness to die for the sake of a religious worldview which, though not anti-technology, depends on the strict control of access to information. Since many young jihadists are recruited from the new class of have-nots that I proposed above, they're not unlike Indian women "recruited" to surrogate "parenthood." They too are disposable labor. Yet such young men are importantly unlike the teenager who networks with other anorexics online or the transgender aspirant who searches the web for package sex-reassignment deals, and it is in part these similarities and differences of status and access that can be illuminated through a feminist perspective—even if the recruiting of young jihadists is not obviously a feminist issue.

Some of the thinkers appearing in the following pages claim feminism as a way of life; others don't, but they have had or may yet have considerable influence on future theorizing and activism. Some are well known within feminism and/or within philosophy; others are less well known but, in my view, deserve greater attention. Several are voices from the sciences. This work, then, is not really about feminism, but aims instead—following the example of Wittgenstein—to exemplify feminism as the critical practice of a life worth living. I am an unapologetic, politically active, ecologically oriented feminist; the following interrogates what such a position might consist of, and in that sense it might offer an example—though surely not an uncontestable one—for my reader. In the end, my project is as traditional as Socrates' exhortation to the examination of conscience, and as radical as Wittgenstein's insistence that we "go look and see."

---

[1] See <http://www.everything2.com/index.pl?node_id=1081711>.

But there's one more thing. While it might be tempting to read the forthcoming discussions of sexuality, gender, race, and economic status as "old hat" for a feminism long engaged with these themes — as if most readers had largely settled all the relevant issues of equality and identity — I think that would be a mistake. Had we settled these issues, a political figure like Sarah Palin would not have gained the attention — even devotion — that she has from the "base" of her party. Indeed, she's wildly popular where I live. "Out here," in rural Pennsylvania, "feminism" is deployed as a term of derision; "not-Christian" is readily translated into "minion of Satan," "pro-choice" means "baby-killer," and "environmentalist" means "whacko-tree-hugger." "Gun culture" isn't merely alive and well in my town; it signals an entire way of life that revolves around a very narrow conception of a Christian god who determines the "place" of each member of "his" creation — and its adherents shop at Walmart for ammo.

My point is that change can count as neither progressive nor enduring until it comes here, that is, to the countless "heres" that characterize the hearts and minds of millions of people who, mostly just trying to get by, don't have a lot of time to think about what "equality" means for women, non-Caucasians, even poorer people — let alone nonhuman animals and the environment itself. This book, then, is not a manifesto — that would be addressed to folks already convinced that the revolution is worthwhile. No, this book is about a modest list of topics that I think matter in ways that touch almost all of us in one fashion or another; yet, understood in the light of a theory and practice devoted from its inception to emancipation — namely, the feminist, gay, environmental, animal-welfare, and civil-rights movements — these topics reveal some new avenues of analysis, and thus some new ideas for forming workable coalitions in pursuit of a more just future.

Chapter II

Sexual Identities: Institutionalized Discrimination, Medical/Technological Possibility, and the (Slow) Death of Binary Nature

THE POLITICS OF SEX, GENDER, AND PRIVILEGE:
THE 2008 PENNSYLVANIA PROTECT MARRIAGE
AMENDMENT

Among the most important contributions of feminist theory to contemporary politics and philosophy has been the critical interrogation of sexual identity, particularly the complex relationship between the politically loaded concepts of "sex" and "gender." My aim here, however, is neither to review the knotty history of, for example, the inclusion of lesbians, transsexuals, bisexuals, or other "gender outlaws" within the feminist movement, nor to elaborate on the debates over the sex/gender distinction. These analyses have been well performed by others. Rather, my aim is to explore the implications of this critical interrogation for the feminist movement given the following:

(1) recent legislation that seeks to constitutionalize—in other words, codify as enforceable by appeal to state or federal constitutions—heterosexuality as the only legitimate expression of sexual desire;
(2) the disruption of heterosexual domination in light of the multiple meanings of sex and gender and, as Donna Haraway (1997) puts it, the

"technoscientific advances" that make possible the reassignment, realization, and reimagining of sexual identity;

(3) the challenges posed by the particular case of transsexual identity in light of these advances to the stability of social and religious institutions such as marriage and "the family"; and

(4) the global marketing of sexual identity which, given what the Internet makes possible in the area of sex-reassignment procedures, for example, offers a new commodity to the culture industry—and reveals a deeper but largely ignored conservatism in how sex and gender are conceived, even by those who reject the domination of heterosexuality.

At bottom, however, my aim is to demonstrate the extent to which sexual identity currently constitutes one of the most hotly contested battlegrounds over how "human being," and hence human life, is to be defined, to what ends, in virtue of what technologically mediated interventions—and by whom.

As Karen Warren (2002 [1990]) persuasively argues, the logic that has tended to dominate this battleground is typically binary, the second member of its contested pairs devalued as inferior with respect to the first: male/female, masculine/feminine, heterosexual/homosexual, straight/queer, human/animal, self/other, white/black, us/them. Just as interracial marriage disrupts the assignment of unequal value according to skin color, so too do queer sexual identities—gay, lesbian, bisexual, transgendered, transsexual—disrupt a heterosexuality institutionally privileged via marriage, family, social status, and access to a wide array of social services. The beauty of such disruptions is that they offer a chance to critically examine this logic of domination in light of some key questions—for example, how marriage instantiates it, whose labor (economic and reproductive) supports it, and who is empowered by it.

Consider, for example, the advantage of such a logic to the supply of labor to an enterprise whose profitability depends on keeping wages as low as possible, that is, any capitalist enterprise. What the logic of domination offers is a "justification" built in to the hiring and firing process in that those devalued by it occupy just those politically and economically disempowered positions that makes them ready candidates for what Alison Jaggar (2002) calls the McJobs: part-time, low-wage, no benefits, and liable to dismissal

(124). The more vulnerable to economic destitution, the more effectively can the logic supply workers to the lowest paying, most oner-
ous, and most dangerous jobs. Insofar, moreover, as heterosexuality
defines the dominant sexual identity, it's not surprising that the patriarchally governed family structure helps to ensure a steady supply of
low-wage workers to the capitalist labor pool.

This is true for at least two reasons: first, because the patriarchal
family defines women as wives and mothers whose proper domain is
the *domestic sphere*, it devalues them as wage-earners. Second, insofar
as "wife" implicitly references the sexual identities of the parties to a
marriage it conforms to the logic's devaluation not only of women
but of sexual identities not captured by the genders presumed to be
designated by "wife," "husband," "mother," or "father." To whatever
extent, in other words, heterosexuality might be best described as a
compulsory or *obligatory* feature of the marriage contract, it renders
those who would resist conformity to it economically vulnerable in
the form of diminished access to basic social goods such as jobs, pro-
motions, the opportunity to perform military service, or job-related
health insurance. As we will see, to whatever extent the patriarchal
family structure is reinforced by appeal to religious doctrine, the
promised consequences for the failure to conform are not merely
economic, but other-worldly, providing yet another "justification" to
the capitalist to discriminate in the interest of keeping wages sup-
pressed. The stakes relevant to the analysis of the relationship
between sex and gender couldn't be higher: it's not only the meaning of "human being" that's at issue but that of the "family" to which
all human beings belong in one way or another.

Because the establishment clause of the first amendment to the
US Constitution requires separation of church and state, the logic of
domination is often veiled—albeit thinly—behind legislation
intended to forward what does in fact amount to a religious mission,
but on grounds that pass constitutional muster. Consider, for example, Pennsylvania Senate Bill (SB) 1250, a bill that, as of this writing,
is making its way through the judiciary and appropriations commit-
tees of the state legislature:

> Proposing an amendment to the Constitution of the Commonwealth of
> Pennsylvania, providing for marriage between one man and one woman.

The General Assembly of the Commonwealth of Pennsylvania hereby resolves as follows: Section 1. The following amendment to the Constitution of Pennsylvania is proposed in accordance with Article XI: That Article I be amended by adding a section to read: § 29. Marriage. No union other than a marriage between one man and one woman shall be valid or recognized as marriage or the functional equivalent of marriage by the Commonwealth.[1]

The Pennsylvania constitutional amendment promises not only to "protect" an institution in its traditional form from those who would allegedly destroy it, but outlaw any union other than that between one man and one woman. It presupposes that "woman" and "man" are clearly delineated categories of sexual identity, and that heterosexuality is the only morally acceptable sexual status, at least with respect to marriage and common-law arrangements ("the functional equivalent of marriage"). The Pennsylvania for Marriage website (www.pa4marriage.org) further elaborates on SB 1250 on a page titled "Questions and Answers Protecting Marriage." In response, for example, to a question about what the amendment claims, it replies: "[w]ith pressure on all sides for same-sex marriage to be legalized, those who believe in traditional families must be vigilant in protecting what we had always taken for granted. Those seeking to drastically redefine marriage will work through the courts and in public opinion to get what they want." Here, of course, "traditional family" would be defined as heterosexual and patriarchal, the unions of gays and lesbians are defined as a "drastic" departure from the normal, and, as the writers go on to point out, any deviation from this definition amounts to "overturning the definition of marriage against the will of the people," a claim which presupposes that "the people" are mostly if not entirely heterosexual *and* committed to a singular view of what counts as marriage.

What is particularly important about SB 1250, however, is its recognition that current Pennsylvania law (Pennsylvania's version of the federal-level Defense of Marriage Act or DOMA) is not immune to, and might not withstand, legal challenge:

---

[1] For the full text of the bill, see <http://www.legis.state.pa.us/CFDOCS/Legis /PN/Public/btCheck.cfm?txtType=HTM&sessYr=2007&sessInd=0&billBody =S&billTyp=B&billNbr=1250&pn=1776>.

It's true that Pennsylvania, like 37 other states, already has a law which limits marriage to one man and one woman. Legal experts agree, however, that in the event of a lawsuit, the DOMA is likely to be overturned or struck down. It is also possible that court rulings at the national level could render such laws "unconstitutional." An amendment to the state constitution is much more likely to withstand such challenges.[2]

In other words, the intent of the amendment is to build a firewall against legal challenge in the form of rendering constitutional what the sponsors of SB 1250 clearly know to be unconstitutional, namely DOMA.

The sponsors of SB 1250, which was tabled in 2008, have renewed the battle to constitutionalize heterosexual marriage in 2009 in part as a response to Pennsylvania senator Daylin Leach's proposed bill to grant "full and equal marriage rights to same sex couples in Pennsylvania." As Leach argues, "There has never been a more propitious time for Pennsylvanians to embrace equality and enshrine the civil rights of all Pennsylvanians to marry."[3] The issue, then, is what the bill's sponsors regard as so threatening about the prospect of same-sex marriage that they are prepared to go to such extraordinary lengths to "protect" the heterosexual institution. Once more, the promotional website provides insight:

If same-sex marriage were permitted, the definition of marriage would be lost entirely. Marriage would no longer be recognized as the crucial, indispensable building block of society, responsible for preparing future generations. Instead, marriage will be one option, no more or less beneficial or acceptable than cohabitation, single parenting, or homosexual households. The next generation would suffer most under this new policy. Our children's psyches are not an acceptable subject for experimentation.[4]

Arguably, the aim of such claims is to elicit fear, or at the very least worry, over the prospect that the legitimacy of "the family" will be

---

2   See the Pennsylvania for Marriage site, <http://www.pa4marriage.org>. The quoted material is in response to question #3, "Is amending the constitution really necessary? Don't we already have a DOMA?" in the section "Questions and Answers on Protecting Marriage."

3   See <http://postgazette.com>, 27 May 2009.

4   The response to question #5, "What's the big deal about same-sex marriage?"

eroded not only by gay marriage, but by any union not proscribed by narrowly construed religious conviction. As the website authors put it:

> Under a court ruling which standardizes same-sex marriage, churches and synagogues could face legal pressure to perform such marriages. Those who refuse could lose their tax-exempt status, lest the government be seen to be "underwriting discrimination." Pastors or rabbis, indeed, anyone who claims that homosexuality is morally wrong, could face legal ramifications. We have already seen this effect in Canada, where teaching these religious moral truths is considered "hate speech," and is punishable by up to two years in prison.[5]

Despite the fact that it is simply false that churches or synagogues would be pressured to perform same-sex marriages (marriage is a civil contract; what the church or synagogue performs is a religious ceremony), and despite the fact that Canada's hate-speech laws have nothing to do with the performance of a religious ceremony,[6] and even despite the fact that the writers conflate legal statute with moral sentiment, the upshot of this passage is likely very persuasive for those already convinced that gay marriage will lead to the erosion of "the family." After all, they appeal to "religious moral truths" that they assume are shared by the citizens of Pennsylvania and those of the other states who've ratified similar amendments (the website provides a long list of such states). That such an amendment violates the establishment clause of the first amendment to the US Constitution appears largely inconsequential to the writers; in fact, they specifically deny that the amendment violates any civil liberty.

What is so striking about SB 1250, then, is that, on the one hand, it seems to nullify decades of work by gay rights and feminist activists; how could so obviously unconstitutional a piece of legislation even potentially make its way into a state constitution? How can representatives elected to represent "the people" be so blind to the second-class-citizen status it creates? On the other hand, SB 1250 acts as a kind of barometer measuring the stormy climate within

---

[5] The response to question #9, "What does this have to do with religious liberty?"
[6] See, for example, relevant documents at the Department of Justice Canada website: <http://laws.justice.gc.ca/en/ShowFullDoc/cs/H-6//en#aSec12>.

which institutions fundamental to the current (re)production of labor, commodities, and social place find themselves under assault by those who would challenge their legitimacy. The difference, after all, between making a law and amending a constitution is that while the former presupposes that questions about what constitutes a citizen are settled, the latter does not. SB 1250 must thus be read not merely as recognizing heterosexuality as privileged, but as an attempt to determine sexual identity as a defining criterion of (at least full) citizenship; it effectively determines what counts as a fully human being who—in virtue of this—qualifies for citizenship. The critical question isn't "What are the bill's sponsors so afraid of that they'd go to such lengths (including tax dollars and legislative time) to amend a state constitution?", but rather "What is so worth the fear mongering required to generate support for SB 1250 that its sponsors are willing to risk the creation of a second-class citizenship in order to establish it?"

The answer, of course, is that SB 1250 is about far more than how fear generates fear mongering (and the reverse). It's about institutionalizing gender roles consistent with a very specific, religiously grounded view of what human beings are, what labor they are to perform within the family, and how they are to behave both inside and outside the family unit. In erecting a firewall against constitutional challenge, SB 1250 (like its analogues across twenty-seven other states) seeks not merely to affirm heterosexuality as the only recognizable sexual identity but to establish it as a moral necessity for "the family," premised on an uncompromising "religious moral truth." State constitutions are thus bestowed with a kind of moral authority no longer tethered to recognizing an equality of rights but rather to defining what counts as an entity worthy of this recognition. By excluding non-heterosexual unions from the marriage contract, the state effectively precludes their members not only from full citizenship, but from a host of material benefits stipulated by the contract—benefits that instantiate marriage as an economic institution first and foremost. In other words, to the extent that benefits such as access to health insurance are critical to the pursuit of life, liberty, and happiness, such benefits empower marriage as the economic engine that conditions the capacity to labor, to participate in the economy, and to consume its products. Contrary, then, to the view that religion discourages, for example, conspicuous consumption, it actually contributes directly to the reproduction of one of the most efficient of its labor-producing "factories": the nuclear family (Lee 2002: 36).

The advocates of SB 1250 know that the promotion of gender roles alone is no guarantee against gays and lesbians seeking the legal recognition of their unions; after all, given reproductive technologies like in vitro fertilization (IVF), gays and lesbians can just as well fulfill the functional role that marriage plays in the reproduction of labor and laborers as can their heterosexual counterparts. Gays shop, have children, drive cars, pay taxes, and vote. No, the aim of constitutionalizing heterosexuality as the necessary condition for entering the marriage contract is to ensure the stability of a social "building block" whose specific economic advantages are reserved to those who "count" as fully human beings and thus citizens. To repeat what the authors of the Pennsylvania for Marriage website claim, "the definition of marriage would be lost entirely."

Entirely lost, in other words, would be the implicit appeal to religious moral authority to define who may occupy which gender roles, and hence who may participate in the material benefits that accrue to marriage. "Preparing future generations," as the authors of the website would argue, is not about preparing good citizens or even good workers; it's about recreating a commitment to a religious ideology that depends for its maintenance on the beliefs of its adherents, as well as on their capacity to reproduce it. Both require as much by way of economic resources as of religious conviction.

To be clear, I'm not suggesting that religion operates merely as a cover story for the maintenance of an economic system (i.e., capitalism). Although the family does function rather like a "factory," and could do so regardless of the sexual identities of its members, the advocates of SB 1250 clearly hold that the psychic stability of future producer/consumers depends on the conformity of sexual identity to gender role—that boys and girls are provided with role models defined in terms of the place they will have in their own future families, including the potential material advantages accorded to its status. Given, however, that upwards of 50 per cent of all heterosexual unions end in divorce, it seems that the stability represented by "the family" becomes a parody of itself. As I argue elsewhere:

Mechanized and commodified, this parody of "family" is a substitutable unit of production and consumption—*a factory*—whose structure is dictated by the manufacture of saleable goods and services. Appeal to the nuclear, racist, heterosexual, and patriarchal maximizes marketability by apportioning extended families into the smallest functional units possible (duplicating need)...and by demanding conformity to *heteropatriarchal* concepts of normalcy and worth. (Lee 2002: 36)

It is ironic indeed that the advocates of bills like SB 1250 claim that the definition of marriage would be lost were the institution opened up to gays and lesbians; the failure rate of "traditional" marriage intimates that its religious and even romantic moorings can be fairly quickly eroded against the harsher economic pressures that define it as a unit of production and consumption. Whether children's psyches are, then, better preserved by this institution seems at least dubious.

One thing, however, is clear: marriage grants access to an array of social services to which children would otherwise have little or no access. Hence the American Civil Liberties Union's opposition to legislation such as this Michigan analogue to SB 1250:

There is significant confusion and disagreement over the interpretation of constitutional amendments that go further than a simple, clear, and concise prohibition on same-sex marriage. The Michigan constitution was amended in 2004 to include this language: "To secure and preserve the benefits of marriage for our society and for future generations of children, the union of one man and one woman in marriage shall be the only agreement recognized as a marriage or similar union for any purpose." Michigan Constitution, Article 1, Section 25. *The Michigan Court of Appeals has held that this amendment bars state entities from providing health care benefits to domestic partners of state employees.* National Pride at Work v. Governor, 274 Mich. App 147, 372 N.W. 2d 139 (Mich. App. 2007). *The court found that "the operative language of the amendment plainly precludes the extension of benefits related to an employment contract, if the benefits are conditioned on or provided because of an agreement recognized as a marriage or similar union."* (ACLU 2008; my emphasis)

Although the Michigan statute is somewhat ambiguous with respect to what it defines as a "domestic partner" for non-married cohabiting adults, it is nonetheless clear that heterosexuality defines the marriage contract. Effectively recreating the status of "bastard" for offspring conceived outside of marriage (regardless of the sexual identities of the unmarried partners), amendments such as SB 1250 go much further—constitutionalizing heteropatriarchal married unions as the only ones that can produce legitimate offspring, effectively penalizing as deviant the offspring of non-married couples—but particularly those of gay and lesbian unions.

This is not to say, of course, that the children of gay and lesbian couples would fare better (or worse) than those of heterosexuals if marriage were to be opened up to the former; the failure rates of heterosexual couples might well be repeated among gays. At least in those US states where gay marriages (or civil unions) are legal, the recency of these statute changes makes such comparisons difficult to draw.[7] Evidence, however, from other nations such as Scandinavia and the Netherlands suggests that gay marriages are about as likely to confront the prospect of divorce as heterosexual ones, and that gay marriage in no way undermines heterosexual unions (Badgett 2004). The really important issue, however, concerns access to benefits like health insurance. The current situation not only discriminates against the children of gay and lesbian couples, but it leaves them doubly jeopardized—first by the second-class status accorded to their parents, and second by opportunities lost due to diminished access to basic human goods such as health care.

Although SB 1250's proponents insist that gay marriage amounts to using children for the purposes of "social experimentation," it seems clear that the real experiment is being performed on an entire class of children who are being denied access to basic human goods. As is forcefully pointed out by the Support Center for Child Advocates (Philadelphia) in its 13 March 2008 testimony to the Appropriations Committee of the Pennsylvania Senate, the same contorted logic to which SB 1250 advocates appeal for the sake of the welfare of children actually entails the denial of benefits to children (Cervone 2008). Such a constitutional amendment, they argue, may in fact function to deny legal protection for partners and their

---

[7]   For information and statistics on gay marriage, see <http://www.loveandpride.com/InformationCenter/Tips.aspx?categoryId=5>.

children in cases of domestic violence (as has occurred in Ohio), and could have direct and damaging effects on an already struggling Pennsylvania foster-care system (Cervone 2008). Additionally, SB 1250 could restrict "[a] child's access to health insurance, medical care, Social Security, and pensions.... At a minimum, domestic partner benefits— and thus the benefits available to the children of the domestic partner—would no longer be available to any state or local government employee, nor the employee of any contract agent, government agency, or recipient of government funds" (Cervone 2008).

There is little reason to doubt that legislation like SB 1250 effectively institutionalizes a permanent state of social and economic vulnerability for some citizens and thus reproduces the logic of domination. Furthermore, such legislation risks the effective dispossession of those against whom it is deployed. In the form of state-sponsored discrimination, it helps to reinforce the existence of an economic underclass—which includes thousands of heterosexual couples, married or otherwise—that live without the benefit of access to health care and other social benefits. Moreover, while not a direct call to violence against gays, lesbians, bisexuals, transgendered, and transsexual persons, and their children, legislation like SB 1250 certainly helps to condone such violence by codifying the second-class status of those who do not fit its definition of personhood and parenthood. That SB 1250's beneficiaries are, first and foremost, economic beneficiaries is made clear by the evidence: its most vulnerable victims are children. This not only exposes the absurdity of such ill-conceived legislation; more crucially, it makes a mockery of any pretense to compassion associated with its proponents' appeal to God.

MERCURIAL HUMAN IDENTITY: TRANSSEXUALITY, INTERSEXUALITY, AND FEMINIST POLITICS

While the political, moral, social, and economic implications of SB 1250 are certainly important, I think that another, perhaps even more pressing issue lies just beyond the horizon of its sanction as constitutional law. Given the alternative possibilities for sexual identity evidenced in homosexual orientations, in transsexual and/or transgendered identities, in bisexuality, and in intersexed identities, to whom precisely does SB 1250 apply? Could there be, even in principle, any way to make this determination? I don't think so. Does the divorce of sexual intercourse from procreation add another dimension of complexity? Yes, and this matters: to whatever extent the complexity of some sexual activities and/or identities disrupts the tidy translation from sex to gender—from biology to behavior defined as "feminine" or "masculine"—it undermines the male–female conception of "human being" that informs the bill's binary logic. After all, it's only because appropriately gendered behavior is presumed to follow sexual identity that the deviation represented by homosexuality, transsexuality, bisexuality, and intersexuality can be cast as *deviance*. This is not to say, however, that non-heterosexual identities dissolve into androgyny. Far from it. As we shall see, sex, sexuality, and sexual identity are in no way done away with by the disruption of their presumed naturalness; instead, I'll argue, they are actually liberated from what turns out to be an incoherent, mostly religious, rhetoric about what counts as "natural."

In her 1997 book *Read My Lips: Sexual Subversion and the End of Gender*, Riki Anne Wilchins argues that the identity politics of the feminist and gay liberation movements in the United States in the late 1990s—that is, the political activism that revolves around identity as a woman or as a gay person—is destined to fail in its current incarnation. The reason for this, according to Wilchins, is that the issues confronting women, gays, lesbians, and many others who share an experience of violence and oppression can no more be identified as exclusively those of women or of gays and lesbians than can issues of race be identified as exclusively those of African Americans, Native Americans, Asian Americans, or Hispanic Americans:

> Feminist politics begins with the rather commonsense notion that there exists a group of people understood as women whose needs can be politically represented and whose objectives sought through unified action. A movement for women—what could be simpler? But implicit in this basic idea is that we know who comprises this group since it is their political goals we will articulate. What if this ostensibly simple assumption isn't true? (1997: 81)

What if, in other words, a movement grounded in the promise of solidarity, itself grounded in the presumed identity of its members, turns out to be inadequately equipped to identify them? Judith

Butler poses a similar question couched in the crucial though often fraught relationship between activism and theory:

> In an understandable desire to forge bonds of solidarity, feminist discourse has often relied upon the category of woman as a universal presupposition of cultural experience which…provides a false ontological promise of eventual political solidarity. In a culture in which the false universal of "man" has for the most part been presupposed as coextensive with humanness itself, feminist theory has sought with success to bring female specificity into visibility and to rewrite the history of culture in terms which acknowledge the presence, the influence, and the oppression of women. Yet, in this effort to combat the invisibility of woman as a category, feminists run the risk of rendering visible a category which may or may not be representative of the concrete lives of women. (Butler 2003: 419)

The worry, then, is that if "woman" is treated as a universal category of experience, the experiences of actual women, and particularly those whose "gender performance" does not conform to cultural expectations (i.e., women who fail to instantiate some stereotypical presumption of what a woman is), will be ignored, potentially contributing to the very oppression that the movement aims to combat.

This, I think, is a profoundly important worry, and one whose implications have yet to be fully appreciated. Why important? Because the presuppositions to which some feminists routinely appeal in the interest of engendering solidarity are, in fact, the very same as those that underlie SB 1250: that there is a stable category called "woman" and one called "man," and that these two and only these two categories can fulfill the criteria for, in the case of the feminist movement, being (or not being) a member of a specific oppressed class, and, for the proponents of SB 1250, being a party to a legally binding contract called marriage. This effectively conjoins feminists and their adversaries at the hip. That we can distinguish "real" women from, say, men in drag seems vital to building a successful movement, since without this "commonsense" category there seems no way to identify who the movement is for. Nor, however, is there any other way to identify the "real" men and women "protected" by legislation like SB 1250. The gender performance that identifies the bodies of some human beings as the victims of oppression identifies those same bodies as those belonging to the sisters, wives, and mothers of the traditional family. What makes gender performative, in other words, is its essentially public dimension: "it is clear," writes Butler, "that although there are individual bodies that enact these significations by becoming stylized into gendered modes, this action is immediately public as well. There are temporal and collective dimensions to these actions, and their public nature is not inconsequential; indeed, the performance is effected with the strategic aim of maintaining gender within its binary frame.... the performance renders social laws explicit" (Butler 2003: 421–22).

Among the testimonials presented, for example, at the 29 April 2008 Appropriations Committee Hearing for SB 1250 was that of a Baptist pastor who made a demonstration of "the social laws" by having his wife and eight young children in the crowded hearing room.[8] His small sons wore awkward suits and his daughters and wife ankle-length dresses; the children were bored, and his wife did her best to keep order. It's hard to imagine a performance more clearly calculated to fulfill what Butler calls "the strategic aim of maintaining gender," but what made his performance particularly troubling, especially from a point of view like that of Wilchins, was that the pastor and his family were African American. The pastor drew no connection between the oppression of gays and that of African Americans, despite the fact that his very position as a pastor defies a history of racism in America; he insisted, in fact, that gay marriage would mean the end to "the family." Yet, as Wilchins and Butler would likely point out, the pastor's own gender performance not only conforms to the patriarchal plan of, as feminist theorist Audre Lorde (1984) has eloquently put it, building and maintaining the master's house (literally and figuratively), but also actively reproduces its "social laws" on the bodies and in the behavior of his children. Although the pastor must have known, given the history of American slavery, that "blackness" is no more discrete or universal a category

---

[8] Senate Appropriations Committee Meeting, 29 April 2008, State House, Harrisburg, Pennsylvania. See also Wendy Lynne Lee, "Testimony on Senate Bill 1250, a Proposed Marriage Amendment to the Pennsylvania Constitution," 9 April 2008. <http://www.apscuf.com/kutztown/documents/SB_1250/TestPA House08_final.pdf>.

than "whiteness," he nonetheless adhered to the notion that "male" and "female" can be so defined. This isn't mere blindness; it's the appropriation of the master's tools to dismantle part of the master's house — namely, that part called racism — while leaving intact all the "rooms" devoted to reinforcing precisely what a history of slavery has denied him — namely, his manhood. What he failed to see is that the master's tools cannot be used to dismantle the master's house, but only to reconstruct it — perhaps in a fashion that renders some aspects of oppression less visible. But the trade-off remains, as the pastor's masculine gender performance epitomizes, the reaffirmation of a compulsory system of sexual identity.

So too, argues Wilchins, is the case with the feminist movement. We are, in fact, trying to use the master's tools to dismantle the master's house by appealing to the same binary logic that undergirds SB 1250. As Butler points out, however, this is a strategy that is destined for trouble: the master's house is a well-constructed edifice that conceals the fact that it's constructed — a human-made institution, not an artifact of nature — behind the "cultivation" of the (hetero)sexual identities that support, maintain, naturalize, and reproduce it:

> To guarantee the reproduction of a given culture, various requirements, well-established in the anthropological literature of kinship, have instated sexual reproduction within the confines of a heterosexually-based system of marriage which requires the reproduction of human beings in certain gendered modes which, in effect, guarantee the eventual reproduction of that kinship system.... My point is simply that one way in which this system of *compulsory heterosexuality* is reproduced and concealed is through the cultivation of bodies into discrete sexes with "natural" appearances and "natural" heterosexual dispositions. (2003: 420; my emphasis)

Just as heterosexuality defines appropriate male and female "disposition" or gender performance, so too does its binary logic define its opposite or deviant in homosexuality. Therefore at one level it is perplexing, but at another perfectly understandable, that gay-rights advocates, like their feminist (sometimes) allies, would themselves pick up the master's tools, that is, adopt the same universalizing strategy: Who else "comes out of the closet"? Hence the question "Aren't we about sexual orientation?" seems as commonsense to ask as does

29

"Aren't we about women?" Yet, argues Wilchins, commonsense may well lead to just the definitional quandaries that confront the endeavor to define "race" and "sex":

> "We're about sexual orientation, not racism." Which is true, unless you're African American and queer, or Asian and queer, or Latina and queer. It [identity politics] says, "We're about sexual orientation, not class." Which is true, unless you're a queer trying to survive on welfare. And it says, "We're about sexual orientation, not gender." Which is true, unless you're a trans or a bisexual or lesbian woman concerned about the right to choose [abortion], about spousal abuse, about the freedom to walk our streets without the crippling specter of rape. (1997: 80–81)

Tethered neither to any particular ethnicity nor to any class, being "about sexual orientation" inevitably intersects with the many other issues that real people confront, including racially motivated bigotry and economic poverty.

The proponents of SB 1250 would not, of course, deny that issues of race or class may affect the stability of marriage. The pastor argued, for example, that it's precisely these kinds of pressures that support the claim that marriage must be protected from additional perils like those represented by gay-rights activists. Indeed, he exploited the history of racism in America to reinforce his argument against gay marriage. Issues of race and class have, however, no particular bearing on the gender roles tacitly promoted in SB 1250; the sponsors of SB 1250 promote the male-headed household as the economic ideal, regardless of race or class. What, however, if this male head of household is a post-operative transsexual? What if he/"he" identifies as a straight male? What if his/"his" gender "performance" includes items like suits and ties, loafers and boxers? The point is that sexual identity, gay or straight, intersects at crucial social junctures with gender expectation: when gender determines social status, choice, sexual vulnerability—or privilege, it does so in part by reinforcing compulsory sexuality. But, for Wilchins and Butler, this isn't about any fact of biology; it's about the reproduction of a binary logic of sexual identity that helps to maintain a system of empowerment and economic privilege. To illustrate this point, Wilchins offers a telling example:

The head of New York City NOW [the National Organization for Women]...informs me that I am welcome, but only to work on "women's" issues. I cannot work on my own, which, by definition, are men's issues. "Do you mean I can work on your access to post-menopausal hormones, but not on my own access to pretransition hormones?" I ask. "Your breast implants after mastectomy but not my breast implants before sex-change? Your danger of ovarian cancer but not my danger of prostate cancer?" She nods, glaring steadily. On the way out she asks me for a hug. (1997: 81)

What does it mean to be told that one may only "work on women's issues," except, at least in this context, that one's body is at odds with the work's purported aims? Why, if Wilchins identifies as a woman, are her issues identified as "men's by definition"?

The easy answer, of course, is that Wilchins is biologically and genetically male, but in light of the very hormones (as well as surgical interventions and behavioral therapies) in dispute in Wilchins's example, this answer is clearly too simple. Defined in opposition to compulsory heterosexuality, NOW's claim is that women's issues are important regardless of gender performance, that is, regardless of whether a woman is heterosexual or lesbian, and regardless of how "lesbian" is itself performed. Yet it's precisely compulsory heterosexuality, that is, the presumed naturalness and moral rectitude of heterosexuality, that is reconfirmed when issues that may confront a masculine-identified lesbian count as "women's issues," but those that confront a feminine-identified pre-transition transsexual don't. Why? Because biology is allowed to govern the determination of whose body belongs to this "work." This is not to say that the prospects of developing ovarian cancer ought to be regarded as any less serious for a butch lesbian than they would be for, say, the pastor's wife. But why aren't the pre-transition breast implants for the male-to-female transsexual a woman's issue? The only answer here seems to imply biology; but to embrace biology as a governing strategy for exclusion is to embrace the binary logic out of which the master's tools are themselves wrought and used. Like the pastor at the Appropriations Committee hearing who rejected the racist logic of white versus black, but embraced the same logic in the form of male versus female, the NOW representative rejects a dichotomy of gay versus straight—but tacitly embraces the same presuppositions on the basis of which the pastor condemns gay marriage. The implications are not merely hypocritical, but in fact self-defeating. Pressing the logic to its absurd conclusions, Wilchins remarks that

> for starters, we'll have to decide who qualifies as a woman for inclusion in our movement. Otherwise we'll find ourselves representing anybody who calls themselves a woman. Now, we know we don't want transsexual women: just taking hormones and having a vagina made doesn't make you a woman. We don't want transsexual men either: they're busy taking hormones, getting hairy chests, and becoming, well…men. We can't have too many stone butches, diesel dykes, or passing women, because they all live as men….And we certainly don't want crossdressers or drag queens: we're not interested in representing the political concerns of men in dresses. And intersexuals who live as women? Oh, please. (1997: 82)

Even, in other words, if we take biology seriously as a criterion of exclusion we are in trouble. What of persons born genetically female —but without ovaries? Or persons born genetically male—but without testes? What about persons whose genetic disposition codes for intersexuality, and who are born with the reproductive equipment of both sexes?

Perhaps biology will help us to exclude some of these groups from having a claim to work on "women's issues," say, male-to-female transsexuals and drag queens. But such a criterion fails to exclude female-to-male transsexuals, lesbians—however male-identified—or women passing as men. Biologically, each member of the latter set is a woman—however she sees it. The real issue, claims Wilchins, is who gets to decide? "Some of us must already have been legitimized as women in order to make this determination to begin with, authorizing us to judge the rest." In so doing, "we're not just keeping the riffraff out; we're creating a hierarchy where 'real women' are separated from the rest of the group" (1997: 82).

Throw in "real men" and you have SB 1250, whose proponents take themselves to "have been legitimized" as judges on the issue of who qualifies for a marriage license. Imagine, then, a post-op transsexual who plans to marry a person whom they now (and perhaps always) perceived to be a member of the opposite sex. Will she/he be able to get a marriage license post-amendment? No doubt, the bill's sponsors do not have this case in mind, but so long as the prospective transsexual groom or bride can provide the altered birth certificate, on what grounds can they be denied entry into the marriage contract—regardless of how SB 1250's proponents see them? Shall we craft another constitutional amendment to exclude transsexuals? Intersexed persons? Note too that few of these claimants are denying the fundamental significance of sexual identity or sexual orientation. The transsexual may well claim to be male/female, have at least the external reproductive "plumbing" to prove it, and claim to be perfectly heterosexual in their choice of a spouse. The intended spouse may, having full knowledge of the hormonal, behavioral, and surgical procedures required to complete this transformation, be fully on-board. To deny this couple a marriage license would thus require denying it to any couple that, say through birth defect, surgery, or cancer, does not have the requisite internal plumbing (whatever that means)—but these are not the "riffraff" the sponsors of SB 1250 intend to "keep out."

While certainly the aims of SB 1250 have little to do with freeing women, and much to do with reinforcing traditional gender roles, the effect of a feminist movement whose own binary logic depends on the same "real" versus "not real" distinction may have little more to offer those who do not conform to its definition of "woman." "Worst of all," remarks Wilchins,

> we started out wanting to liberate women….Yet our first act has been to fence off all the things they cannot and still be considered women [such as become men]. Our message is no longer, *You are free to become whatever your talent and heart allow*, but rather, *You are free to become whatever your talent and heart allow as long as it's not too masculine and you continue to look and act like a woman*. And it appears that the woman you will look and act like is based on the traditional, limiting, heterosexual-based model we had hoped to chuck for good. (1997: 82–83)

The question, of course, is whether Wilchins's withering criticism of feminist identity politics fairly and charitably represents the movement, and, if so, takes fair aim at its weaknesses. Are feminists— at least with respect to defining "woman"—in bed, as it were, with their conservative opponents? Yes and no. It turns out that for Wilchins—like many feminists, gay-rights advocates, and others—the answer to this question is as much about a movement in transition as it is about sexual identity itself. In her 1994 *Village Voice* article about the Michigan Women's Music Festival, Wilchins describes a gradual but progressive transformation of feminist, and particularly lesbian feminist, consciousness from the exclusionary politics that had dominated the "Womyn Only" dynamics of the festival since its incarnation in the 1970s, to the somewhat more open dynamics of a festival that, while still struggling to define its intended audience, has begun to rethink its criteria for inclusion. She describes the first time that she and some of her allies were allowed to enter the Michigan campsite:

> We have checked with Festival Security about this [entering the festival site] and have been told that [the] "womyn-born womyn only" policy stands. Unlike past years, however, each of us must interpret it for ourselves. And that is how the six of us—three pre-operative transsexuals, two post-operative, one intersexed individual—happen to be there. I suspect our lives and identities are far more complex than any policy could possibly anticipate.... After what seems like forever, we head up a short rise to the Avengers' meeting area. This is the first time a mainstream, national lesbian group has supported transsexual women, and the scattered applause, growing to a real ovation as we come into full view, is an incredible rush. I have never seen so many young, hip dykes with good hair and straight teeth in one place, and they are all, for gosh sakes, clapping for us.... I am suddenly aware, clearly and precisely, that lesbian politics is changing—fundamentally, irrevocably, right before my eyes. (114)

Remarkable it is, then, that even though the feminist movement—as far back as 1994—began to reconsider and revise its own view of whose emancipation it champions, another movement—one that effectively acts to repeal these gains—is now building its own momentum. How can this be? How can bills like SB 1250 buck this tide toward greater enfranchisement, more open institutions, and the gradual falling out of favor of the binary logic that supports its codification of heterosexuality as the only appropriate sexual identity for human beings?

SEXUAL IDENTITY, THE FUTURE OF MOVEMENTS, AND "POSTMODERN" HUMAN BEING

No doubt, there's much truth to the claim that what accounts for the backlash against the feminist challenge to compulsory heterosexuality (and the gender roles it supports) is the realization that with emancipation comes the potential loss of unearned privilege for many (though certainly not all) men and some women. This, however, is not by any means the end of this story, and if I'm right, it's not wholly clear what a contemporary feminist and/or gay-rights movement to fully enfranchise women, gay men, lesbians, bisexuals, transgendered and/or transsexual persons, and intersexed persons would look like. That SB 1250's sponsors have gone to such lengths—aiming to *constitutionalize* heterosexuality as foundational to marriage—intimates not only the fear that accompanies the loss of political, social, and economic privilege, but also the deeper and perhaps more visceral fear that what such loss really means is the loss of the prerogative to define human sexual identity, and hence human identity, *per se*.

I say "human identity, *per se*" because what *is* made clear in the backlash represented by legislation like SB 1250 is that sexual identity is both conceived of and experienced as intimately bound to what it means to *be* a human being. Even the confusion or distress that can accompany the discovery of intersexuality (whether in oneself, in others, or in one's newborn) testifies to the rudimentary significance of sexual identity.[9] Moreover, the fact that some transsexuals seek hormonal and surgical intervention in order, by their own accounts, to realize their full humanity as male or as female implies the magnitude with which we all experience sex and gender as indispensable to our conceptions of ourselves as persons. This is not to say that human identity is reducible to sex or gender, but rather that since every aspect of that identity makes some reference, implicitly or otherwise, to one or both, sex and/or gender is essential to the private and public experience of being human. Indeed, no one's experience makes this clearer than the transsexual's. As Wilchins recounts,

---

[9] An excellent fictionalized example of the many and complex permutations of intersexuality is explored in Jeffrey Eugenides' Pulitzer Prize–winning novel *Middlesex* (New York: Picador, 2002).

When people started reading me as a woman, I had to very consciously learn how they saw me in order to use the restroom. I had to learn to recognize my voice, my posture, the way I appeared in clothing. I had to master an entire set of bathroom-specific communicative behaviors just to avoid having the cops called. In essence, I had to build an elaborate mental representation of how I looked and was read. And in spite of all this effort, sometimes it didn't work. The cops would humiliate me, checking my ID as publicly as possible, making sure everyone got a good, long look at the gender trash being put back in its place—which was out of sight. (1997: 151)

That it's possible to master appropriate "bathroom-specific" gender behavior—however difficult and imperfect—implies that, as Wilchins puts it, "the body may not be a stable basis for recognition" (151), and yet, as she makes equally clear, it needs to be. Otherwise it cannot function as one's own body. "To navigate in a society of human beings," writes Wilchins, "to think oneself at all, one must have a self: a specific organization of flesh, soul, and meaning, a mental sign which stands for 'this person' having certain properties and characteristics" (133).

Being able to master gender-specific behavior shows that the body can be sufficiently "stabilized" or disciplined, as Judith Halberstam puts it, to "pass" (1999: 127). In the context of "trans," however, "passing" and "being" are neither in opposition to each other nor synonymous, and this is surely the source of the very visceral fear that drives legislation like SB 1250. It's as if its sponsors believe that they can eradicate the definitional ambiguity that fuels this fear by writing heterosexuality into the constitution; they aim to prescribe whose gender performance is to be legitimized through the creation of its opposite, the "fake" who "merely" passes. This "fake" can then be stigmatized, harassed, even criminalized for being "the wrong kind of person" in the wrong place, like a bathroom. But the bathroom, of course, is really just a metaphor for everywhere. Consider, for example, the highly gender-scripted performance epitomized in weddings: it encodes not only a public affirmation of what counts as "real" women and "real" men, but serves to reinforce within ourselves that we, too, "fit" (or don't, but should try harder). If only it were this simple; but, as Wilchins remarks,

[i]f it is true that at this point in human development [as we become aware of ourselves *as* selves] we must have a "self," perhaps the single most profound and private thing we can create on our journey through this life is our sense of who or what we are. This is not a problem for most of us. We inherit meanings for ourselves which are more or less acceptable.... For others, the self which resonates within us is entirely at odds with what culture works to inscribe on our flesh. And this inaugurates a lifelong battle. To be so taxed with a cultural body whose meanings not only fail to resonate, but which actively militate against our deepest sense of what is meaningful, consequential and true at every turn, to have this experience is to feel a unique kind of discomfort and pain. It affords little respite. For it is not just there in the shower, in dating situations, before strangers on the street, when applying for a job, undressing, in the act of making love, and in the eyes of family and friends, but it is also in our heads whenever we think about what constitutes "me." (1997: 134)

To be faced, in other words, with the very possibility that there exist human beings whose "parts" are identical to one's own, but whose experience and identity bear the stamp of difference at every level—public and private—is to be faced with the possibility that one could discover oneself in the throes of such a "lifelong battle," that one may know others who are so embattled (but not know *that* they are so), and that one might not be able to recognize them—to know whether they are *passing*—no matter what laws are erected, what constitutions are altered, or what religious proscriptions are exhorted.

My simple point here is that the effort to mandate "real" heterosexuality (and the gender roles that go with it) by tethering it to the institutionalized benefits, economic advantages, and social recognition of marriage is not so much a consequence of a worldview driven by the long history of heterosexual (and ultimately patriarchal) privilege. Rather, it's a symptom of the anxiety created by the possibility that the sex of a person can be transformed in such a fashion that we could be mistaken in our judgment about what a person is, a mistake that is not necessarily made out of a hasty miscalculation of cosmetic or behavioral clues, and that is not necessarily one we know we've made—or will ever know. Indeed, it may not even count as a mistake to the transsexual person we've identified as male or female. For Wilchins, after all, such "mistakes" aren't mistakes at all; they're confirmations that she's gotten something right. The unprecedented effort undertaken to fix sexual identity by defining who will be rewarded, and under what circumstances, in effect, for having sex is, I think, symptomatic of the worry that gender performance can no longer be reliably read to reveal sexual identity, experience, or desire. Like at no other time in this history, sexual identity can be chosen and realized in a battery of ways: hormonal treatment, behavioral therapy, and especially surgical sex reassignment. Choosing, however, is not equivalent to passing. Indeed, many transsexuals may not see themselves as choosing at all, but simply as realizing the sex they were "meant" to be. As the very possibility of a transitional sexuality shows, the basis for sexual identity is experience—that is, "what I say I am regardless of genetics"—so the real/passing distinction is destined to remain as mercurial as sexual identity itself.

The possibility that not only gender but sex is a socially constructed performance, that both can be detached from sexual orientation and procreation, that each can be performed in opposition to genetic fact—and still counted by a particular self and some reaffirming others as real—threatens to upset the notion that "human being" is a fixed category of nature (or God). It is at least unclear that "human nature" can be fixed in such a dependable way that some— heterosexual (especially white) men—are rightly and naturally empowered to define the lives, opportunities, and liberties of others. Note that I've not denied that there is some fact of the matter about genetic identity, that is, some specific and unalterable genetic "fingerprint" that identifies me as this entity in the world. The point is that it doesn't necessarily matter to *personal* identity as it is experienced privately or publicly (and can be rightly identified as *inter*-sexual)— especially when the very "flesh" we associate with this identity can be altered. Halberstam makes the point succinctly:

> We are all transsexuals except that the referent of the trans becomes less and less clear (and more and more queer). We are all cross-dressers but where are we crossing from and to what? There is no "other" side, no "opposite" sex, no natural divide to be spanned by surgery, by disguise, by passing. We all pass or we don't, we all wear our drag, and we all derive

a different degree of pleasure—sexual or otherwise—from our costumes. It is just that for some of us our costumes are made of fabric or material, while for others they are made of skin; for some an outfit can be changed; for others skin must be resewn. There are no transsexuals [if we are all transsexuals]. (1999: 126–27)

It is hardly surprising, then, that those for whom a fixed sexual identity is morally or ideologically essential to human being would find so much to dread in the suggestion that they too are "passing." Nonetheless, legislation like SB 1250 can be described as "trans" in that, not unlike the transsexual who goes to great lengths to make "real" her or his sexual identity, the effort to constitutionalize the "real" is simultaneously recognition and creation. Butler reiterates the point: "[t]hat gender reality is created through sustained social performances means that the very notion of an essential sex, a true or abiding masculinity or femininity, are [sic] also constituted as part of the strategy by which the performative aspect of gender is concealed" (2003: 423). Not only, in other words, are gender and sex socially constructed—but so too is the effort to conceal this fact. We can readily conceive of all three as projects aimed at stabilizing the performance of masculine or feminine roles, even where the substance of those roles has undergone considerable transformation, thanks especially to the feminist movement. As the case of transsexuality shows, however, sexual identity is destined to remain a site for contested meanings, for anxiety about the real.[10]

Even for those transsexual persons who claim that their experiences inform them of their essential sexual identity as male or female, that there exists "an essential sex," the link between sex and gender is still broken. After all, it cannot be the case that this "essential identity" has been determined by genetic fact. So we're all transsexuals—at least in the sense that whatever we *believe* about the purported essential nature of sexual identity, however important it is to believe it, whichever "side" we're on with respect to defining marriage, whatever we experience, it seems that "essential" actually captures

---

[10] Note, too, that each of these aspects of achieving the final product involves other corporate enterprises, including pharmaceuticals, cosmetic companies, and clothing manufacturers. For an illuminating account of how these dynamics played out during the 1980s and 1990s in the United States, see Clark (1993).

little beyond conviction. The SB 1250 effort to "refasten" sex to gender through legislation *is* a construction project. This, however, is precisely what's concealed, as Butler shows, in the arguments made by the bill's proponents, and especially by those who appeal to the intentions of a god. Perhaps the support necessary to such an enormous undertaking requires the supernatural to justify it. Be this as it may, a rearguard appeal to "religious truths" might also be seen as a form not only of anxiety but also of desperation. Haraway captures this when she remarks that

> [t]he distinction between nature and culture in Western societies has been a sacred one; it has been at the heart of the great narratives of salvation history and their genetic transmutation into sagas of secular progress. What seems to be at stake is this culture's stories of the human place in nature…. It is a mistake in this context to forget that anxiety over the pollution of lineages is at the origin of racist discourse in European cultures as well as at the heart of linked gender and sexual anxiety. The discourses of transgression get all mixed up in the body of nature…. The line between the acts, agents, and products of divine creation and human engineering has given way in the sacred-secular border zones of molecular genetics and biotechnology. (1997: 60)

Although Haraway's focus here is genetic engineering and the development of biotechnologies, her remarks speak just as forcefully to transsexuality. To whatever extent the realization of "becoming a woman/man" involves the use of therapies, medications, technologies upon the body—to whatever extent it is the body that becomes the site of transformation—the nature–culture distinction is "polluted" or "transgressed."

If Haraway is correct, and "the discourses of transgression get all mixed up in the body of nature," this is because nature is effectively "denatured" whenever the body can be altered to create a "new" identity or function in a different way. Whether what's experienced as "new" is the realization/creation of an alternative sexual identity, or being free of cancer, or momentarily released from the tremors of Parkinson's disease, "[t]he line between the acts, agents, and products of divine creation and human engineering has given way." We too, it seems, can play God. That we applaud some forms of transgressing

the body—treating cancer and Parkinson's—and condemn others—
sex reassignment surgery—reveals rather precisely the source of our
anxieties. Haraway continues: "The techniques of genetic engineering developed since the early 1970's are like the reactors and particle
accelerators of nuclear physics: Their products are 'trans.' They themselves cross a culturally salient line between nature and artifice, and
they greatly increase the density of all kinds of other traffic on the
bridge between what counts as nature and culture…" (1997: 56).
Although Haraway is referring in this case to genetically engineered
mice, the point that the products of such engineering are "trans"
applies just as usefully to Wilchins's discussion of a workshop at Camp
Trans called "Our Cunts are not the Same" where she invites atten-
dees to conduct a hands-on examination of her engineered vagina.
Wilchins's description of one attendee's reaction tells the story:

> Another participant discovered her friends from home were so grossed
> out that she had touched a transsexual cunt, "a man's cunt!"…that they
> stopped speaking to her. She related all this to me through tears, because
> they were people she had come to the festival with and had known since
> childhood. She was astonished to discover how transphobic they were
> toward me, and correspondingly quick to turn on her, as if I were con-
> tagious. What was even stranger was that her outraged friends were so
> deliciously and completely butch, they made me feel like I was an extra
> in petticoats straight out of Gone with the Wind. (1997: 117)

It might be tempting to think that "trans" in this case is meant
metaphorically, not literally, or that "transphobia" is more about a
perceived political sell-out of butch lesbianism than it is about the
actual transformation of Wilchins's body. But Wilchins insists that her
audience take the concept "trans" more seriously—and literally:

> Another interesting thing happens when I ask all participants, in the
> strongest possible terms, to refer to the area in question as my penis. I
> remind them that many trans vaginas are actually constructed by invert-
> ing the penis, so I would prefer if they refer to mine by its original name.
> It's not important that this is not the particular surgery I had. The point
> is, *they are unable to follow my instructions.* Nearly all the participants do
> three things while exploring my penis: first, they exclaim about the

41

wonders of modern surgery; second, they invariably refer to it as a cunt; and third, they declaim about how it's just like theirs. (1997: 117; my emphasis)

It seems that the participants cannot quite comprehend what is literally transformed, that a penis can *be* a vagina. They recognize the transformation made possible through highly sophisticated forms of surgical technique and yet can't quite recognize that, as Wilchins puts it, "not all cunts are the same."

Not unlike the anxiety evinced by SB 1250 proponents, the "trans" represented by what can be accomplished through surgery, genetic manipulation, nuclear fission, and other forms of technology elicits anxiety along those very fissures where our conception of human being is most vulnerable—and most vital to our *self*-conception. "[W]hen starting with the assumption that bodies are always gendered and marked by race," writes Anne Balsamo, "it becomes clear that there are multiple forms of technological embodiment that must be attended to in order to make sense of the status of the body in contemporary culture" (1999: 278). Quoting from Haraway's "Manifesto for Cyborgs" (1990 [1985]), philosopher of science Katherine Hayles agrees that

"[a]ny objects or persons...can be reasonably thought of in terms of assembly and reassembly; no 'natural' architectures constrain system design".... From one perspective this violation is liberating, for it allows historically oppressive constructs to be deconstructed and replaced by new kinds of entities more open to the expression of difference. The problem, of course, is that these new constructs may also be oppressive, albeit, in different ways. For example, much feminist thought...has been directed toward deconstructing the idea of "man".... To achieve this goal, another construction has been erected, "woman." Yet, as it has been defined in the writings of white affluent, heterosexual, Western women, this construct has tended to exclude the experiences of black women, Third World women, poor women, lesbian women, and so on. (1990: 282–83)

Echoing Wilchins's criticism of feminist identity politics, Hayles acknowledges the potential peril of "denaturing" human (sexual) nature, the sheer riskiness of trying to organize a movement without the appeal to identity. "What is left to organize around," queries Wilchins, "if we don't use identities?" (1997: 85). Hayles puts the point eloquently: "If denaturing the human can sweep away more of the detritus of the past...it can also remove taboos and safeguards that are stays, however fragile, against the destruction of the human race. What will happen to the movement for human rights when the human is regarded as a construction like any other?" (1990: 285). However just and necessary an undertaking it may be to challenge these "safeguards," the "stays" of SB 1250, it nonetheless remains an open question what comes after "trans." But, as Wilchins's examples show, this bridge has already been crossed.

The issue, I suggest, is how to take responsibility for, as Hayles describes it, this "postmodern" human being, for such a human being's "trans" world of living things. One option, the one advocated by the proponents of SB 1250, is to reclaim the concept of an essential nature that defines sexual identity. Or, as Wilchins attributes to Butler, we could "allow identity to float free"; we could "stop barricading the gates of gender and encourage everyone to define themselves as they wish, even change their identity or invent new ones" (Wilchins 1997: 85). "Instead of merely tolerating this gender fluidity as a necessary evil," we could, writes Wilchins, "accept the inherent instability of all identities and make it work for us" (85). But *how*? How can we craft a movement that "works for us," whose core values include emancipation, mutual respect, tenacity, compassion, and joyfulness, on the fluidity of identity? A daunting task indeed. It's Haraway, however, who poses the central question:

> [w]ho are my kin in this odd world of promising monsters, vampires, surrogates, living tools, and aliens? How are natural kinds identified in the realms of late-twentieth-century technoscience? What kinds of crosses and offspring count as legitimate and illegitimate, to whom, and at what cost? Who are my familiars, my siblings, and *what kind of livable world are we trying to build*? (1997: 52; my emphasis)

Perhaps, in other words, movement building must become less about identity and more about imagining a livable world regardless of the stakes we hold in being women, or men, or gay, or black, or white, or indigenous, or abled, or trans. This, however, creates its own worry

CONTEMPORARY FEMINIST THEORY AND ACTIVISM

in that it seems to dismiss the pressing issues represented by these stakes, namely, the subjugation of human beings, and among them those who occupy bodies that fail to conform to the binary logic of SB 1250. A livable world, we might ask then, *for whom?*

MARKETING "TRANS": GLOBALIZING A MOVEMENT/COMMODIFYING ITS VALUE

For Haraway, "monsters, vampires, surrogates, living tools, and aliens" are not necessarily other human beings; they may be nonhuman animals, cybernetic organisms, transgenic creatures, or even altered molecular entities. Blurring the lines between natural and technologically generated "kinds," these "monsters" reinterpret what it means to be "trans" in order to embrace other bodies, other "resewn" skins, other genetic codes. She asks, "What kinds of crosses and offspring count as legitimate and illegitimate, to whom, and at what cost?" (1997: 52). Daunting questions all, especially given the fluid and dynamic feel of the notions of "cross" and "offspring," which, like "trans," cannot be dismissed merely as metaphorical wordplay. Balsamo raises similar issues when she observes that "[t]he availability of manufactured body parts has subtly altered the cultural understanding of what counts as a natural body. Even as these technologies provide the realistic possibility of replacement body parts, they also enable a fantastic dream of immortality and control over life and death" (1999: 285). In light of such a "fantastic dream," the question "a livable world for whom?" takes on a particularly urgent feel.

But it's "To whom?" and "At what cost?" that raise the most contentious issues. The first reiterates precisely those questions of authority and power that have been our focus thus far; the second also raises an old question—but in a radically new context: What networks of exchange are implicated such that it makes sense to refer to cost? Cost to whom? What in the conceptual economy of "trans" or "cross" counts as a commodity in the world of economic exchange? Body parts? Cells? Genes? Feminine and/or masculine appearance? Identity itself? What's the relationship between those authorized to define the "legitimate" or "real" and the networks of exchange that market "trans" in the form, for example, of cancer research, gene therapy, nanotechnology, cloning, surrogate pregnancy, and sex-reassignment surgery (among a growing number of procedures involving the transmutation, transfer, or transformation of bodies)? To what extent does "real," despite its SB 1250-style detractors, become translated as the marketable? Who bears the cost of the production of what "monsters"? Who decides what is a monster, as opposed to a miracle?

With respect to the technoscientific economy of breast-cancer research, Haraway argues that the meaning of "trans" cannot be divorced from the reality of corporate funding, the potential marketability of trans-products and services, and the potential implications of the use of such products for the ways in which we define, for example, disease, cell, gene, sex, identity, and so on. Consider, for instance, transgenic OncoMouse™, an animal and a patented invention, fully enmeshed, says Haraway, in the economy of capitalist exchange value:

> One of a varied line of transgenic mice, s/he is an animal model system for a disease, breast cancer, that women in the United States have a one in eight chance of getting if they live to old age…, OncoMouse™ is an ordinary commodity in the exchange circuits of transnational capital. A kind of machine tool for manufacturing other knowledge building instruments in technoscience, the useful little rodent with the talent for mammary cancer is a scientific instrument for sale like many other laboratory devices. Above all, OncoMouse™ is the first patented animal in the world. By definition, then, in the practices of materialized reconfiguration, s/he is an invention. (1997: 79)

It might seem incongruous to compare transgenic mice to transsexual persons, or to the "parts" at issue in sex-reassignment surgery. But consider this: the technoscience—that is, the technologically motivated medical/biological science—responsible for producing OncoMouse is not conceptually different from that which makes sex-reassignment surgery possible. Both produce "cyborgs," that is, technologically altered and/or enhanced biological entities, and both are wholly commodifiable as long as they have audiences ready and willing to pay the cost of their service. Sex reassignment simply markets a different set of "saleable instruments"—for example, breasts, labia, pared-down Adam's Apples, etc.—which, like OncoMouse, are technologically tailor-made to specific purposes. The fact that one is legitimated as cancer research (a "miracle") and the other disparaged as immoral (a "monster"), mentally ill, or queer is irrelevant to the fact that neither would be possible without the commodification of the material body as an instrument manipulable according to market interest.

Not unlike OncoMouse, sex-reassignment surgery not only produces capacities—like the capacity to develop breast cancer or the capacity to function as a woman/man—but also (re)creates the transsexual person as the product of a menu of technoscientific options. One example, from the Dr. Chettawut Plastic Surgery Clinic, an international sex-reassignment practice in Bangkok, Thailand, includes the following options and prices:

Trachea Shave: $1,800
Secondary Labiaplasty: $3,000
Breast Implant Surgery: $3,500
Sex-Reassignment Surgery (SRS) with Scrotal Skin Graft: $10,200
SRS with Groin or Abdominal Skin Graft: $11,200
Combination options: $11,800–$16,400[11]

On this extremely well presented website, the prospective transsexual patient can investigate a cornucopia of surgical procedures, educate himself with respect to precisely what such an undertaking will involve (including what documents and proofs must accompany the patient on arrival at the relevant medical facility), plan for both pre- and post-operative expectations, and schedule his journey to Bangkok. Indeed, patients can even read testimonials from other, successful patients. The site is highly user-friendly and aimed at a global market. Its surgical "team," headed by Dr. Chettawut Tulayaphanich, advertise their credentials as a key aspect of their product/ service. Dr. Tulayaphanich advertises globally, but he knows his market is likely to be composed of English-speaking Westerners. Hence the site's primary language, unsurprisingly, is English.

This site epitomizes Horkheimer and Adorno's observations concerning the mass-scale reproduction not merely of products, but of a culture of affluence, chic, and wealth. The promised transition is a "product" that not only (re)produces the trans-body as a Western-

---

[11] See <http://www.chet-plasticsurgery.com/index.html>. The prices given here were listed in July 2009 as being effective until December 2009.

stylized configuration of feminine/masculine attractiveness, but also reproduces that body *as* a commodity—a "purchasable"—available to anyone. It's not, then, simply the desires of the transsexual that become inscribed as post-operative "skin"; rather, skin itself becomes a site (literally) of cultural transcription, a cybernetic medium for the translation of the bodies of individual consumers into a culture whose markets remain as molded by gender as ever. As a salient category of marketability, in fact, gender goes as unchallenged here as it does in bills like SB 1250. Consider, for example, a testimonial on the site from a post-operative transsexual who identifies herself as DeeDee:

> I have been very busy, but I am doing great. The dilation is going great. It is beautiful and sensitive. I am very happy. I am so glad that my higher power and spiritual guardians led me to you. I never doubted for a moment about my surgery or my choice in you. I had an amazing time over there in Bangkok, and your staff was fantastic. I would be more than happy to talk to any of your prospective patients. The few people I have shown, transsexual and non-transsexual, have said it is the best they have seen in person or on the Internet. I am still amazed when I look down there. Thank you so much for making my already good life better.

DeeDee closes with "I miss you guys," and she includes a picture that depicts a smiling young woman who, posed in very feminine fashion, in lipstick and eye makeup, offers a gender performance that the architects of SB 1250 would find hard to criticize; indeed, they probably would not realize she was a transsexual if they met her on the street. She is quite the satisfied customer.

DeeDee, however, is even more the whole package than her gender performance implies; she refers to a higher power and credits spiritual guidance with her decision. She identifies as heterosexual. It's easy to imagine her aspiring to reproduce the very family structure that traditional marriage advocates want to see constitutionalized. She's the "woman" ready to fill the role prescribed by SB 1250—and this is, of course, just what makes her a "monster" for its proponents—if they were in a position to know her previous birth certificate information. But DeeDee's far more than a monster; she's SB 1250's worst nightmare because, much like "getting it right," "ready to fill" locates DeeDee not only as (trans) gendered, but as a

47

"gendered-member-of-a-family-structure" outfitted for maximal production and consumption. DeeDee, in other words, epitomizes the economic ideal built into the family structure that SB 1250 advocates, but, given the advent of corrected birth certificates, its proponents are in no position to know that DeeDee does not fulfill the criteria the bill intends to codify with respect to either sexual or gender identity, at least not as they clearly envision the aim of the bill's passage into law. The proponents of SB 1250 assume that being male or female is a fixed fact that determines to whom one may become married, and hence who may enter an institution whose production and consumption form an essential component of a capitalist economy. But DeeDee represents a profound subversion of the bill's intentions. She not only reproduces many or all of the roles built into the "traditional" family, she also provides a market for a range of products and services that help her to maintain just that role. DeeDee *is* a culture industry in the sense that her gender performance requires very specific products — including sex-reassignment surgery itself — whose aim it is to reproduce a status quo. Her purchases confirm the reality of a femininity that is the same for DeeDee — given her assumptions — as it is for every (real) woman. As Horkheimer and Adorno describe these social dynamics, products marketed as opportunities for individuality, for difference, become desirable — even popular — precisely because what they really guarantee is a comforting sameness, a "generality" that could be just as well described as a "getting it right":

> What is individual is not more than the generality's power to stamp the accidental detail so firmly that it is accepted as such. The defiant reserve or elegant appearance of the individual on show is mass produced.... The peculiarity of the self is a monopoly commodity determined by society; *it is falsely represented as natural*.... On the faces of private individuals and movie heroes put together according to the patterns on magazine covers *vanishes a pretense in which no one now believes*; the popularity of the hero models comes partly from a secret satisfaction that the effort to achieve individuation has at last been *replaced by the effort of imitation*, which is admittedly more breathless. (1972: 154–55; my emphasis)

Does "getting it right" have something to do with the "power to stamp the accidental detail so firmly that it is accepted as such"? Arguably, it does. After all, the "details" of sex reassignment are, at one level, not accidental at all, but rather the carefully planned (re)construction of a "new" sexual identity identified with what may be conceived to be the opposite of some original (at least genetic and anatomical) fate.

But at another level, the aim of an ideal surgical, hormonal, behavioral transition is that the (re)construction be perceived by (especially anonymous) others as an accidental detail in the sense that "getting it right" means going unnoticed; it means that the way one straightens one's skirt or zips one's pants is perceived as nothing more than an "accidental detail" in the style of the individual. It means that once a birth certificate is altered such that the reassignment of sexual identity is essentially elided, the advocates of bills like SB 1250 would have no recourse but to allow transsexuals recognition as marriageable—so long as they did not identify as gay or lesbian. A peculiar state of affairs indeed. Insofar, however, as all such "stamps" are acquired as commodities—mass-produced and mass accessible—the best their consumers can achieve, according to Horkheimer and Adorno, is a kind of "pseudo-individuality" (1972: 155). DeeDee *is* the product of her own manufacture, an "imitation" of a "woman," her individuality a stylistic assembly of "details" that nonetheless define her as female. She is at once a technoscientific creation and the realization of her "essential" self, a "pretense in which no one now believes" (since we could in theory *all* have undertaken the procedure) and that everyone—especially the crafters of SB 1250—takes entirely for granted as "natural." But—and such is the unmistakable upshot of Horkheimer's and Adorno's analysis—so aren't we all?

Such analyses, however, are not without criticism. For example, do Horkheimer and Adorno presuppose that there exists some "original" identity? The one lost in translation, as it were, to the pseudo-individuality of the culture industry? The one that's forfeited in the quest for the stylized "self" made available through the markets? DeeDee, of course, also assumes something like a real or original self. But here the comparison ends in that DeeDee must contract for the realization of her "self"; she has to buy her own technoscientifically mediated transformation. There is for her no "original" in the sense that she could simply claim to be this self and live it out as such. Were such the case, it seems highly unlikely that she would go to so much trouble to transition. DeeDee thus puts the lie to Horkheimer and Adorno's apparent presupposition that there exists nothing other than the potential to become something that accords with desire — desire itself manufactured via the culture industry. Of course, DeeDee probably doesn't see it this way at all. Contrary to the concession of some original authenticity implied by Horkheimer and Adorno's references to "the pretense no one now believes," DeeDee has undertaken her transition to her real and original "self" at substantial personal risk and expense; and the fact that she's willing to do so implies — if little about whether there is any such thing as an original self — a good deal about the exploitability and commodifiability of that belief.

In one sense, what DeeDee accomplishes is a "generality" — a passing — so successful that her self-conception is reinforced every time she looks at her feminized face in a mirror, or is "mistaken" for a "real" woman, or "looks down there." But she is also "trans," a cyborg created out of the marketing of technoscientific possibility. So we're all "trans" in another sense as well: insofar as we all epitomize the "generality" or "individuated sameness" that characterizes our inevitable participation in the global market, we are transcribed with its logo, its brands, its style no more or less so than DeeDee. But we're also not DeeDee, and this isn't just because she has likely confronted discrimination, possibly even violence, that many of us will never experience. Accounts like Horkheimer and Adorno's fail to account for the fact that DeeDee's "self" is not merely a "monopoly commodity determined by society" (even if DeeDee found this acceptable) *since it is precisely that society that may have driven her to seek outside the West for the surgical procedures she needed to realize this self.* Moreover, it cannot be lost on DeeDee, any more than it is on Dr. Tulayaphanich who advertises Bangkok as the global capital of sex reassignment surgery and facial feminization, that going outside the United States might be part of what makes his practice attractive.[12] Going "out-

---

[12] A limited exception to this claim in the United States would include the practice of Marci L. Bowers, M.D., Trinidad, Colorado: <http://marcibowers.com/grs/gender.html>.

side" may contribute to its feeling safe, and hence to what's of paramount importance, "getting it right": "[t]he few people I have shown, transsexual and non-transsexual have said it is the best they have seen in person or on the Internet," writes DeeDee of the Thailand service.

It is, then, doubly ironic that Dr. Tulayaphanich's practice itself depends on the maintenance of both gender role and compulsory heterosexuality to provide the models on the basis of which sex-reassignment can be sculpted; gender to provide the femininity or masculinity transcribed onto the body's features, heterosexuality to instantiate fully the conviction that one was born into the "wrong" body that must be "fixed" by realizing its *opposite*. Heterosexuality can thus be divorced from sexual preference since it's neither preference nor desire that defines being in the "wrong" body but rather deeply held conviction. Hence DeeDee might identify as straight or gay with respect to sexual desire; she might desire the same others with respect to sexual interaction post-reassignment, and she might define those others in light of her "new" bodily configuration; or she could comprehend her "new" body as an opportunity for an alternative adventure. The point is that there's nothing here that determines sexual desire other than the post-operative transsexual's interests—and they may be identical to the preoperative transsexual's interests—or not. And it's only if DeeDee identifies as gay/lesbian that she becomes the target of legislation like SB 1250.

We come, then, full circle back to SB 1250 in that, however, rocky a marriage, the union between the culture industry and the rise of fundamentalist strains of Christianity make for albeit wary but undeniably promising bed-fellows. Dr. Tulayaphanich's practice depends just as much on the rigidity of gender roles and our desire to fulfill them as does the Christian Right; that he can turn this desire into a profitable business is not in the end different than, for example, a wedding industry marketed to "traditionally minded" couples. It's ironic, but not inconsistent with this observation that were it not for the primarily religious censure experienced by transsexuals in the United States, practices like those found in Thailand would not likely be thriving. This observation is, however, an old one found in Karl Marx's argument that religion can advantage the capitalist in that, because religion stands to the ready in the supply of hard-working, but otherwise complacent labor looking to purge sin and earn heaven-bound reward, it's highly useful to the maintenance of those institutions which guarantee this supply. Compulsory heterosexuality is just such an institution, and it in turn subserves the reproduction of that optimal unit of labor called the (nuclear) family. It's at just this juncture, then, that the example of transsexuality would seem to pose a real danger to the status quo.

The thing is, however, is that as we have now seen, it doesn't. Not really. So perhaps a central question raised by these observations for contemporary feminists is this: given the relatively insignificant threat posed by transsexuals, gays, lesbians, and other "gender outlaws" to the marriage of capitalism and religion, what's driving the colossal and often violence-inducing rise in religious fanaticism not only among Christians, but among Muslims and Jews? Why are "gender outlaws" the target (other than their vulnerable convenience)? Why scapegoat those who present no real danger? What ideological motives are promoted through this fabrication of an enemy? Is it as simple as a "turf war" over who gets to define "human being"? Of course not, but that this prerogative should form one crucial element of contemporary forms of religious fundamentalism certainly raises a vital question for *any* emancipatory movement: whose vision of the "livable world" includes Wilchins? DeeDee? Whose "fantastic dream of immortality and control over life and death" of the technoscientific future will prevail? Who gets to *be* the postmodern human being?

Chapter III

Reproductive Technology and the Global Exploitation of Women's Sexuality

CHARTING A FEMINIST RESPONSE TO THE FUTURE OF REPRODUCTIVE TECHNOLOGY

In light of feminist analyses of the politics and economics of gender, sexuality, and sexual identity, it's hardly surprising that technologies appearing to offer women greater control over their fertility would be applauded as liberating; and indeed in many ways they are. More recent feminist critique, however, raises a number of issues concerning not only whether the pill, for example, is as liberating for women as it is for their male partners, but whether the price of this liberation in increased vulnerability to cancer and other forms of disease is worth it. Others query whether locating the responsibility for contraception solely within the domain of the private, allegedly autonomous decision making of the individual provides an adequate picture of the conditions under which women choose and use birth control. And few—feminist or otherwise—would deny that access (or the lack thereof) to abortion was one of the most morally and politically divisive issues of the twentieth century, at least in the United States.

Control over the conditions of childbirth, however, represents only one aspect—albeit a vital one—of feminist responses to the burgeoning array of reproductive technologies beyond the pill, the intrauterine device (IUD), or sterilization. With the advent of technologies whose aims are not contraception but conception, especially in vitro fertilization (IVF), a daunting array of new political, moral, philosophical, and environmental questions have become the focus of sophisticated analyses, particularly by feminists critical of the liberal tradition in philosophy. As Kathryn Russell remarks in her 1994 "A Value-Theoretic Approach to Childbirth and Reproductive Engineering," "[i]n advanced capitalist societies today, reproduction is undergoing revolutionary change. Heated social debates echo new relations among people as we engage in practices that bring childbirth more and more under human control. Industry, hospitals, lawyers, insurance companies, social services, and a burgeoning cadre of professionals are increasingly involved in the central relation between a birth mother and her child" (328). Theorists such as Donna Haraway and Irene Diamond, and feminist bioethicists such as Susan Wolf, Rosemarie Tong, Helen Bequart Holmes, Debora Diniz, Ana Christina Gonzalez Velez, and Susan Sherwin have begun to explore the implications of these revolutionary technologies in light of a number of aspects which, as Wolf shows, have been largely ignored in the traditional, male-dominated bioethics literature.[1]

In her essay "Erasing Difference: Race, Ethnicity, and Gender in Bioethics," Wolf documents the extent to which, although "born of outrage at scandals in which [racial, ethnic, or gender] difference figured large ... bioethics has until recently ignored the significance of these differences" (1999: 65). Bioethics, she writes,

> has emphasized that Tuskegee[2] teaches the need for disclosure and consent, with less analysis of the detailed workings of racism in research. The field has similarly construed the Nazi physician's experimentation on concentration camp victims as a case of human subjects abuse, with less focus on how that experimentation functioned as a part of the attempted extermination of an ethnic and religious group. Bioethics has too often

---

[1] See, in particular, in addition to Wolf, Sherwin (2000a, 2000b), Diniz and Velez (2000), Holmes (1999), Diamond (1994), and the various sources by Haraway.

[2] For more information on the Tuskegee experiments, see Borgna Brunner, "The Tuskegee Syphilis Experiment," <http://www.tuskegee.edu/Global/Story.asp?s=1207586>.

recast these and other events as problems between generic subjects or patients and generic doctors.... Even when the racism, ethnocentrism, and sexism haunting key events have been acknowledged, they have usually been treated as a layer of extra insult added onto the more fundamental harm. (65)

Wolf goes on to trace a history of medical practice, research, and in some cases grotesque abuse, saturated by racist and sexist assumptions which, she argues, are not adequately remedied by calls for equality of treatment, but which demand more thorough going analyses of medicine as an institution itself that is dominated—like other Western institutions—by the prerogatives of primarily white Christian males (67–71). To treat racism and sexism merely as an "extra layer of insult" is, from this perspective, to effectively participate in the reproduction of the assumptions that perpetuate injustice within medicine, most importantly that of the generic patient whose allegedly raceless and sexless status as a medical subject conceals the role that underlying stereotype plays in the diagnosis of disease, appraisal of pain, consideration of circumstances, or respect for patient autonomy (66–67).

Further complicating the role that race, ethnicity, sex, and sexual identity play in health care—but only recently garnering serious attention in the bioethics literature—is the extent to which economic status determines access. Wolf notes that "the individualistic patient-by-patient way in which bioethics has applied principles such as autonomy and beneficence has obscured patterns of stereotyping and prejudice that are *themselves* ethical problems" (1999: 70; my emphasis). Indeed, but I suggest that an exclusive focus on these factors fails to tell the whole story, even when we include factors like "poor" in our descriptions of those whose health care is consistently inferior. No doubt, poverty often accompanies the race and/or sex of particular patients, but not always, and to assume that it does is to treat it like the "extra layer of insult" that merely reproduces stereotype. Among the more than 48 million Americans without access to health care, an increasing number are white and/or male. Insofar, then, as discussions of truth telling, confidentiality, and informed consent make little sense outside the assumption that patients have access to health care, lack of access defines many US citizens as "different," and effectively precludes them—regardless of race, ethnicity, or sex—from counting as medical subjects at all.

What this complex brew of factors makes clear is the need for more discerning analyses not only of health care as an increasingly profit-driven enterprise that defines its "generic" subject in terms of economic access, but also of who counts as patient, research subject, or exclusion. Consider, for example, a transsexual aspiring to the completion of her/his transition via sex-reassignment surgery. Since such a procedure is excluded from virtually all health-insurance policies and programs, she/he is effectively defined not only as different, but as a non-patient at least with respect to a particular medical procedure. And this is not because such procedures are excessively risky (heart bypass surgery, for example, is risky, but often covered), but because the surgery itself is defined as "elective," that is, unnecessary to maintaining the health of the (non-)patient, or "merely" cosmetic. The transsexual can, of course, pay out of pocket for the surgery and accompanying therapies (hormonal, behavioral, etc.), but this assumes that the transsexual's objectives are not as important as other procedures covered by insurance, and that the economic status of members of this group bears no relevance to the significance of their medical needs.

Feminist bioethicists have responded to the fact that groups under-represented in the health-care system are not composed of the same people—that they are defined in fact by difference—in a number of important ways. Dorothy Roberts's essay, "Reconstructing the Patient: Starting with Women of Color" (1996), for example, centralizes the experience of women, and particularly poor women, of color. Roberts argues that poor women of color whose health care is accessed via public settings such as clinics are often subject to special problems, particularly with respect to the observation and advocacy of central bioethics tenets, namely, confidentiality, truth telling, and respect for patient autonomy. Roberts demonstrates this claim by showing that when women are suspected of drug use during pregnancy, they are rarely afforded access to confidentiality with respect to their medical information. Many, but especially women of color, are also often not told about the option to abort a pregnancy, and the failure to respect women's refusals of cesarean sections is, argues Roberts, well established (1996: 116–19). Raced, sexed, and economically disempowered, difference does not merely define the relationship between doctors and their patients; it determines the conditions under which patients are understood *as* patients, that is, as embodied, medically relevant (or irrelevant) subjects.

Notice, too, that in Roberts's account the treatment of poor African American women corresponds directly to their capacity for sexual reproduction. This is hardly surprising in light of a history rooted in the marketing and control of women's sexuality (including sexual slavery, forced sterilization, and pregnancy resulting from rape), but it does raise serious questions about how difference affects and is affected by newer, more expensive, and more sophisticated reproductive technologies such as IVF. How, for example, should we evaluate the conscription of IVF for the outsourcing of surrogacy to nations in the developing world? Can approaches like Wolf's adequately capture the racial, sexual, and economic aspects of baby making made possible via the export of IVF to nations such as India? IVF offers an avenue for exploring what I consider some of the thorniest issues for feminist bioethicists, precisely because it raises questions about the use of reproductive technologies beyond contraception or even abortion, questions that intersect with women's sexual identities and social status, the marketability of their capacity for reproduction, and their access to health care well beyond the private sphere of pregnancy and delivery, parents and infants. Consider, for example,

(1) the specific kind of labor and time-intensive work undertaken by women and women's bodies in the voluntary conception, gestation, and delivery of offspring, and

(2) the fact that the specific reproductive labor facilitated through IVF is made possible only through an expensive and generally uninsured advanced technology mediated by experts via

(3) national and international agencies that contract as for-profit businesses with aspiring "parents," who themselves are in a position to pay substantial fees for such a service,

and "difference" takes on a whole new dimension: women typically targeted for derision by virtue of their allegedly uncontrolled reproduction are now solicited as the ideal candidates for surrogate "parenthood," and for largely the same reasons—because they are vulnerable, by virtue of sex, race, social status, or poverty, to perform work they would probably not choose otherwise.

Not altogether unlike the reasons why some women choose prostitution, the surrogate's rationale may have very little to do with wanting to help another woman become a mother—indeed, as we'll see, she may never see as much as a photograph of this other woman—and much more to do with factors directly or indirectly connected to her social and economic status. Consider a recent example from an Associated Press news item written by Sam Dolnick, "Pregnancy Outsourced to India: Infertile Couples Look Overseas for Surrogacy":

> Anand, India—Every night in this quiet western India city, 15 pregnant women prepare for sleep in their spacious house they share, ascending the stairs in a procession of ballooned bellies, to bedrooms that become a landscape of soft hills. A team of maids, cooks, and doctors look after the women whose pregnancies would be unusual anywhere else but are common here. The young mothers of Anand, a place famous for its milk, are pregnant with the children of infertile couples from around the world. The small clinic at Kaival Hospital matches infertile couples with local women, cares for the women during pregnancy and delivery, and counsels them afterward. Anand's surrogate mothers, pioneers in the field of outsourced pregnancies, have given birth to roughly 40 babies. (2008: 5)[3]

It's certainly tempting to read the article—complete with photograph of the smiling fertility clinic coordinator, Dr. Nayna Patel; the happy couple, Asian Americans Karen and Thomas Kim, who make their home in California; and their cheery-looking newborn, Brady —as a kind of "everyone wins" story of what IVF can make possible. Indeed, the description of "spacious houses" and "bedrooms that become landscapes of soft hills" and the depiction of surrogate mothers as "pioneers" evoke an image of a kind of resort for these surrogate "mothers."

As we read further, however, a number of interrelated questions begin to take shape. Ought, for instance, corporations whose locus of production involves women's reproductive capacities be understood in the same way as other corporations with respect to their moral

---

[3] All subsequent references to Dolnick relate to this article.

responsibilities to their workers? Are surrogate workers like other workers—despite the fact that the site of production is the womb? What about the consumers of IVF-facilitated reproductive services? What are they buying? A service? If so, whose? The surrogate's? The agency's? To whom, in other words, are the consumer-"parents" responsible? Are they buying a baby or adopting one? Can the latter make any sense when the baby is the couple's genetic offspring? Is the baby a product? Does the global nature of the transaction or the portability of the technology alter the use of IVF in any important way? Should we think of reproductive technologies in the same way we think of other technologies, for example, the robotics of automotive manufacture or the cash register at the grocery outlet? Where does the outsourcing of surrogacy fit into the globalized "free" market?

Perhaps the most important question, however, is this: Why are couples from wealthy countries such as the United States or Great Britain contracting with agencies from developing countries such as India to secure a surrogate to make babies? A panoply of related questions follows from it, highlighting the extent to which outsourced surrogacy offers a metaphor for the complex relationships between so-called first-world women and developing-world women— especially around issues of reproduction and basic human rights with respect to the disposition of one's body. For example, does the possibility that the surrogate and the contracting couple are likely never to meet each other deflate the notion that surrogacy is typically done out of a desire to help a couple become parents? In what sense, if any, is the outsourcing of baby making consistent with motherhood? In what sense (if any), in other words, is the surrogate a mother? How should we think about technologies whose bearing on human life, desire, and decision making is so intimate, when the context of their use is mediated primarily by market forces, across international borders, under circumstances that have about as little to do with the feelings associated with sex, parenthood, or love as paying taxes? Dolnick reports that "[m]ore than 50 women in this city [Anand] are now pregnant with the children of couples from the United States, Taiwan, Britain, and beyond. The women earn more than many would make in 15 years." But what is the relevance of this economic fact? What role, in other words, does economic vulnerability play in the choice to become a surrogate mother?

Dolnick points out that Patel's surrogacy program in India "raises a host of uncomfortable questions that touch on morals and modern science, exploitation and globalization, and that most natural of desires: to have a family." Yet even the language of the report betrays an important assumption, namely, that the desire to have genetically related offspring is a natural one and not socially constructed. But is it? Cultural taboos that prohibit carrying the offspring of others as a violation of the sanctity of the marital union are clearly capable of being suspended where it is desirable—and it turns out, profitable—to do so. Indeed, the technology itself ameliorates any sense of violation by removing sexuality or sexual interaction from its marketing as a resource for income. But if sexual reproduction can be reinvented as the (antiseptic) marketing of a service whose production site just "happens" to be a woman's body, then can the notion that the desire to have a baby is a natural one really remain immune to the dynamics that remove the desire from the actual "manufacture"? Is it "natural" to "desire" the production of a baby via IVF?

Surrogate mothers are not, of course, merely incubators. Twenty-six-year-old Suman Dodia, a surrogate mother in Patel's program, already has three children for whom she's going to buy a house with the $4,500 she earns carrying the child of a British couple. However, her remarks about the process of surrogate motherhood are telling. Dodia points out that her "own" children were delivered at home without the benefit of modern medicine: "'It's very different with medicine,' Dodia said... 'I'm being more careful now *than I was with my own pregnancy*'" (Dolnick 2008; my emphasis). Does Dodia's word choice imply that *someone else's pregnancy* can take place in her body? How does the use of IVF encourage such dissociation? What role does the context play—the fact that it's globalized, that Dodia does not know the genetic parents, that her compensation is monetary, that the alternative is poverty for herself and her children—in her self-conception as a surrogate?

Arguably, this self-conception is aimed at preserving the "sanctity" of marriage (for both the surrogate and the contracting couple) by divorcing sex from reproduction, surely a safer view than one that retains any thread of connection between sexuality and pregnancy, especially for the surrogate. But if this is true, the surrogate may be best considered simply as a part of the reproductive technology, and thus as property of the servicing agency. After all, she is in effect simply the machinery through which the product is produced; that both machinery and product are living beings is irrelevant to the substance of the transaction, since a failure to meet the conditions of the contract is likely attended by consequences identical to the failure of any contract—however much more seriously they are felt by the surrogate. Yet Patel strives to maintain her program's human face. Many, if not most, of the surrogate mothers in the program are married and "receive their children and husbands as visitors during the day when they're not busy with English or computer classes," and Patel insists that "she only accepts couples with serious fertility issues like survivors of uterine cancer." But does this apparent compassion indemnify Patel's agency as a money-making enterprise against some of the criticism it receives? Or is the appeal to the cancer survivor an advertising strategy? Or a veneer painted over the fact that outsourcing is significantly less expensive than contracting surrogates in the wealthy West? "Critics say," continues Dolnick in his article, that "the couples are exploiting poor women in India—a country with an alarmingly high maternal death rate—by hiring them at cut-rate cost to undergo the hardship, pain and risks of labor." But does this assessment offer a complete picture?

Although not exclusive to the global context of this enterprise, the economic and social status of women like Dodia is surely a factor in evaluating agencies like Patel's. The major risks, after all, are borne almost exclusively by the most vulnerable of the developing world's women, women who face possible death having their own offspring yet—and precisely because they are too poor to afford their own healthcare—are in a position to receive top-shelf care so long as "their" baby is born for someone else. One critic, John Lantos, of the Center for Practical Bioethics in Kansas City, Missouri, refers to operations like Patel's as "baby farms" and points out that "[i]t comes down to questions of voluntariness and risk" (cited in Dolnick 2008), that is, whether agreeing to become a surrogate is really voluntary and whether the surrogate mother is in a position to understand the risk she may be taking. Patel, however, adamantly denies that the relationship between the contracting couple and the contracted surrogate is exploitive. Indeed, she captures this relationship not only in terms with which many of us can readily identify, but also in a way that highlights the emotional volatility of the issues:

"[t]here is this one woman who desperately needs a baby and cannot have her own child without the help of a surrogate. And at the other end there is this woman who badly wants to help her [own] family.... if this female wants to help the other one... why not allow that? It's not for any bad cause. They're helping one another to have a new life in this world." (Dolnick 2008)

The article goes on to give an example of a desperate Los Angeles couple, "emotionally and financially exhausted," who turned to Patel. For $20,000—a far cry short of the $280,000 the couple had already spent—they "are now back home with their four month old baby, Neel." The couple remarks that "Even if it cost $1 million, the joy that they had delivered to me [the mother] is so much more than any money that I have given them.... they're godsends to deliver something so special."

But who exactly is "they"? Patel's agency? The combination of the agency, the inseminating doctors, the surrogates? Because each of the relevant relationships is technologically mediated via IVF, the language to which one would typically appeal to define mothers, fathers, bodies, babies, and contracts is ambiguous—particularly across the kinds of cultural and economic divides represented in stories like that of Patel's agency. No doubt, feminist work in bioethics like Wolf's offers an invaluable ally in coming to understand what is at work and what is at stake with respect to race and sex in practices like the global outsourcing of baby making. I suggest, however, that the high-tech commodification epitomized by the use of IVF in this context demands an analysis that is sensitive not only to the potential alienation produced by the divorce of sexual embodiment from conception, surrogate mothers from infants, and contracting mothers from the experience of pregnancy and delivery, but also to the more pervasive role played by reproductive technology in altering the very way in which we imagine bodies, mothers, fathers, and babies—especially given the lucrative ventures it makes possible. The outsourcing of baby making is not, in other words, just about the practical consequences—however important—of surrogacy for vulnerable women in the developing world; like the political wars over who can marry, or what constitutes sexual identity, it's about what/ who gets to count as a fully human being.

THE "GLOBAL FETUS": REPRODUCTIVE TECHNOLOGY AND THE FEMINIST ANALYSIS OF ALIENATED LABOR

Anticipating the extent to which "capital has pushed itself into what was once thought to be one of the most intimate—even sacred—of human activities: conception, gestation, and birth," Kathryn Russell argued in 1994 that reproductive technologies like IVF were ripe for appropriation, transforming childbearing into a "new" form of exploitable labor (329). Contrary to liberal pronouncements touting the emancipatory potential of a technology that can help to produce a genetically related child without the involvement of the genetic mother's womb, Russell argues that what might be experienced as a godsend for some depends upon conditions of alienated labor for others, that is, labor estranged from the conditions that lend it meaning and value. Though surely this is not the first time the perceived freedom of some women (in this case to have their "own" babies) has been secured through the exploitation of others, the conditions under which childbirth is transformed into a variety of wage labor, argues Russell, may be particularly dehumanizing:

> The commodification of childbearing represents a further loss of women's control over birth as well as over other aspects of their lives.... Contrary to the American Fertility Society and its allies, selling body parts and procreative labor power will not free women, just as liberal contract law will not protect people from exploitation. The subsumption of childbearing labor into capitalist market relations represents an extreme example of dehumanization and alienation, and it may be laying the groundwork for new forms of exploitation. (1997 [1994]: 342)

Although the appropriation of women's procreative labor is no less "new" than the selling of body parts—and both are geared toward the production of labor power—its marketable value is forever altered at the moment conception is divorced from gestation.

Effectively producing two "new" products—the fertilized, portable ovum and the surrogate incubator—the conditions of procreative labor are primed for conversion into wage labor, especially given allies like the American Fertility Society. As Russell makes clear:

> [i]n a sense, a process similar to deskilling is taking place in reproduction. These biological processes are being isolated and assigned to different people: the provision of gametes, fertilization and the acquisition of the embryo, implantation, and gestation and birth. All these can be separated from social parentage.... Individual women are to a great extent interchangeable; within certain medical parameters, one uterus or egg is as useful as another.... we see that reproductive engineers are engaging in productive consumptions, expending their labor power in uniting the raw material (egg and sperm) with a functioning uterus (means of production) to create a product. (335)

Russell's view hearkens back to Karl Marx, who argued that where the conditions of labor are controlled by interests that are not the laborer's, and where those interests, namely, the capitalist's, convert the value of labor into the wage, workers inevitably come to identify the value of labor not with a quality or creativity that reflects on themselves, but with the wage. The wage, moreover, comes itself to reflect the value of the labor *and* that of the worker, whose significance to the production process can be measured in terms of his or her replaceability or substitutability (Marx 1964: 109–14; Lee 2002: 25–29).

These dynamics, however, take on an especially oppressive character, as Chandra Mohanty makes clear, in the context of women's wage labor as it intersects with other axes of segregation in the developing world. Citing Maria Mies's 1982 study of lacemakers in Narsapur, India, Mohanty argues that caste plays a key role in the sexual domestication of Indian women, some of whom are destined to become agricultural labors and others—by virtue of their higher caste—are segregated to the task of lacemaking:

> The caste-based ideology of seclusion ... was essential to the extraction of surplus value [i.e., profits]. Since ... the seclusion of women is a sign of higher caste status, the domestication of Kapu laborer women where their [lacemaking] activity was tied to the concept of "women in the

house" was entirely within the logic of capital accumulation and profit....
Domestication works...because of the persistence and legitimacy of the
ideology of the housewife, which defines women in terms of their place
in the home, conjugal marriage, and heterosexuality. The opposition
between definitions of the "laborer" and of the "housewife" anchors the
invisibility (and caste-related status) of the work; in effect, it defines
women as nonworkers. (2003: 150)

Given the mutually reinforcing effects of sex and caste in the production of "women in the house," it is not surprising that among the first
to offer comparatively inexpensive "one-stop" surrogacy would be
agencies operating in India—and that among the first to take advantage of these would be couples from wealthy Western nations. Like
the lacemakers of Mies's study, the surrogate mothers in Patel's program in Anand (Dolnick 2008) are likely to be drawn from higher
castes, in part because such women are more likely to be seen as
healthy, but also because as housewives defined by sex *and* caste they
are ideally situated for a variety of labor that exploits their domestication. Just as the beneficiaries of the lacemaking, moreover, are not
the "housewives" who produce it, but rather their husbands who
"defined themselves as exporters and business men" (Mohanty 2003:
149), those who primarily benefit from the surrogate mother's labor
include the surrogate only marginally, with the lion's share of the surplus revenue going to the agency and its partners.

Russell argues that procreation is commodified when "[w]omen
are estranged from the product of their reproductive labor—ova,
fetal tissue, or infant—if it is taken over by others who decide who
will use it and how and when it will be used. They are alienated from
the process of reproductive labor when they have no control over the
course of their own pregnancy" (1997 [1994]: 342). Granted, but what
makes this "taking over" possible is a complex brew that includes not
only sex, or even sex combined with economic status, but culturally
established expectations defined in terms of caste, class, familial relations, health, and geographic location, among other factors. Control
is thus not merely appropriated, but manipulated through the exploitation of the implicit threat of destitution as it is defined within a specific set of cultural mores; such threats—however concealed and
nuanced—are institutionalized through agencies like Patel's via the

ideology of the "housewife," and mediated through an involved, compensated, set of other workers largely invisible to the surrogate mother. Russell argues that

> during in vitro fertilization or surrogacy the relationship among the different people involved is not direct. Parents, biological and social, are brought into contact by the activity of technicians, agency workers, and often lawyers. These services must be paid for. The social character of the activity of joining egg, sperm, uterus, surrogate mother, or future parents comes about through the introduction of money. (1997 [1994]: 336–37)

It is easy to see, given these dynamics, how women like Suman Dodia come to dissociate their surrogate pregnancies from themselves as women and as mothers, despite the fact that their bodies function as the central site of product manufacture. With reproduction converted from (ideally) a creative, sexual and intimately familial activity to a variety of wage labor, Dodia is likewise transformed from a birth mother into a replaceable incubatory extension of a culturally mediated industry, whose product is not first and foremost babies, but rather a specific set of patriarchal, cultural, and economic relationships that define the place of Indian men and women. Dodia, her fetus, and her labor, to put it simply, are the product of a culture industry.

Outsourced pregnancy can be described in Horkheimer and Adorno's (1972) terms as being located squarely within Western "free" market conceptions of the body as replaceable, manipulable, and disposable property. Seductively promoted to Indian women (and their husbands) as an avenue to economic advancement and elevated social status, surrogacy epitomizes Donna Haraway's discussion of the transformative effects of "technoscience" on the ways in which we comprehend bodies, the natural, the technological, and conditions of exchange. On this view, outsourced pregnancy alienates women (and men) from the processes of conception, gestation, and birth, and transforms the entire constellation of baby-making agents into a techno-organic machine or—a notion I introduced in the previous chapter—a cyborg:

> Cyborg figures—such as the end-of-the-millennium seed, chip, gene, data-base, bomb, fetus, race, brain, and ecosystem—are the offspring of

implosions of subjects and objects and of the natural and artificial. Perhaps cyborgs inhabit less the domains of "life," with its developmental and organic temporalities, than of "life itself," with its temporalities embedded in communications enhancement and system redesign. Life itself is life enterprised up, where, in the dyspeptic version of the technoscience soap opera, the species become the brand name and the figure becomes the price. (1997: 12)

The cyborg prefigures a notion of "life itself" no longer mediated exclusively through either organic processes or technologies like IVF, but through agencies of "communications enhancement" like Patel's.

For Patel, however, such enhancement is not represented as baby brokering—even less so as alienating for the parties involved—but as facilitating a relationship between women who (naturally) want to help each other. Or at least that is how her service advertises itself. As cited above, Patel sees no problem with "allowing" the parties in a surrogacy relationship to help each other "to have a new life in this world" (Dolnick 2008). Taken at face value, Patel's remarks seem to capture what many feminist care ethicists recommend as a model for moral decision making: the empathetic assistance an individual is willing to offer to another in the interest of preserving caring human relationships—of "enhancing communication." Feminist bioethicist Rosemarie Tong describes this approach: "An ethics of care is directly concerned neither with doing duty for duty's sake nor with maximizing the good of the aggregate; rather, it is focused on attending to the specific needs of particular individuals and on weaving thick webs of human relationships and responsibilities" (1999: 33).

The creation of "life itself" (to use Haraway's phrase) might be said to instantiate just such a web, "thickened" both by the empathy epitomized in women's desire to help one another, and by the technologies, technicians, and facilitators that make this particular web possible. From this point of view, it doesn't really matter whether the processes involved in realizing the essential relationships are organic or cybernetic. The surrogate and the contracting mother; the mother and her husband; the prospective parents and the facilitating agent; the agent, surrogate, and the necessary technicians; the technicians and the fertilized embryo; the embryo, the implanting technology, and the surrogate; the surrogate's husband and family; the family and the community—all can be said to participate in this moment of the web of "life itself." Technological assistance need not be experienced as alienating, but rather simply as a "redesign" of a long respected institution, namely, the family; and it's not really redesigned at all, but merely modified in the interest of fulfilling desires long associated with it.

The difficulty, as Russell would surely make plain, is that such a characterization belies the fact that no such relationships would be facilitated were it not for agents like Patel whose motives are, at least in the first place, hardly consistent with "weaving thick webs of human relationships," but are better described in light of Haraway's reference to "brand names" and "price." Patel's role is thus not properly described as one of "allowing," since it's highly unlikely that any of the participants, human or technological, would interact without the intervention of such an agent. Indeed, "Patel's center is believed to be unique in offering one-stop service. Other clinics may request that the couple bring in their own surrogate.... But in Anand the couple just provides the egg and sperm and the clinic does the rest, drawing from a waiting list of tested and ready surrogates" (Dolnick 2008). The entire price for Patel's unique one-stop service is also very competitive: "Most couples end up paying the clinic less than $10,000 for the entire procedure, including fertilization, the fee to the mother and medical expenses."

To the extent that the images of caring, voluntariness, and mutual concern solicited by Patel's description function to advertise her agency, they aid, as Haraway might put it, in the reenactment of the liberal "soap opera" wherein economic coercion, gender expectation, oppressive caste, and cultural mores are artfully concealed behind a rhetoric of free choices, free markets, and feminine empathy. Perhaps Patel really does see herself as empathetic, as helping women help other women. But the fact remains that, acting as vehicles of communicative exchange and troubleshooting moral spin, agencies like Patel's symbolize not only the (cross-)cultural industry of technologically created offspring, but also the extent to which the future of "life itself" departs from the past—however much the past remains necessary to justifying future relations of power. "One-stop" solicits empathy for the couple who have waited possibly years for "their" child, and who can now count on an efficient, successful process;

and it simultaneously captures the complete commodification of a process that, like shopping at a Walmart, capitalizes on the "cut-rate" labor made possible through the globalized job market. "The off-spring of these technoscientific wombs," writes Haraway "[literally and metaphorically] are cyborgs—imploded germinal entities, densely packed condensations of worlds, shocked into being from the force of the implosion of the natural and the artificial, nature and culture, subject and object, machine and organic body, money and lives, narrative and reality" (1997: 14).

Embodying an entire industry devoted to the cultural (re)production of relationships that maintain male bloodlines, capitalist control, and hierarchically organized social status, the offspring of the global surrogate epitomize the ultimate product: techno-humanity. Ironically, twenty-first-century entrepreneurs like Patel in some ways do realize the aspirations of feminists like Mohanty when the latter argues that her "most simple goal was to make clear that cross-cultural feminist work must be attentive to the micropolitics of context, subjectivity, and struggle, as well as to the macropolitics of global economic and political systems and processes" (2003: 223). Patel's one-stop business model is, after all, unlikely to be successful in many other contexts. It's her savvy understanding of the micro and macro politics of the Indian sex and caste system that "reveals how the particular is universally relevant" to turning a profit (223). Mohanty would, of course, reject such an interpretation of her call to avoid the Westernizing of the issues of women in the developing world—and she's right. The point, however, is that given the appropriation by agencies like Patel's of "technoscience" such as IVF, there are no unambiguous distinctions to be drawn between Western and non-Western cultures (Patel's adoptive parents in the story's case are, for example, Asian-American), reproductive technologies and embryos, gestational mothers and ova-contributors, the sites of exchange and the resultant product. "Ideologically powerful" images of helpful women, happy couples, and babies evoke a past rooted in the trusted institutions of the traditional patriarchal family, science, and medicine. Yet these same institutions are also "imploded" through the global marketing of "the" family (Haraway 1997: 174), their images hijacked to Internet sites advertising the fulfillment, legitimacy, and happiness that only a baby can make possible (Lee 2002: 36).

As Marx foresaw long ago in the *Communist Manifesto*, and as I expand on in my own analysis of the family, "the more vital or consequential an institution is to human experience, the more commodifiable it becomes" (Lee 2002: 34), and thus the more it can become an unwitting parody of itself, as I note in Chapter II (see pp. 22-23, above). Gestated by the developing world's surrogate "mother" whose motives are the survival of her own family, and contracted by the affluent Western couple seeking to establish theirs, this "global fetus" reproduces a techno-organic unit of consumption tailor-made for the replication of a "need" for "normalcy." Yet at the same time it remains essentially symbolic of the living and unspoiled. The "global fetus," argues Haraway, "provoke[s] *yearning* for the physical sensuousness of a wet and blue-green Earth and a soft, fleshy child" (1997: 174; my emphasis). Hence, the possibility of such a child is ironically fulfilled *and* displaced by the mechanics of IVF. Such images "signify the immediately natural and embodied over and against the constructed and disembodied" (Haraway 1997: 174), but they also cannot fail to signify how the constructed and disembodied make the embodied possible — at least for some.

If yearning implies the alienation from which we desire escape (or denial), it's hard to imagine what could more effectively symbolize it than the fetus who re-enchants our connection to the natural, the embodied, the sense of "ours." Woven into race, sex, culture — and our increasingly technological interface with the world — "the fetus functions as a kind of metonym, seed crystal, or icon for configuration of person, family, nation, origin, choice, life, and future" (Haraway 1997: 175). The fetus functions, in other words, as a conduit for future forms of human exchange across many axes of identity (and anxiety). Nonetheless, the yearning solicited by such images is as much a product of slick advertising as it is of any unambiguously "natural" sentiment; indeed, the increasingly nostalgic appeal to the "natural" just may be the most powerful advertising tool of the twenty-first century.

FEMINIST BIOETHICS AND THE APPEAL TO HUMAN RIGHTS

While socialist feminist analyses like Russell's, Mohanty's, Haraway's, and my own emphasize the extent to which we may be laying the technologically lubricated groundwork for future forms of exploitation along the very old rails of sex, race, and economic vulnerability, how we—as feminists—might respond to this challenge remains a subject of considerable debate. One avenue involves the recent attention paid to the concept of human rights by feminist bioethicists such as Rosemarie Tong, Anne Donchin, and K. Shanthi. Donchin, for example, defends a specifically feminist approach to human-rights discourse as a viable alternative to a care ethics whose "virtually exclusive emphasis on interpersonal relationships and its neglect of the political dimensions of social connection" offers little with which to address the institutionalized injustice epitomized in practices like the outsourcing of pregnancy to India (2004: 35). Moreover, despite feminist objections to the propensity of rights advocates to characterize their bearers as generic, thus failing to account for differences that can affect the exercise of a right, "rights talk has been integral to both academic bioethics and feminist activism for decades," many having appealed to it to argue for the right to be free from bigotry (Donchin 2004: 35). "[T]he value of rights," argues Donchin, "needs to be assessed not only from the privileged position of those who already have them but also from the position of those to whom they have been denied. Once human rights are understood as the moral rights of all people in all situations, the central issue is transformed from whether human rights claims should be included within moral discourse to how to identify and characterize them" (39).

It's hard to imagine anyone other than the most hard-boiled racist, sexist, or elitist raising serious objection to Donchin's equation of moral rights and human rights. The issue, as Donchin rightly points out, is "how to identify and characterize" these rights. This, however, is a truly daunting task in the case of contract pregnancy, given the experiential, embodied, and technological—as well as social, economic, and political—intimacy of the relevant relationships. To what (or to what combination) do rights attach in this case? What does autonomy of decision making mean in a context of such complex interrelationships? For feminist bioethicist Elisabeth Boetzkes, these questions are not answered adequately within human-rights discourse. She observes, for example, that

> if being autonomous for the pregnant woman means engaging in an
> ongoing dialectic among the experience of pregnant embodiment, an

examination of the cultural meaning of pregnancy and maternity, and the shaping of a personal and bodily perspective, then contractual restrictions actually preclude autonomous choice. The preconception contract binds a woman to a particular self-understanding, uninformed by the pregnancy she will undergo and compromised by the dominant... romanticized public images of maternity. (1999: 129)

Contract pregnancy, in other words, pits a right to the autonomy of how a pregnant women interprets her experience and its potential bearing on her decision making against a contract that precludes this experience if it conflicts with giving up the baby.

"Change of heart" clauses could be built into surrogacy contracts (Tong, cited in Boetzkes 1999: 129), making them more like adoptions. However, argues Boetzkes, it is doubtful whether such clauses would be seen as adequately empowering—especially to women already vulnerable to social and economic pressures:

Would the "change of heart" option be seen as a true option by the gestating woman? Within the practice of adoption, the legitimacy of the gestating mother's claim to her child is never in question. At the same time, the adopting couple is seen as relatively weak and certainly not as sufficient for a grievance against the birth mother.... Feelings around contract pregnancy, however, are quite different.... there is almost always a genetic connection to one or both social parents. This connection has been seen as strong enough to cast doubt on the claims of contract birth mothers. Second, the fact that there was an understanding prior to conception that the child would be handed over generates a moral expectation that is absent in the adoption case. These perceptions will be internalized by the contract mother, thus providing both internal and external pressure to forfeit the change of heart provision. (1999: 130)

Such pressures are no doubt exacerbated in the case of agencies like Patel's, due not only to geographical distance between surrogate and contract parents, or even language barriers, but due to the social (caste) and economic positions that define their relationship, locating them as prospective surrogates or as contract parents.

K. Shanthi makes a similar point in her essay "Feminist Bioethics and Reproductive Rights of Women in India." She argues that even where there exists a commitment to democratic institutions like the vote, government programs that promote reproductive freedom but focus primarily on population control, combined with a culture whose preference for sons encourages the abuse of technologies like ultrasound for sex selection, effectively ensure the continuation of conditions inconsistent with women's practicable autonomy. It is difficult, in fact, to fathom the freedom necessary to a change of heart where, "because the majority of Indian girls marry at a very young age, about 10%…become mothers before their skeletal and reproductive systems are fully developed, and 43% of all deaths of girls between the ages of fifteen and twenty are due to complications associated with pregnancy" (2004: 128). If anything, agencies like Patel's contribute to the erosion of women's autonomy under such conditions by exploiting the language of reproductive rights to ends that, because their effect is to reinforce the inferior status of women and girls, hardly instantiate it.

The facts are that 50 to 80 per cent of young Indian women suffer from anemia due to becoming mothers too early, and girls are systematically underfed and less well cared for than boys (Shanthi 2004: 128). Who then, we must ask, are appropriate surrogates for Patel's service? Are they in a position to enter a contract, one that concerns their body and has an impact upon their health? Even if they have undergone pregnancy before, is this a guarantee that they are in a position to comprehend its risks? What role does education about IVF play? Can consent to it be informed? If the exercise of a right presupposes knowledge about the risks and possible benefits of that exercise, what guarantees that women who would otherwise not have access to it have access in this case? The issue is that even if it makes sense to treat the surrogate as a rights-bearing agent distinct from the contracting couple, the IVF procedure, or the agency, it is not clear whether "rights-bearing" can gain any practical traction within a culture so deeply rooted in the preservation of its sexual, racial, and caste/class mores.

Given, then, the additional role that hunger and marginal health may play in decision making, both the rhetoric of "women helping women" and that of the exercise of a right to enter a contract seem better suited to the advertising and public relations of agencies like Patel's than they do as a representation of the surrogate mother's real

73

CONTEMPORARY FEMINIST THEORY AND ACTIVISM

desires. In any case, it's not obvious that the rhetoric of either care or rights is reflected in the reality of Indian women's lives, or that human-rights discourse, at least by itself, is adequately prepared to respond to the questions posed by the socialist feminist critique of alienation and exploitation. Nor is it merely a matter of reclaiming caring or respect for rights as substantive values, for given the intimate role played by the culture, the economic status, sex, race, and technology in the construction of the relevant agents, conceiving of them as fully autonomous, rationally calculative, self-interested agents makes little sense. It's also not a matter of becoming disentangled from or rejecting the technology, not just because such a monumental task could not be successful (or even clearly conceptualized), but because our self-conception is mediated by and through an array of technologies we take largely for granted as the users of everything from refrigerators to cell phones to automobiles. We may, as Haraway claims, really be most usefully conceived as cyborgs.

We are faced, then, with a dilemma. If the critique leveled by socialist feminists is correct, and if human rights discourse fails to offer an adequate way forward, where can we find direction? How ought we to respond to the reconstruction of the human body entailed by reproductive technologies like IVF? How can we prevent the appropriation of human-rights discourse as sales propaganda? These are crucial questions for feminists, not only because such technologies are unlikely to disappear from the global landscape, but also because there are good reasons why we should not want them to. "My own negotiation," remarks ecofeminist Irene Diamond, "through the world of baby-making... has impressed on me once again that there are no straightforward answers for individual women" (Diamond 1994: 112). What we need is a way to craft a coherent feminist response beyond the socialist critique, beyond a care ethic whose focus on empathetic relationships ignores institutionalized injustice, and beyond the limitations of a human-rights discourse focused too narrowly on the "individual." Is there such a way? I think so.

REPRODUCTIVE TECHNOLOGY: AN ALTERNATIVE STANDPOINT

Irene Diamond's *Fertile Ground: Women, Earth, and the Limits of Control* (1994) reflects an approach to technology common to ecologically oriented feminist discourse (ecofeminism or ecological feminism): exploited by "free" market capitalism, technological innovation results in the alienation of human beings from nature, from other human and nonhuman beings, and—particularly in the case of technologies that directly involve the body—from the self. However much heralded by some feminists as an avenue of choice and control over fertility, the extent to which reproductive technologies are implicated in the patriarchal commodification of women's bodies is the primary focus of feminist criticism, and, as we have seen, for some very good reasons. "[N]ew reproductive technologies and genetic engineering," argues Diamond, "are themselves fully implicated in the stability of industrial practices.... Today, women's birthing bodies are reconfigured in gynecologists' offices and hospital wards, every facet of procreation commodified and monitored in the name of health and choice" (92).

Diamond argues that because reproductive technologies are implicated in the alienation of women from the natural processes and experience of menstruation, pregnancy, and birth, they cannot deliver on their promise of improving reproduction:

> [t]he contemporary technical mastery of biological fertility, which the dominant culture promotes as a blessing and relief from the unwieldy sorrow and turmoil of the uncertainties of life, is the final point of instrumental thinking and economic logic. For when fertility is taken over by the specialist, isolated from the cyclical processes of the "natural world," patented and commodified, the cultural tissues that sustain life's vibrancy and joy are mutilated and destroyed. (56)

It is significant that Diamond equates "instrumental thinking" with "economic logic," that is, technology and its capitalist appropriation. It is also significant that, although she frames it in quotation marks, Diamond positions the "natural world" as that from which women are "isolated," that is, alienated in the quest—appropriated now by medical experts and their technological tools—for the "perfect" baby. Diamond's apparent presuppositions, however, raise some difficult questions: Must technology inevitably be "implicated in the stability of industrial practices"? Are the sciences, their technological applications, and their capitalist markets inescapably connected?

Must technological advance necessarily occur in opposition to nature? If so (and if we can make sense of it), is this always bad? Is "instrumental thinking" necessarily implicated in capitalist exploitation? Is it always alienating?

The answers to these important questions are not as obvious as arguments such as Diamond's make them out to be. As Haraway shows, the equation of "instrumental thinking" and "economic logic" may raise some important questions about the specific ends to which we put "technoscience." Aren't, for example, "the cultural tissues that sustain life's vibrancy and joy" some of the same tissues that support oppressive patriarchal structures, themselves sustained by the "economic logic" that Diamond rejects? Is technological mastery necessarily a precondition for patriarchal domination? Don't some technologies actually contribute to sustaining human life? What about those involved in climate modeling, pollution reduction, wilderness restoration, water filtration, and emissions control? Admittedly, these technologies are a response to the environmental destruction produced by industrial excesses, but this doesn't diminish their value to human and nonhuman life. But, and ironically, Diamond's own tendency to universalize "technology," "science," and "industrial practice" is itself potentially implicated in the tendency to see the world in the predominantly Western terms associated with this destruction. The point, of course, is that given the extent to which technology, both "high" and "low," is woven into the very fabric of human life, it's not clear whether we can make any sense of what a rejection of it would mean. Whose return to nature, after all, would this be? Who is in a position to find this attractive, or insist that such a return embodies what we ought to do?

I don't think these issues can be adequately sorted either by opposing nature to technology, or by merely identifying the latter with its capitalist appropriation. Consider IVF: in its simplest form, it offers a technological intervention on behalf of facilitating an otherwise "natural" process without which the latter would not likely be possible in a particular case. But, as Haraway shows, where the "natural" leaves off and the technology intervenes is not obvious. Is it in the tools used to extract ova? The process of fertilization? The process of implantation? The soap with which the physician washes her/his hands? The fertility clinic? The vitamins taken by the surrogate? Every aspect of IVF is technologically mediated, but not more so than the process for people who conceive in the "ordinary" way. We wear industrially manufactured perfumes to be attractive; we drive cars to facilitate a date; we buy "sex toys" to enhance sexual activity; we have sex on beds, kitchen tables, against walls. These are *all* technologies, but we're just so accustomed to their presence that we don't think of them in that way. IVF is not more technological than is perfume production, and it's no more patriarchally oriented either; perfumes are overwhelmingly aimed at a female market cast as in need of disguising female scent (whatever that is). It seems, then, that we're "cherry-picking," that is, we're picking out one variety of technological mediation, IVF, and subjecting it to critical interrogation—all the while ignoring the myriad other ways in which technology mediates everything from the most quotidian of chores to the most sophisticated of scientific production, much of which involves the human body in equally intimate ways (consider kidney dialysis, or prosthetic limbs, for example). But unless we can give good reasons for singling out IVF from other technologies that may be involved in baby making, it seems groundless to treat it as alienating *per se*. Are there such reasons?

One possibility is that couples who resort to IVF are going out of their way to have their own genetic offspring, and this is certainly true. But "going out of their way" isn't about what technologies facilitate their desires; it's about their commitment to fulfill them. In other words, while IVF makes a certain kind of "going out of their way" possible, its use demonstrates the value that a couple ascribes to the desire to have their own genetic offspring. Hence, the proper focus of critique is not the technology, but a desire that can, for example, rationalize the outsourcing of pregnancy to a nation whose maternal and infant mortality rate is as high as India's. Slavery is alienating, exploitive, and slavers go out of their way to acquire slaves; it also involves a battery of technologies. But we would be quite reluctant, I think, to blame the ships, chains, harnesses, and weights for the injustice of this institution; we go, and rightly, to the slavers and to all those who benefit from their human trade. Few doubt that technologies like ships, weights, chains, and harnesses may have morally defensible—even very good—uses. Hence it seems that just because we might go out of our way to avail ourselves of their use is not in itself a reason to single them out as alienating.

Another response is that certain technologies are just more alienating in their use than others, for example, those that involve the body intimately. IVF certainly does so, and hence it may be especially alienating. But, as Diamond's own account of technologically mediated baby making shows, the specific situations in which real people find themselves make this alienation far from apparent:

> But after I miscarried and became pregnant again, I was six months older [than forty-one] and found it more difficult to dismiss the numbers that seemed to be stacked against me.... I was beginning to struggle with these new thoughts [concerning the potential for having a special-needs child], when the doctor asked again about amnio[centesis]. By this time we had our prepared response, but the doctor's paternal advice about what *his* wife would do, in the midst of my own doubts, left me emotionally vulnerable and confused. The tests now seemed reassuring if not necessary. Yet how could I live with myself given my condemnation of the system? I finally decided I could go ahead because my criticisms concerned the routinization of screening, not the technology *per se*. The "system" wouldn't sustain itself if it had only the business of women my age. (1994: 109)

What makes Diamond's situation radically different from that of the women of Patel's clinic is not whether amniocentesis is merely routine screening; after all, it is a technology, it can be exploited to ill-conceived or morally suspect ends, and it can certainly be imposed as part of a contract coerced via economic destitution. Amniocentesis is not routine in all cases, and even where it might be (say at Patel's clinic), it might still be experienced as alienating, exploitive, coerced, and painful. Moreover, that Diamond's social status and economic position is substantially different from the conditions confronted by the Indian surrogate's is less about the technology and more about the conditions under which it is utilized. "The system" cannot sustain itself without the "business" of younger women, but this should alert us to the fact that Diamond's conditions are not typical. After all, Diamond is older and occupies a far more empowered position than many younger women, Indian and otherwise. She rationalizes opting for amniocentesis as "routine" because she's condemned "the system" and wants to avoid hypocrisy. But it's only because she fails to distinguish the technology from its alienating potential under certain conditions, namely, the capitalist exploitation she largely ignores, that she's forced into this position. Similar to the "going out of one's way" objection, just because amniocentesis can be experienced as "routine" doesn't make it less technological, just more accessible. Diamond's reasoning is inconsistent; she can't hold that technology necessarily alienates us from nature, others, or ourselves *and* that amniocentesis is "reassuring."

Fortunately, Diamond's inconsistency is resolvable in that we have very good reasons for distinguishing the critique of the uses to which technologies like IVF are put and the technologies themselves. And, as I'll show, this is true even though drawing distinctions between technology and its users cannot be made precise. A benefit, however, of drawing this distinction is that it encourages us to examine use in particular contexts, and thus avoids, as Mohanty advocates, the universalizing of women's experience as if that of some Western women's reflected all women's (Mohanty 2003: 1–42; 222–24). After all, those who can afford solar panels, hay-bale houses, hybrid SUVs, and microbiotic diets are not bucketing water from a Ganges threatened by global warming. Whether we're referring to the high-tech of the hybrid SUV or the low-tech of a water-bucket, achieving lower carbon emissions or relieving thirst, what defines our relationship to technology in the first place is not whether it alienates us from nature, others, or ourselves; were this true, alienation would constitute an existential condition rendering any discourse devoted to technology's defensible uses moot. The issue is its use in accomplishing human objectives in particular contexts. I don't doubt that Diamond would agree that context matters; what she misses is the extent to which context is defined not by the technology itself, but by our relationship to it, and by the extent to which that relationship is itself not merely permeated by technological artifacts, but controlled by institutions that regulate our access to it (as well as our conception and understanding of it).

Peter-Paul Verbeek offers useful insight concerning this relationship in *What Things Do: Philosophical Reflections on Technology, Agency, and Design* (2005). Appealing to fellow theorist Don Ihde, Verbeek argues that there are three different ways in which human beings can relate to technological artifacts. In the first, our perception is mediated by the technological artifact. In such a *relation of mediation* we are not directly related to the world but only are so via an artifact—as for instance whenever we wear glasses or watch television. A second kind of relation, which Ihde calls an *alterity relation*, is a relation not via an artifact to the world but to an artifact itself, as for instance when operating a machine. The third kind of human-technology relation Ihde calls a *background relation*, in which technological artifacts shape our relation but do so by remaining in the background, as do thermostats that automatically switch the heat on and off without our intervention or even awareness. (123)

Like Haraway, Verbeek resists the temptation to characterize our relationship to technology in one-size-fits-all terms, offering instead a more nuanced account that can accommodate for alienation without simply presupposing that the role played by exchange necessarily determines every aspect of that relationship. I, for example, did pay for my current pair of glasses, but the impact of this fact is more than compensated for by the gain I experience in wearing them. Because they mediate my perceptual experience by correcting my vision, I am arguably less perceptually alienated from the world, and in any case, my relationship to this particular technology clearly depends on other aspects of my experience, perceptual or otherwise: for example, that I have access to an optometrist, that I am virtually disabled without corrective lenses, that I have a job that lends itself to eye stress, that I have insurance, and so on.

The important point is that we can articulate, as Verbeek does, aspects of our relationship to technology not (at least solely) tethered to its use in just one context (capitalist labor and/or consumption), or even in just one mode (mediating perception, instrumentally, or regulating a feature of the background). Ihde's distinctions open a door to conceiving technology in light of the specific circumstances of our experience. This is not to say that capitalist values don't permeate every context (I paid for my glasses); they do. Rather, it's to suggest an approach to our relationship to technology that aims to account for how it mediates our experience in light of the many axes which inform the context(s) in which it mediates perception, presents itself as an "other" (an alterity), or structures a background. Such an approach should be highly attractive to feminists who take seriously how these axes interact with technology in its particular uses. We do not then have a relationship to technology, but rather multivalent relationships depending upon what place(s) it occupies in the lives of individuals, families, or communities under specific conditions, some of which may be oppressive — but others potentially liberating.

How, then, might we consider technologies like IVF, given the different ways in which we may experience it? Verbeek offers a clue in his discussion of alterity relations: "Technology appears in alterity relations as quasi-other because while we may encounter technologies in ways in which they seem to behave as 'other,' they can, of course, never be present as a true person.... The reason that technologies in alterity relations are experienced as quasi-others is that on the one hand they possess a kind of independence and on the other hand they can give rise to an 'interaction' between humans and technologies" (2005: 127). Technology, in other words, presents itself to us as *not* us (my corrective lenses are not my eyes), yet our relationship to it is interactive (my lenses improve my vision; in fact, I can't fathom the world without them). Such relationships can be very intimate; I need my glasses and am reminded of their "otherness" (and my own vulnerability) the moment I cannot locate them. They can be mediating (correcting my capacity for visual perception) and quite "other" simultaneously (it's frustrating to have to depend on them). They are not "true persons," but I can *anthropomorphize* them, that is, I can ascribe to them human characteristics, especially since they "help" me see, "age" along with the rest of me, and "want" to sit evenly on the bridge of my nose.

Similarly, the implanted embryo can be fitted into this framework as a "quasi-other" in that "it" is not genetically the surrogate's, and "its" insertion into her body involves a highly technological process. Yet as her interaction with "it" is interactive, the embryo cannot be adequately described as merely "other" either, even though (at least in the United States) it has no legal standing until the end of the first trimester. Indeed, it is hard to imagine a more profoundly intimate relationship than that between a pregnant woman and the embryo/fetus within her body. And the implanted embryo is not "other" *at all* to the contracting parents but, at least a quasi (if not a "true") person, namely, *their* baby. In fact, they may be all the more encouraged to see the surrogate herself as "other" in order to conceive the fetus growing in her body as theirs.

From the contracting parents' point of view, then, describing the embryo as (part of the) technology may seem odious, yet this is what the surrogate is encouraged to believe in order to avoid attachment. In any case, what Ihde's conceptual distinctions allow us to do is show how the technologically mediated interface between the couple, the surrogate, and the developing fetus can be a source of experiential ambivalence. What about the surrogate's body? We could describe it as a mediating technology in that, like a television, it mediates the contracting couple's desires. Unlike a television, however, the surrogate is a "true person" even if the contracting couple, in virtue of the luxury that distance affords them, never has to confront this fact, and even if, like a television, her death in childbirth could be understood in terms of "malfunction." This is not to suggest that contracting couples are unfeeling, or even that agencies like Patel's encourage this attitude (though they well might); rather, it does suggest that our relationships with other human beings are so fully permeated and mediated by technology that alterity relationships do not exhaust them. We do not merely use technology; we live in it—and, in some cases literally, it lives in us.

Perhaps Verbeek would object that we ought to restrict our application of Ihde's conceptual framework to IVF to its nonhuman or non-living components, the tools used in implantation, for example. As Verbeek claims, in an alterity relationship the other is only a quasi-person. But here too there is much about which to be ambivalent. The surrogate mother's body does not simply function *as* an incubator; it *is* an incubator, and not just because it is appropriated via capitalist exchange (though this may emphasize the point), but because it is arbitrary to exclude living or conscious things from Ihde's framework. (Consider, for example, clones, androids, or persons fitted with prosthetic limbs.) Moreover, the externally fertilized and implanted embryo can certainly be considered to be a technology, and not just because its existence is technologically dependent, but because the point at which it becomes an independent living thing—the "global fetus"—is irrelevant to its being a living thing. Whether it's living or not, in other words, is only relevant to what it's produced to accomplish insofar as that conforms to the contracting couple's desires; we could imagine, after all, a world where an android—living (or "living"), but composed of entirely non-natural parts—would do just as well with respect to the fullfilment of desire.

Verbeek himself makes way for such possibilities when he observes that "[t]echnologies can even open up new ways for reality to manifest itself" (2005: 134). Indeed, and to the extent that this reality is composed of living and non-living things, technology can offer us new ways to consider what we mean by "mediation," "use," and "background." Ihde cites as an example the capacity of infrared photography to reveal tree disease better than the naked eye reveals reality— not a reality that is other than the one we ordinarily experience, but one that in virtue of technological mediation is made more comprehensible (134). Is our altered concept of the diseased tree a concept of tree-as-mediated-via-technology? Yes, but unless we're committed to a notion of a "pure" reality perceivable and unmediated by any technology, this point is not especially significant. What is significant is that just as the diseased tree is not fully distinguishable from the technology utilized to reveal it, neither the fertilized embryo nor the surrogate womb is fully distinguishable from the technologies that realize them *as* developing fetus or incubator. Bruno Latour makes a similar point when he argues that "[a]s soon as we add to dinosaurs their paleontologists, to particles their accelerators, to ecosystems their monitoring instruments...we have already ceased entirely to speak of nature; instead, we are speaking of what is produced, constructed, decided, defined, in a learned City whose ecology is almost as complex as that of the world it is coming to know" (2004: 35). This "learned City" is a reference to the sciences through which what is known can come to be so known, where new realities can be both revealed and at the same time constructed via the technologies that inform our interface with them—technologies that make dinosaurs and particles and ecosystems possible as objects of knowledge.

It makes sense, then, to agree with Verbeek that if we conceive of technology only as "a storehouse of raw materials that lies ready for human manipulation," the world will "appear only in a very limited respect" to us, namely "under the guise of control and domination" (2005: 135). The world cannot be revealed other than when it is mediated through *some* conceptual framework: "Human beings are what they are," writes Verbeek, "by virtue of the way in which they realize their existence in the world, and their world is what it is by virtue of the way in which it can manifest itself in the relations humans have to it" (163). Control and domination describe one such framework, one within which technology appears not only as raw material, but one in which it is conceived as radically distinct from and inferior to its human users. What we have seen, however, is that this distinction can be preserved only at the cost of assigning some human beings (not to mention all nonhuman animals) to the "raw material" side of a conceptual framework within which "reality" is divided exclusively into users who dominate and tools that are controlled (wielded, deployed, and discarded). Surrogate mothers are thus readily imagined as contracted incubators, "storehouses of raw materials" that function to expedite a "free market" venture (and relieve agents like Patel of moral culpability). The user–instrument distinction assumed by this conceptual framework solicits the critique that it is alienating. What else could our relationship to technology be? It seems that there is no escaping alienation if this is the only conceptual framework possible for constructing our relationship to technological advance. And worse: such a relationship is not only alienating; it helps to facilitate and entrench an alterity. Those who are empowered to control its uses are also those in a position to define what—and who—counts as "other."

REPRODUCTIVE TECHNOLOGIES AND A FEMINIST VISION OF SOCIAL JUSTICE

Fortunately, this is not the only framework within which to consider the interface of human objectives and technological means. What analyses like Verbeek's offer to feminist theory and practice are ways of radically re-imagining this interface in light of emancipatory and social-justice goals. We need to craft frameworks that take the following factors seriously into account: (1) the feminist critique of the appropriation of technology to the exploitive ends of the culture industry; (2) the fact that technologies are not simply tools, but mediums of experience without which we would have little or no conception of a human world; (3) the fact that the contexts within which particular human beings experience and navigate their worlds, including their own technologically mediated interface, vary widely across sex, gender, race, economic and social status, religion, value, and culture; and (4) the fact that such an alternative must take seriously the emancipatory potential of (some) technology in light of more sophisticated and contextualized analyses offered by theorists like Ihde and Verbeek. Verbeek remarks that among the implications of his view is that technologies are "more ambivalent than alienating with respect to the interpretation of the world with which they are linked" (2005: 135). This may be true, but we may well want to see it as a virtue—or at least a call for ongoing critical reflection and revision of the assumptions that govern our technologically mediated relationships.

Verbeek offers a first clue to such a re-conceptualization in his discussion of "multistability," when, following Ihde, he argues that

> technologies are never "in themselves" but are always related to the human beings who are engaged with them. Technologies receive "stability" only in their use; they are then interpreted as "artifacts-in-order-to…." Such multistability exists not only within a single use context, but always has a cultural index as well…. The multistability of artifacts implies not only that artifacts can have different meanings in different contexts, but also that specific goals can be technologically realized in different ways by a range of artifacts…. Human ends, therefore, can be realized in many different ways, depending on the cultural context in which they play a role. (2005: 136–37)

That the advance of technology creates what Verbeek calls a "decisional burden" by virtue of the potential choices it makes available depends upon the ways in which its uses are "stabilized," that is, valued and interpreted to particular ends by particular agents within a context itself governed by a variety of factors. He remarks, for example, that "[h]aving children … is no longer something that simply befalls us but has become a conscious decision" (138). This is certainly true for many. Even Verbeek, however, does not quite seem to grasp that this "us" describes that what is a "decisional burden" for some is, for others (say, Patel's surrogates), hardly a burden, but a strategy for survival, or that for others there is no "decisional burden" because there is still no opportunity to make real choices about reproduction. He continues: "[f]or those who are eager to have children but are unable to conceive, there are a steadily increasing number of technologically assisted options available....All of these technological developments create ever more instances, as well as kinds of choice. And we no longer have the choice to shirk them..." (138).

Many do, of course, have a choice, if not exactly to shirk choices as such, at least to choose for or against what they offer under relatively un-coerced conditions. But for others, the decisional burden has little to do with too many choices—but rather with too few, or with choices between the lesser of two evils. Decisional burden, in other words, is itself conditioned by the multistability of context, and while this no doubt creates the conditions for the ambivalence to which Verbeek refers, it also lends itself to a consideration of what the technologically mediated future might look like in a context whose guiding assumptions are not control and domination, but relative freedom, compassion, and justice. Such contexts are not exempt from decision making, but to the extent that they take the multiple stabilizing relationships between human objectives and technology seriously as an ongoing call for critical reflection, they need not be necessarily oppressive. Donna Haraway remarks, for example, that she

> strongly believe[s] that there are too many people on earth, not just millions, but billions too many for the long-term survival of ourselves and incomprehensible numbers of other species. That belief in no way softens questions of justice and freedom about who survives and reproduces and how. The individual human being matters; communities matter. Counting matters. Further, reducing population growth rates and absolute numbers in every class, race, ethnicity, and other category on Earth will not necessarily reduce habitat destruction, urban or rural poverty, pollution, hunger, crime, agricultural land devastation, overcrowding, unemployment, or most other evils....The story of interrelationship is much more complex, and is hotly contested. I am convinced that the success of comprehensive freedom and justice projects would do a much better job of alleviating suffering and reducing resource and habitat devastation than population limitation policies.... (1997: 205)

Because technology has been cast by some feminists as being on the side of the evils Haraway names, its potential for being put to the service of the alleviation of "evil" has, I think, been underappreciated. If Haraway is right that reducing human population growth rates will not necessarily lead to environmental improvement or the reduction of crime rates, this is not because the technologies implicated in pollution and crime are themselves necessarily evil, but because the specific stories of their particular use—the ways in which they are realized in particular contexts—elicit a conceptual framework of domination and control. Questions concerning who reproduces and how focus not primarily on whether the technologies involved are themselves alienating, but under what conditions they could become so—a substantially different question since it leaves wide open the possibility for conceiving of alternative conditions which may or may not include a technology in question.

Haraway continues, that "[i]n a time of crushing overpopulation, the perverse fact is that there are too few living babies among the poorest residents on earth, too few in a sense that matters to thinking about technoscience studies and reproductive freedom. These missing and dead babies are, of course, intrinsic to the ongoing production of overpopulation" (1997: 205). Observations like these pose one of the greatest challenges to a twenty-first-century socialist feminism and, read through Verbeek's approach to technology, also intimate a significant opportunity. The challenge is to undertake a thoroughgoing evaluation of the conceptual underpinnings that fuel this seeming contradiction between overpopulation and too few babies born to poor women. On its face, human-rights discourse seems inadequate to the task: What, for instance, does reproductive freedom mean in a developing nation such as India, whose dead babies are the product of the very economic system that makes poor women "available" to clinics like Patel's? Freedom—to enter exploitive contracts? The feminist critique of alienation, however, is also not fully adequate. If technology is an inevitable source of alienation, it's hard to imagine any "freedom and justice project" other than a "return to nature," which, from the point of view of many (especially poor) women, might seem incoherent, if not simply cruel. "Nature," after all, is likely to seem quite real to people whose acquaintance with starvation and disease is intimate.

The opportunity, then, is to radically rethink technology from the point of view of emancipatory social justice. Because women and girls are so often the bearers of the most egregious forms of injustice, such a project is certainly a feminist one; because, as Haraway makes

CONTEMPORARY FEMINIST THEORY AND ACTIVISM

clear, such projects are deeply interwoven with environmental issues that are themselves the product of technology misappropriated to short-sighted market ends, they invite coalition with other movements. Verbeek's (and Ihde's) conceptual framework offers a way of distinguishing the various complex and overlapping roles that technology plays, and in so doing it evokes a caution against conceiving it solely as the instrument of human alienation. The question is not merely how there can be too many babies *and* too few babies that survive poverty, or how there can be human overpopulation amidst starvation, but what role technology—including but not limited to reproductive technologies—has played in the production of this injustice. But the very next question—one that tethers the feminist movement to others, especially the environmental movement—is this: "How can we think about contemporary technologies as tools with which to confront oppression and injustice?" If the human world is mediated by the technosciences, how can this mediation be made to serve the good? What revolution in the way we think about technology would this require? This, I suggest, is one of the most important questions contemporary feminism needs to address more aggressively—and one whose answers can, I think, be more promising and hopeful than we have so far surmised.

Chapter IV

Economic Disparity and the Global Market: Institutionalized Inequality

THE SOCIALIST FEMINISM OF ALISON JAGGAR'S
FEMINIST POLITICS AND HUMAN NATURE

In her groundbreaking 1983 work *Feminist Politics and Human Nature*, Alison Jaggar argues that, revised in light of feminist analyses of the status of women within patriarchal institutions such as the family and the church, Karl Marx's biting critique of capitalism can help to illuminate the economic oppression not only of workers generally, but also of women theorized in terms of sex and gender, as well as class. Consider the potentially decisive role played by economic status in, for example, the transsexual's access to sex-reassignment surgery or the Indian woman's decision to contract to be a surrogate mother in an outsourced pregnancy. Heteropatriarchal—male-dominated and -privileged—prerogative determines in both cases, and for largely the same reasons, this status in the very concrete terms of access to health insurance in one case and to health care (including basic life necessities) in the other. Following Zillah Eisenstein's claim that "[i]f women's existence is defined by capitalism and patriarchy through their ruling ideologies and institutions, then an understanding of either capitalism alone or patriarchy in isolation will not deal with the problem of women's oppression" (1990: 131), Jaggar argues for a feminism that is capable of articulating the mutually advantageous relationship between patriarchy and capitalist enterprise:

> On the socialist feminist analysis, capitalism, male dominance, racism, and imperialism are intertwined so inextricably that they are inseparable; consequently, the abolition of any of these systems of domination requires the end of all of them. Socialist feminists claim that a full understanding of the capitalist system requires a recognition of the way in which it is structured by male dominance and, conversely, that a full understanding of male dominance requires a recognition of the way it is organized by the capitalist division of labor. Socialist feminists believe that an adequate account of "capitalist patriarchy" requires the use of the historical materialist method developed originally by Marx and [Friedrich] Engels. (1983: 124–25)

Although, as historian Isaiah Berlin points out, "[n]o formal exposition of historical materialism was ever published by Marx himself," Marx regarded it as "a practical method of social and historical analysis, and as a basis of political strategy" (1963: 101). In a feminist context, showing how heteropatriarchal institutions such as the family and capitalist enterprise (outsourced pregnancy or Internet-accessible sex-reassignment surgery, for example) are mutually dependent and mutually advantageous, with respect to their exploitation of human material need, offers a foundation for the analysis of oppression and commodification. The method includes both an evaluative component concerning how well human institutions meet material need and a political component aimed at reforming or overthrowing those institutions that fail this moral imperative.

Most significant for a socialist feminist account is that the method begins with what Marx referred to in the *Economic and Philosophic Manuscripts of 1844* as "species being," namely, the notion that "human beings are a species of animal who, like other sentient creatures, have real physical needs, are capable of suffering, live for a finite time, and eventually die" (Marx 1964: 112–14; Jaggar 1983: 52–60; Lee 2002: 1). Since it is grounded, in other words, in the material or embodied conditions of human existence and experience, the aim of the method is to evaluate human institutions, including family structure, the organization of labor, the drafting of civil law, the practice of medicine, and the system of economic exchange in light of the success or failure with which each contributes to meeting human need. Indeed, it is precisely because capitalism, according·to Marx, not only fails to meet human need but does so in the process of empowering the few at the expense of the many, that the historical materialist method offers something more than merely analysis, namely, the impetus to revolution.

What socialist feminism contributes to the historical materialist account, then, are answers to key questions concerning who is empowered by capitalist exchange, whose labor is responsible for creating wealth, how the division of labor is organized, and what defines relationships between workers and capitalists.[1] Unsurprisingly, Jaggar argues, the system's primary beneficiaries are *some* men, namely, white, Western (or Westernized) men whose dependence on the labor of a proletariat or working class composed of "others," as well as on the "private" or unpaid domestic labor of housewives, is well-concealed behind the sexed, gendered, and racialized stereotypes that reproduce the division of labor—public or private. As Jaggar says, "On the traditional Marxist view, the organization of work under capitalism subjects housewives to a form of oppression that is even deeper than the direct oppression that they may suffer from their husbands. No matter how gentle and respectful their husbands may happen to be, housewives are oppressed by their exclusion from public life" (1983: 220). It would seem, as Marx and Engels themselves advocated, that the solution to this form of oppression would be found in the introduction of women into the active labor force (Jaggar 1983: 200–01). As recent US Census Bureau statistics make clear, however, hundreds of years of women's contribution to wage labor offers little more than cold comfort to pay equity, despite arguments that competition is the remedy for inequality.[2] We can, of course, point to examples of union organizing (especially in the textile industry) or to the creation of regulatory agencies such as the

---

[1] For additional elaboration of this theme, see Ehrenreich (1997).
[2] See the National Women's Law Center website: <http://www.nwlc.org/pdf/ PayCheckFairness>.

Equal Employment Opportunity Commission (EEOC), whose charge it is to address claims of sex- and race-based inequality. It is nonetheless telling, however, that "[a]t the time of the EPA's [1963's Equal Pay Act's] passage, women earned just 58 cents for every dollar earned by men. By 2006, that rate had only increased to 77 cents, an improvement of less than half a penny a year. Minority women fare the worst. African-American women earn just 64 cents to every dollar earned by white men, and for Hispanic women that figure drops to merely 52 cents per dollar."[3]

From this point of view, efforts to reform patriarchal capitalism's essential structure can never be fully adequate, and the key, once again, lies in the concept of species being. Species being "cannot be defined as an unchanging given attendant on species membership, but rather must be conceived *dialectically*, that is, as an evolving work or project whose relationship to nature is both material and rational, physical and psychological" (Lee 2002: 1; also see Marx 1964: 112; my emphasis). A dialectical process "is one in which progress or change occurs through the overcoming of some initial set of conditions itself the product of some earlier set overcome, and so on. To claim that species being is dialectical, then, is to claim it as a product of a continuous progress of overcoming those material conditions through which change for it is made possible" (Lee 2002: 2; also see Marx 1981: 47). Institutions that encourage dialectical progress through what Marx calls "praxis" or "creative labor" are those which meet human need and support human flourishing; institutions that hinder or stifle human creativity in the interest of creating wealth regardless of cost (environmental, human, time) are, as Marx puts it, "alienating"—that

---

[3] For an alternative but complementary feminist argument whose aim is to analyze reasons given for the wage gap, see Schultz (1992). Schultz argues that among the most common reasons given for the wage gap is that women prefer "women's work," even though it pays less than "men's work," because it allows them to do more of what they really want—to be wives and mothers. She then goes on to demonstrate that the ways in which we define and inculcate gender actually reinforce the patriarchal and heterosexist attitudes that influence women's and men's "choices" of occupation. Despite critiques like Schultz's, this view is reiterated in a number of contemporary conservative critiques of feminism, for example, Warren Farrell's *Why Men Earn More* (2004). Ironically, it is at least arguable that Marx's own conception of the division of labor actually reinforces a very similar viewpoint. For an analysis in support of this claim, please see Lee (2002: 12–17, 63–68, 74–79) and Jaggar (1983: 69–72).

is, they result in the estrangement of the individual from her or his own creative potential (Marx 1964: 107–9; Jaggar 1983: 208–15).

Socialist feminists, argues Jaggar, share this fundamental conception of human being:

> Implicit in the socialist feminist conception of human nature … are certain social values. Chief among these is the value of productive activity or work. Since socialist feminism shares the basic Marxist conception of human nature, it is inevitable that it should share the Marxist belief that human fulfillment is to be found in free productive activity [praxis]. But because socialist feminism has a broader view than traditional Marxism of what counts as distinctively human productive activity, its conception of freedom is very different. (1983: 304)

If, as Marx argues, capitalism places premium value not on human welfare but on profit making, its entrepreneurs must be willing to accept manufacturing or service-producing conditions that subordinate the welfare of workers to the generation of profit. The results are predictable, as I have argued elsewhere:

> The laborer's very wish to exist is thus (and necessarily) the capitalist's victory, for it not only insures the conditions of exploitation, but insures *against* the emergence of those conditions whereby the laborer can … compete with … the capitalist. As Marx puts it, "the worker sinks to the level of a commodity and indeed becomes the most wretched of commodities … in inverse proportion to the power and magnitude of his production" [Marx 1964: 106]. The more the laborer works to increase "his" own wage, the more the profit accrues to the capitalist whose reinvestment in production augments "his" wealth and hence "his" power over not only the conditions of labor but over those social and political conditions most conducive to the production, promotion, and mass consumption of product or service. (Lee 2002: 26)

Among these social and political conditions are those whose fulfillment socialist feminists include in a "broader" view of praxis, specifically, those that bear on the reproduction not only of labor but also of laborers. The worker who "sinks to the level of a *commodity*," a saleable good, is doubly significant for women in that women are commodified both as laborers and as the producers of laborers (Jaggar 1983: 69–79, 307–17; emphasis in original). Jaggar also makes the point that "[m]uch, though never all, of women's energy has been consumed in sexual and procreative labor—and most of this labor has always been forced rather than free" (305). That women—unlike men—are exploitable in this double fashion helps to clarify the different meaning of freedom that Jaggar suggests: institutions that deny reproductive choice—for example, the traditional patriarchal family—cannot adequately address what it means to engage in "free productive activity" *and* be female.

Consider again the Indian woman who contracts with the American couple for the production of a baby via IVF through an agency that acts as paid broker and financier. From a socialist feminist point of view, not only is she vulnerable to economic exploitation in that she likely comes to the contract disempowered by poverty, but she is also doubly jeopardized by that fact that she is likely to have children for whom she's at least partly responsible in her own family. To be emancipated from economic vulnerability, then, requires being emancipated from its primary beneficiaries—the mostly male agents of the relevant institutions. But this can be made possible only through the exercise of real control over fertility. The freedom, in other words, to make reproductive choices is fundamental to being in a position to control every other aspect of one's life. Because a Marxist account, argues Jaggar, is firmly grounded in the material conditions of human being, its central categories—the meaning and meeting of human material need—are readily translatable into the terms that define labor as work *and* labor as sexual reproduction. Lack of control over body and labor within the patriarchal family structure readily translates into an exploitable and relatively disempowered commodity for the market. This is not to say that capitalism necessarily depends on any particular family structure to ensure its supply of expendable labor, but rather that it is hardly surprising that the beneficiaries of women's labor in the home are largely the same as those who benefit from women's labor in the workplace, namely, mostly white, mostly Christian, mostly Western (or Westernized) men (Lee 2002: 34–37). Donna Haraway sheds further light on the significance of existing social relations in the context not only of sex, but also of race:

For American white women the concept of property in the self, the ownership of one's own body, in relation to reproductive freedom, has more readily focused on the field of events around conception, pregnancy, abortion, and birth because the system of white patriarchy turned on the control of legitimate children and the consequent constitution of white females as women.... Black women specifically—and the women subjected to the conquest of the New World in general—faced a broader social field of reproductive unfreedom, in which their children did not inherit the status of human in the founding hegemonic discourses of US society. (1992: 95)

As the examples of slavery and racial segregation make pointedly clear, the mutually reinforcing relationship of capitalism and patriarchy is a kind of marriage,[4] but this is not because capitalism is sexist (or racist) in and of itself, but because it's opportunistic; whatever social, racial, and/or sexual divisions can be exploited to the purposes of production count as justifiable, given the value attributed to goals driven by profit over welfare. That sexual reproduction should epitomize commodification is thus hardly surprising; converting all value into exchange value, such an economic system effectively converts being female into the *sine qua non* of all resources—the mechanism for the reproduction of labor itself, and hence the first form of property.

THE CONTEMPORARY CHALLENGE TO SOCIALIST FEMINISM

While Jaggar's contribution to the feminist analysis of heteropatriarchal capitalism offers key insight into the history and mechanisms of the oppressive economic conditions faced daily by millions of women, it may not be as well suited to the issues confronting contemporary theorists and activists. I think this is so for at least four reasons. First, while corporate exploitation, the export of Western standards of culture via the culture industry, and the continuing exhaustion of environmental resources are hardly new to the twenty-first century, each in its own way has been transformed by the globalizing of labor in tandem with the advances of technology—or, as Haraway puts it, *technoscience*. Analyses of the relationship between capitalism and

---

4   See Hartmann (1976, 1981) and Young (1997).

patriarchy must, then, include these factors, particularly as they bear on the rapidly changing conditions of women in the developing world, and as the economic gap between Western and developing nations grows ever wider.

Second, however perceptive they were, few writers in Jaggar's 1980s were in a position to foresee the consequences of the global-ized market, and hence of the virtually exponential growth of the culture industry into the twenty-first century. More than merely an instrument for the export of Western values, and revolutionized by the Internet, the culture industry appropriates the value associated with creative labor or praxis and transforms it into the desire to imi-tate the popular, well heeled, sexy, and powerful. Given the commod-ification of sexuality and reproduction already deeply rooted in Western culture, it is not surprising that the impact of the culture industry on women and girls is disproportionately exploitive, or—contrary to the Internet's liberating potential—that it may actually reinforce patriarchal institutions including the traditional family, prostitution, pornography, and masculinist (male-centered) religion.

Third, although there is little doubt that Western values permeate the global culture industry, it would be naïve to suggest that these are the only values whose influence is felt on this global scale. As the recent resurgence of religiously motivated terrorism amply illus-trates, other systems of value—even systems purportedly anti-capital-ist—have had significant impact on the ways in which Westerners understand their increasingly fragile cultural hegemony. Terrorism, moreover, may be "merely" the most extreme example of the possi-ble effects of alternative and competing systems of value. As Chandra Mohanty argues in *Feminism Without Borders* (2003), a number of other factors have begun to play crucial roles within the global exchange not only of currency and labor, but also of power realized in other (though enduringly patriarchal and racist) ways:

> Economically and politically, the declining power of self-governance among certain poorer nations is matched by the rising significance of transnational institutions such as the World Trade Organization and gov-erning bodies such as the European Union, not to mention the for-profit corporations. Of the world's largest economies, fifty-one happen to be corporations, and Amnesty International now reports on corpora-

Mohanty

ECONOMIC DISPARITY AND THE GLOBAL MARKET

tions as well as nations.... The rise of religious fundamentalisms with their deeply masculinist and often racist rhetoric poses a huge challenge for feminist struggles around the world. Finally, the profoundly unequal "information highway" as well as the increasing militarization...of the globe, accompanied by the growth of the prison industrial complex in the United States, poses profound contradictions in the lives of communities of women and men in most parts of the world. (229)

For Mohanty, this potentially volatile brew of global corporatism, religion, militarization, lack of access to cyberspace, and the prison industrial complex—that is, the relationship between the threat of imprisonment (especially for minorities), the pressure to accept low-wage jobs, and the exploitation of prisoners themselves to perform low-wage (or even unpaid) labor—raises serious questions about the extent to which non-Western nations are influenced by Western values. But it also raises questions about the effects of non-Western values, religious convictions, economic disparities, and political struggles on Western hegemony. That Amnesty International, for example, counts corporations as independent economies (in effect, as sovereign nation-states) hints at the antiquated nature of geographical borders and thereby once again raises questions about what characterizes the relationship between "West" and "Non-West," or "North" and "South." The fact that ultra-conservative moral systems like Sharia law (or its Christian Identity Movement analogue)[5] have resurged in some factions of Islam (or in the religious right in the United States), not restricted by geography, language, or economic status, raises serious issues about the roles that both men and women play in the increasingly violent conflicts between religion and the power of the state.

Fourth, although Marx's analysis of the role of religion in the creation of the guilt that can be assuaged only through the penance-performance of wage labor (a third party to the "marriage") is persuasive, it nonetheless seems poorly equipped to respond to, for

---

[5] We will explore the relevance of fundamentalist religious belief to the future of the feminist movement more fully in chs. V and VI. For a comprehensive definition of Sharia Law, please see <http://www.religioustolerance.org/islsharia. htm>, particularly with respect to that version of Sharia practiced in Saudi Arabia. For a comparison of Sharia and fundamentalist forms of Christianity, please see <http://www.religioustolerance.org/reac_ter9.htm>.

example, the attack on the World Trade Center. After all, the WTC appears to have been chosen as a clear opportunity to *reject* capitalist values on specifically religious grounds. At their fundamentalist extremes, the place of women in Islam, Judaism, Hinduism, or Christianity presents a challenge to the marketing of Western values, but this is not because religion offers emancipation from patriarchy, but because it offers escape from the culture industry. As the culture industry has come to be identified with greed, avarice, and exploitation, what especially fundamentalist incarnations of religion proffers is the opportunity to live a less status- or possession-driven life. A woman who chooses a fundamentalist identity may identify this choice with emancipation from male domination—as her choice—and with its Western face epitomized in capitalist consumption. The relationship between religion and capitalism is thus far more complex than Marx accounts for. The role women play in the politics of navigating their own status at once as subservient to religious proscription and as consumers marketed to *as* Christian (or Islamic or Jewish, etc.) wives, sisters, and mothers is as essential to the maintenance of this relationship as it is fragile. And as these politics begin to take on the characteristics of global religious movements, that role becomes even more fractious—and significant. Mohanty, once again, offers important insight, situated not in any single religious tradition, but in the central role that the control of women's labor and sexuality plays in each:

> Religious fundamentalist constructions of women embody the nexus of morality, sexuality, and nation—a nexus of great importance for feminists. As in Christian, Islamic, and Jewish fundamentalist discourses, the construction of femininity and masculinity, especially in relation to the idea of the nation, are [sic] central to Hindu fundamentalist rhetorics and mobilizations. Women are not only mobilized in the "service" of the nation, but they also become the ground on which discourses of morality and nationalism are written.... One of the central challenges Indian women face at this time is how to rethink the relationship of nationalism and feminism in the context of religious identities. (2003: 132–33)

Among the most daunting tasks for twenty-first-century socialist feminists, in other words, is to understand not only how Western capitalism has an impact upon women in developing nations, but also how as a response to these dynamics women are configured in the resurgence of religious fundamentalism and religious nationalism. This task is made particularly daunting in light of the increasing antiquatedness of the concept of a national border, a notion itself endangered by the global corporatism of the culture industry and by the competitive proselytizing of Christianity and Islam, if not of other religions. What "nation" and "nationalism" mean in such a context is itself unclear, yet one thing remains constant: the economic status of women, especially—but by no means exclusively—in the developing world, remains the lynchpin for substantive change.

THE GLOBALIZING, "CASUALIZING," AND FEMINIZING OF LABOR

With respect to the globalizing of labor, Marx did foresee to some extent the colonizing expansion of capitalism to markets, natural resources, and labor pools beyond the West, and he did have some notion that the geographical borders of nation states would gradually be made obsolete by corporate interests (Mandel 1994: 63–70). He could not, however, have foreseen the toll this expansion would take on workers (as he conceived them, Western and male), or on the domestic and subsistence-farming labor traditionally performed by women, or on the environmental resources polluted if not wholly exhausted by mass production (Lee 2002: 89–91). In her 2002 essay "A Feminist Critique of the Alleged Southern Debt," Jaggar points out that

> [l]arge-scale cash crop development has displaced women's subsistence farming and thereby contributed to famines, especially in Africa. In India, the destruction of forests for large-scale agriculture has resulted in an increase in the time women must spend collecting firewood and fodder, which in turn means they have less time available for crop production; their income is reduced and their nutrition suffers. (126)

Moreover, while Marx had high aspirations that technology would replace at least the most arduous of labor, he did not foresee what feminist writers like Swasti Mitter describe as the "casualization" of labor:

A significant yet grossly underemphasized aspect of the current global restructuring is...the emergence of an acutely polarized labor market. In such a market...a small number of core workers is going to exist with a vast array of peripheral workers. There are many names for these peripheral workers: flexible workers, casual workers, or...temporary or part-time proletariat. All these terms have the same or similar connotations, and conjure up invariably the image of a worker who is a woman, and whose status as a wage-earner does not necessarily carry with it an automatic prospect of career progression. Nor does the image imply job security or other employment-related benefits such as a core worker enjoys.... [These workers] provide the base of a growing "shoe-shine" economy even in the affluent West. (1997:163)

Mitter, who wrote her article in 1986, goes on to note the distinctively sexed and racialized character of this expansion, as well as the technologically mediated reality of its factories and assembly lines. The "casualized" working class, writes Mitter, is "not only ignored by the mainstream labor movement, but by most writers on economic and political issues," by virtue of the fact that it is composed primarily of women, persons of color, indigenous peoples, and children (164). "Whereas literally thousands of articles have been written on the labor-replacing aspect of new technology," she concludes, "only a handful have been written on the casualization of work, and these mostly by committed women scholars" (164).

As the trend toward casualized labor continues into the twenty-first century, its hallmark, as Jaggar shows, is the extent to which it has become feminized both nationally and globally:

In the global North, women, especially women of color, are disproportionately impoverished by the economic inequality resulting from "free" trade, which has resulted in many hitherto well-paid jobs being moved from the North to low-wage areas in the global South. These jobs have been replaced in the North by so-called "McJobs," "casual," contingency, or part-time positions, often in the service sector, which are typically low-paid and lack health or retirement benefits.... The feminization of poverty was a term coined originally to describe the situation of women in the United States, but the United Nations reports that [it] has now become a global and growing phenomenon, with women comprising 70 percent of the world's 1.3 billion poor. (2002: 124; my emphasis)

For Jaggar, like Mitter, globalization represents less the economic development with which it is typically associated than, as Vandana Shiva puts it, the "maldevelopment" that leads, on the one hand, to tremendous wealth for a lucky—mostly Northern (Western)—few, and on the other to an ever-deepening poverty for the many, particularly women, nonwhites, indigenous peoples, and children. By highlighting the environmental consequences of this restructuring of labor, however, Shiva adds another dimension to the meaning of "globalization," namely, the relationship between human beings conceived of in terms of species dependence (species being) and the fragile integrity of the environment itself:

> The displacement of women from productive activity by the expansion of development was rooted largely in the manner in which development projects appropriated or destroyed the natural resource base for the production of sustenance and survival. It destroyed women's productivity both by removing land, water, and forests from their management and control, as well as through the ecological destruction of soil, water, and vegetation systems so that nature's productivity and renewability were impaired. While gender oppression and patriarchy are the oldest of oppressions, they have taken on new and more violent forms through the project of development.... Development, thus, is equivalent to maldevelopment.... (1994: 274)

With the development of the global marketplace having seriously jeopardized the relationship between human agents, subsistence labor, and the natural resources upon which it depends, development, argues Shiva, is at least for some women—and disproportionately so —maldevelopmental, if not simply toxic: harmful for those whose productivity is imperiled by its potential ecological consequences. While it is no wonder that women bear the brunt of the destruction of resources through the destruction of their own opportunities to engage in productive (and reproductive) labor, Shiva's analysis highlights the fact that casualization begins in the displacement of those forms of productivity more directly associated with soil, water, and vegetation. It begins, in other words, not only with the destruction of a variety of labor—subsistence farming—performed primarily by women, but also with the alienation of a primary element of women's cultural, gendered, and even personal identity: *the provision of food*. Work that was once valued as essential to family and community is now displaced by casualized labor, itself ironically characterized as "women's work," that is, as feminized (Lee 2002: 89). Because the conditions for food production are themselves jeopardized through the destruction of soil and water, the pressure to enter the paid labor force increases as a way to secure food—even though it is grown and packaged elsewhere. For Shiva, "maldevelopment" offers a metaphor for the complex dynamics of the displacement of subsistence farming, the introduction of wage labor, and its feminization by means of wages that ensure the preservation of the labor pool. It is hardly surprising, then, from the point of view of those who benefit, that the imposition of Western capitalist values looks like "development," but for those whose lands are polluted and whose labor is devalued, it can hardly be said to be so.

One significant dissenter from this point of view is global economist Jagdish Bhagwati, who argues in his *In Defense of Globalization* (2007 [2004]) that globalization has actually helped women toward economic independence. He offers as an example the experience of Japanese women and children who accompany their executive husbands to the United States:

> In the aftermath of the great outward expansion of Japan's multinationals in the 1980's and early 1990's, Japanese men executives were sent to the United States, England, France, and other Western nations.... These men brought with them their Japanese wives and children.... And the wives saw at first hand that Western women, though they have some way to go, were treated better. So did the young children become not docile Japanese who are taught the value of social conformity and harmony but rambunctious little Americans who value instead the individualism that every immigrant parent confronts when the children return home from school and say, "That is the way *I* want to do it.".... The women and children who then returned to Japan became agents for change. (74)

He offers as evidence for this improved agency the number of Japanese students entering American universities such as Columbia: "Just a decade ago at Columbia where I teach the largest nationality in an entering class of over four hundred in the School of International Affairs was Japanese" (75). However, Bhagwati doesn't specify how many of these students were women, or to what extent financial aid figured into their admission—a peculiar omission for a section entitled "Globalization Helps Women."

Indeed, from a feminist point of view, Bhagwati's claims raise far more issues than they address. Can we really generalize from the experience of affluent Japanese wives who accompany their husbands to America to that of women from the developing world, when the brunt of the "McJobs" and their oppressive consequences fall disproportionately on the latter? Can we fairly compare the experience of privileged Japanese women to that of women in the developing world? Can we compare postwar Japanese economic development to that of the economic South? Why assume that the improved agency of children whose families are already wealthy enough to send them overseas to Columbia will have a positive effect beyond their class and culture? Bhagwati appears to assume as unproblematic that women accompany their husbands—even if it means permanent emigration—to an assignment in a Western country. But isn't this among the sexist assumptions a feminist analysis is intended to address? Bhagwati makes clear that his aims are neither the "documentation" nor the "explanation" of "discrimination against women" (74). Fair enough; but he still must provide an argument for the implicit causal connection he draws between the "rambunctious individualism" he thinks immigrant children visit upon their harried parents and the liberation he implies this will offer to women. For, as feminist analyses show, this ideological connection not only is far from obvious, but often comes at an astoundingly high cost for women.

Unwittingly, Bhagwati himself provides an apt and instructive example of this cost when he argues (in a section entitled "Women's Fears") that so long as the choice to migrate is made voluntarily, the psychological costs to women who leave their children behind in order to work for wealthy Westerners is outweighed by the benefits of working in the West. Remarking on a study of migrant women conducted by Arlie Russell Hochschild, Bhagwati argues that

> even if these sentiments [namely, of psychological distress at having left one's children to the care of others for an extended period and across a long distance] had emerged from a proper sample rather than from interviews of not necessarily representative migrants, they would have to confront the fact that as long as the choice to migrate had been made voluntarily, the psychic costs—and possibly gains, as in the case of our own maid of many years from Haiti, who escaped from an abusive husband—were outweighed by the psychic and economic gains. It is important to emphasize also the fact of psychic gains that can accrue because the migrating woman enjoys the liberating environment, both economic and social, that working away from her family, in a feudal and male-dominated environment back home, will imply. I have seen it with our maid, who has grown over the years in self-respect and dignity. (77)

Dismissive of what is in fact a very carefully documented study of immigrant women's painful feelings and experiences, Bhagwati insists that because the decision to migrate is voluntary, the experience overall must be good—or, at least, that it *ought* to be. He continues: "even if attention was paid naïvely only to psychological consequences, it is more likely that many women in the global care chain are better off rather than suffering from emotional 'deficit' and distress. The migrant female worker is better off in the new world of attachments and autonomy; the migrant's children are happy being looked after by their grandmothers, who are also happy to be looking after the children; and the employer mothers, when they find good nannies, are also happy that they can work without the emotionally wrenching sense that they are neglecting their children" (77–78).

Bhagwati assumes that "the world of attachments and autonomy" just is better than the world from which female workers migrate—or rather that such a world is better *because* it offers attachments and autonomy. Hence women ought to feel better. But Bhagwati provides neither an argument that "attachments and autonomy" are the primary motives for women to choose to migrate nor evidence that this is what is achieved (or realistically can be achieved). Again, he raises more questions than he answers—especially given how recent is his writing. First, why describe as "naïve" Hochschild's attention to psychological consequences? Does he regard these as irrelevant because work in the West ought to be experienced as liberating? Why? Because migration is voluntary? Is it? Certainly this answer is not as obvious as Bhagwati makes it out to be, and even he hints that he knows otherwise when he points out that employer mothers are happy to find good nannies because then they don't have to feel guilty for "neglecting their children." In other words, he credits the Western woman's feelings of guilt while simultaneously dismissing the migrant woman's—intimating in effect that the latter should feel grateful for the opportunity to be a wealthier woman's nanny. This is precisely the hypocrisy that analyses like Jaggar's and Mitter's expose. The fact, moreover, that the Western woman is more than likely to be white and the migrant a woman of color is wholly ignored by Bhagwati, even though, as he acknowledges elsewhere, racial dynamics play a key role in the opportunities and effects of globalization (2007 [2004]: 79–80).

Second, Bhagwati's appeals to voluntariness are betrayed by the fact that given the close familial and community ties women experience with respect to their children—even in otherwise patriarchally oppressive cultures—they do not merely leave their families in pursuit of a "world of attachments" (Hochschild 2000: 144). In fact, they send the lion's share of their wages home, and, as Hochschild's discussion of the psychological distress they experience in being away shows (2000: 136), such women would not leave if they had alternatives (Bhagwati 2007 [2004]: 76–77). That Bhagwati's maid *may* be better off having left an abusive husband does not necessarily imply that her present circumstances are liberating; she works as a maid, and it is at least arguable that her subservience works to preserve the very class system within which women remain oppressed and husbands—including abusive ones—are empowered. Deny it though he surely would, from a socialist feminist point of view Bhagwati is the one who benefits from the abuse meted out against his maid by her husband. After all, her "voluntary" migration provides Bhagwati with a cheap and reliable source of labor. That she should be grateful for this liberation both ignores everything else she had to leave behind in Haiti and, assuming she is of African descent, reinforces a long-standing and racialized class system—in the United

States. I wonder whether Bhagwati asked *her* whether she felt an increase in self-respect and dignity—or whether he is rationalizing his own participation in the exploitation of women of African descent.

Perhaps I am being unduly harsh on Bhagwati or am misrepresenting his argument without giving him a chance to respond, but I don't think so. His discussion of unpaid domestic labor is just as instructive. Bhagwati acknowledges that unpaid domestic labor affects resource allocation in an economy: "This is because child care and child rearing have socially desirable spillover effects for which the market does not reward women as it should" (2007 [2004]: 79). He even goes so far as to point out that because women should have a choice to participate in the workforce, a good argument can be made for subsidized childcare. Then he claims the following:

> But these and other implications of women's unpaid work are matters of domestic policy. It *defies common sense* to attack either the WTO [World Trade Organization] or the freeing of trade for the absence of such policy initiatives by nation states that are members of the WTO or that are seeking gains from trade by freeing trade. Yet Women's Edge [a US-based NGO] and other groups do make *that illogical leap*, and others, when they make assertions such as "Trade agreements need to recognize women's competing demands and ensure that women benefit from trade to the same extent men do." The same extent? Can we manage to achieve such parity of results from trade liberalization for any group, whether women, Dalits (India's untouchables), or African Americans or Hispanics in the United States? (79–80; my emphasis)

Why does it "defy common sense" to agitate for a WTO policy that acknowledges the economic and social value of domestic labor? Why is it an "illogical leap" to work toward economic equality? Why is it, as Bhagwati implies, merely utopian to aspire to parity for India's untouchables, African Americans, or US Hispanics? That such aspirations will be difficult to achieve is surely true, but if Bhagwati is serious about the "socially desirable spillover effects" of child rearing, why chastise NGOs like Women's Edge for taking these effects—not to mention the moral value of human equality—seriously? Note too that Bhagwati offers no argument here. He simply calls organizations like Women's Edge "illogical," and lacking "common sense";

that is, he resorts to just the language that some men have deployed against women for centuries, and that some white men (or their honorary representatives—like Bhagwati himself) deploy against nonwhite "others," in the interest of promoting a globalized trade whose trickle-down effects result in the "McJobs" of Jaggar's and Mitter's analysis.

What seems clear from these examples is that, for Bhagwati, the value of women's liberation is to be measured in the currency of men's economic success (signified by the entrance of their children into Ivy League schools—or their capacity to retain a maid), and to this end lack of compensation for domestic labor is "logical." Given this "reasoning," it is hardly surprising that women remain responsible for the unpaid domestic labor required to reproduce the capacity in others as well as themselves to work the "McJobs." As Jaggar remarks, "[o]ne frequently noted problem is that conventional economics generally fails to recognize the enormous value of much of women's work because it ignores unpaid work done outside the market.... Women are especially likely to perform the routine daily work of maintaining infants, children, the sick, the aged—and men" (2002: 129). Indeed, women's unpaid domestic labor is essential to the reproduction of men's capacity to work, and hence it is essential to the substantial material benefits that men—including some men in developing nations—have the opportunity to realize. "Because women take on the bulk of the necessary domestic labor," Jaggar writes, "men have more time and energy for paid work and thus are enabled to advance their careers, whereas women's career options are limited by the limited time and energy they have available for paid work" (129).

This fact, however, places women in the developing world (including the many developing pockets of Second- and First-World countries, such as Native American reservations) in an untenable economic position. Like their sisters in the North/West, women in the developing world are responsible for ensuring the labor productivity of their patriarchally structured families; they remain, in other words, responsible for the provision and preparation of food and for other forms of domestic service. The consequent constraints on time and energy, however, make women, especially in developing nations, even more vulnerable to low-paid, casualized jobs—that is, to precisely the jobs whose resource depletion and waste products are responsible for the destruction of the environment upon which they likely still depend for food and clean water. Accomplishing the provision of food, then, inevitably becomes more and more difficult, even as expectations associated with the patriarchal family remain unchanged and, in fact, *cannot* change without altering the fundamental justification for feminizing labor—namely, that "McJobs" are suitable for women who (a) cannot be (and may not want to be) maximally productive workers given their domestic responsibilities, and (b) do not need to be more productive than the McJob requires, given the support they are likely to receive from men in marriage.

INTERNATIONAL LOAN DEBT, FEMINIZED POVERTY, AND MUHAMMAD YUNUS'S BANK FOR THE POOR

Far more than merely an extension of Marxist concepts to the global market, what Jaggar's, Mitter's, Mohanty's, and Shiva's analyses show is the extent to which those who produce the lion's share of its labor benefit from less than a fraction of its wealth, and that these laborers are disproportionately female and/or a member of an indigenous population, and/or a minor. By showing, for example, how casualization exploits already gendered divisions of labor embedded in developing world cultures, their analyses expand the meaning of commodification to include the distinction between the affluent global North (West) and the (mal)developing South (non-West). Shiva (1994) adds to this picture the vital link with the feminization of labor, the phenomenon that, as Jaggar points out, has led to enormous and escalating debt owed by developing nations to wealthier Western ones by virtue of loans made to their governments for economic development projects. Jaggar, then, may raise the most important issue when she asks whether citizens of developing nations can be said to owe their Northern/Western creditors for loans made to their governments to develop capitalist ventures. Her answer is "no":

> The people who bear the overwhelming burden of paying the Southern debt are the poorest citizens of the poorest countries of the world— especially Southern women. These citizens are held economically responsible for debts undertaken by their governments, often before they were born.... In the most heavily indebted countries, however, electorates were uninformed about the meaning or even existence of foreign

loans. Debts were often assumed by local elites who spent the money on unproductive prestige projects or siphoned it into personal foreign bank accounts.... Given this history, it is plausible to argue that poor people in the global South have no responsibility to pay back money that they did not ask to borrow, from which they enjoyed no benefits, and through which they were even repressed. It is especially unreasonable to expect Southern women to be responsible for the debts because even if they had the formal equality of the vote, they had even less input than men into taking on the loans and benefited even less from them. Southern women as a group receive even less food, health care, and education than Southern men. (2002: 128–29)

There is no question that international loan debt imposes a significant burden on many men in developing countries; Shiva would certainly include it within the ambit of maldevelopment, the environmental consequences of which we are only now beginning to grasp. However, it also benefits some men, particularly given their dominant numbers in government office or on the boards of multinational corporations (or "local elites"), insofar as debt provides a mechanism to justify the casualization of labor, and hence its continuing feminization. International loan debt creates pressure to keep wages as low as possible in the interest of generating proceeds toward paying off the loan (or, at least, its interest). Because poor women (and many poor men) provide a ready-made pool of labor, they are among the most likely to be hired into the casualized "McJobs" whose production of goods and services then provides leverage for developing nations' governments to negotiate (or renegotiate) loans and interest. The cycle thus created contributes to the reinforcement of existing social divisions precisely because these divisions are profitable—at least for employers, loan agents, and government agents, many of which, as Jaggar notes, are corrupt.

Jaggar's question captures the relationship between a heteropatriarchal capitalist North/West and a feminized South whose only recourse, like that of its female citizens, may be to refuse to participate in the reproduction of conditions whose benefit for some comes at so high a cost for others. Yet the likelihood of such a revolt is improbable in the extreme, given the importance for developing nations of appearing economically (and thus socially and politically) progressive to the international community. Another possibility, however, is offered by "banker to the poor" and Nobel Peace Prize–winner Muhammad Yunus, whose Grameen Bank in Bangladesh provides modest loans—"microcredit"—to small business enterprises, especially those featuring women's traditional occupations, in the interest of empowering the poor against poverty and starvation. Although such enterprises are "capitalist" in the sense that they are intended to generate profit over investment, their primary aims are not defined by profitability alone, but by its potential benefits for the families, communities, and ultimately nations empowered at the grassroots level to make more deliberate—and less economically coerced—decisions aimed at the improvement of human life (Yunus 2007: 118–30).

Yunus describes in rich detail the daunting challenge of convincing poor women to form a small business cooperative in the Bangladeshi village of Jobra in 1977:

> There were about twenty-five women peeking at me through the cracks in the bamboo [of a hut] when suddenly the pressure on the partition grew too great and part of it collapsed. Before they knew what had happened, the women were sitting in the room listening and talking directly to me. Some hid their face behind a veil.... That was the first time I spoke with a group of Jobra women indoors. "Your words frighten us, sir," one woman said hiding her face with the end of her sari. "Money is something that only my husband handles," said another, turning her back to me so that I could not look at her directly.... "I wouldn't know what to do with money," said a woman who sat closest to me but averted her eyes.... It was easy to see the crushing effects of poverty and abuse in these faces. As they had no power over anyone else, their husbands would vent their frustrations on these women by beating them. In many ways the women were treated like animals.... [I] understood why none of these women wanted to get involved in an area reserved traditionally for men—the control of cash. (76)

Yunus goes on to describe a progress that is "[v]ery slow" (77), and made even slower not only by the cultural and religious obstacles that systematically disempower women, but also by the bureaucratic obstacles created by a government dominated by a very small (male) elite group, resistance from other Bangladeshi banking institutions, and the stereotypes that accompany poverty (117–19). But the Grameen project did make progress, in large measure because, contrary to stereotype, recipients of the Grameen loans achieved a nearly perfect repayment record: "To date [1989], we have extended a total of $190 million in loans to build more than 560,000 houses with near-perfect repayment in weekly installments. The housing programs of the commercial banks cannot boast such success" (130).

Part of what makes Yunus's capitalism a radical departure from its competitors (Bhagwati's *Defense of Globalization*, for example) is its unflinching focus on social benefit over profitability for its own sake; in other words, the Grameen Bank incorporates a fundamentally socialist or collectivist vision of what a project involving human labor and capital is supposed to accomplish. "A social business," Yunus writes, "is a non-loss, non-dividend enterprise, created with the intention to do good to people, to bring positive changes to the world, without any short-term expectation of making money out of it" (265). This vision—really a way of life—is captured in what Yunus refers to as the Sixteen Decisions:

We shall follow and advance the four principles of the Grameen Bank —discipline, unity, courage, and hard work—in all walks of our lives.

Prosperity we shall bring to our families.

We shall not live in a dilapidated house. We shall repair our houses and work toward constructing new houses at the earliest opportunity.

We shall grow vegetables all the year round. We shall eat plenty of them and sell the surplus.

During the plantation seasons, we shall plant as many seeds as possible.

We shall plan to keep our families small. We shall minimize our expenditures. We shall look after our health.

We shall educate our children and ensure that they can earn to pay for their education.

We shall always keep our children and the environment clean.

We shall build and use pit latrines.

We shall drink water from tube wells. If they are not available, we shall boil water or use alum to purify it.

We shall not take any dowry at our son's weddings; neither shall we give any dowry at our daughter's wedding. We shall keep the center free from the curse of dowry. We shall not practice child marriage.

We shall not commit any injustice, and we will oppose anyone who tries to do so.

We shall collectively undertake larger investments for higher incomes.

We shall always be ready to help each other. If anyone is in difficulty, we shall all help him or her.

If we come to know of any breach of discipline in any center, we shall go there and help restore discipline.

We shall introduce physical exercise in all our centers. We shall take part in all social activities collectively. (Yunus 2007: 135–36)

It is important to note the extent to which sexual equality is presupposed by, as well as explicitly incorporated into, the Sixteen Decisions. References, for example, to "our children" indicate that offspring are not the sole responsibility of single families, much less of isolated women, but of a community whose Grameen projects are a reflection of both its collective and individual ambitions. Decision 11's rejection of dowry, moreover, is not merely symbolic, but a repudiation of the very idea that the worth of a daughter (mother, wife) can be calculated in terms of exchange value. Throughout *Banker to the Poor*, Yunus, like Jaggar, Mitter, Shiva, and Mohanty in their respective works, demonstrates the critical significance of gauging the social and economic status of a people in terms of how its women are faring, particularly with respect to attempts to control global population growth:

> UN studies conducted in more than forty developing countries show that the birth rate falls as women gain equality. The reasons for this are numerous. Education delays marriage and procreation; better-educated women are more likely to use contraception and more likely to earn a livelihood. I believe that income-earning opportunities that empower more women... will have more impact on curbing population than the current system of "encouraging" family planning practices through intimidation tactics. (134)

The best birth control, in other words, is equality of opportunity and the dignity of social status that comes with education. As an advocate of these goals of development, Yunus is surely to be counted among the best of feminist allies.

The Grameen Bank is not, however, without its detractors, among them economists Drucilla Barker and Susan Feiner. In *Liberating Economics* (2004), they point out, for example, that among the reasons the repayment rate for Grameen's microcredit loans are so high is because "[i]f one women in the circle [of those responsible for the loan] does not repay her loan, the others in the circle are ineligible for future loans. In this way the collective liability of the group serves as collateral" (125). Moreover, "[t]he interest rate on the loans is 16 percent" (125), which Barker and Feiner consider to be rather high. They continue:

> Despite its rosy aura the reality [of Grameen microcredit] is less appealing, and the situation is more complex. It is certainly true that microcredit has been a success for many of the banks that have adopted it. The loan repayment rates are extraordinarily high. We must remember, however, that lending to the poor has long been a lucrative enterprise. Pawnshops, finance companies, and loan sharks profit handsomely when poor people find themselves desperate for cash and unable to secure regular

credit. In these conditions they are forced to pay higher interest rates. One would be shortsighted, indeed, to think that profitable lending to the poor was a new innovation. The real questions about microcredit are these: Does it reduce women's poverty, or does it exploit the poor? Does it empower women, or does it make them dependent upon lenders? (125)

No doubt, some of this criticism is fair. The Grameen Bank is still an enterprise whose main objective is profitability, and not human welfare, and to the extent that this is true, Barker and Feiner's observations illustrate the inherent limitations of *any* capitalist enterprise with respect to the inevitable conflict between, for example, the vulnerable conditions of those who seek microcredit, especially women, and the objectives of the lending institution to maximize profit. In this respect, then, we might consider whether any capitalist system of economic exchange is morally defensible.

I am not convinced, however, that Barker and Feiner's comparison of the Grameen Bank to traditional pawnshops and loan sharks is entirely fair. It is, for example, unlikely that any pawn shop would have posted on its walls anything like Yunus's Sixteen Decisions, and while it is doubtless true that the women who secure these high-interest loans are vulnerable to economic exploitation, they are in other ways very unlike the people likely to appear in pawnshops. In the first place, what women have to offer in exchange for Grameen Bank's microcredit loans are not things like wedding rings or other family heirlooms, but rather skills like weaving or cooking. They are not, in other words, already engaged in the capitalist venture but rather are outsiders to it. At one level, this may make them even more vulnerable to exploitation by virtue of their economic naïveté, but at another it may empower some women to bargain more vigilantly because of the high value of their skills. In the second place, while desperation may well characterize the situations of women seeking microcredit loans, it is markedly different from the desperation of those who are typically drawn to pawnshops in that it is less likely to be complicated by, for example, drug abuse, and far more likely to be caused by conditions such as lack of access to birth control. What accounts for desperation, in other words, matters — particularly when the poor in the case of Grameen Bank loans are virtually all women, and the victims of pawnshops and loan sharks primarily men. Unless we take the Sixteen Decisions entirely cynically—as if they were simply a manipulation to convince women (and their families and villages) to sign onto microcredit loans—it seems a stretch to compare Yunus to a loan shark.

Still, as Barker and Feiner themselves point out, the evidence for this version of capitalism-with-a-human-face is "mixed":

> Proponents of microcredit usually offer stories of its individual success—women whose lives were transformed after they purchased a market stall or some simple inputs that allowed them to start handicraft production. There is no doubt that many individual poor women and their families have been helped through microcredit. There is also no question that when women take out loans, the whole family is likely to benefit and the impact on child welfare will be greater than when men take out loans. At the same time, there is little evidence that microcredit has any impact on poverty rates in the developing countries. (2004: 125)

Whether we opt to see this glass as half empty or half full depends, of course, on a number of other factors that determine what counts as successful. If fulfilling Decisions 4 and 5 lead, for example, to topsoil erosion, we might hesitate to count an aggressive farming project as successful in the long run. It is hard, however, to imagine anything but good coming from the health-oriented provisions of Decisions 9 and 10. Perhaps the central question is not whether the Grameen Bank and its Sixteen Decisions empower women, but whether its loan program empowers women in the most effective way possible. Barker and Feiner suggest that the evidence here too is "ambiguous":"According to the World Bank, microfinance empowers women by allowing them more control over household assets, more autonomy and decision-making power, greater access to participation in public life, and more control over household resources" (126). Nonetheless,

> [o]ther findings suggest that microcredit increases women's dual work burdens of market and household labor. Microcredit can also increase household conflict when men rather than women control the loans. Men sometime use women to get the loans and make women responsible for paying the loans back. (126)

It's hard to imagine a clearer example of the sheer durability of the material relationship between heteropatriarchy and capitalism than if a program explicitly intended to empower women were hijacked by men as a means of exploiting their wives, daughters, and mothers — *and* the lending bank.

For Barker and Feiner, what the vulnerability of microcredit to such abuses implies is that, although it can be empowering,

> it does nothing to change the structural conditions that drive women to the informal sector [street vendors, domestic laborers, and other "fringe economy" labor]....As an antipoverty program, microcredit fits nicely with the prevailing neoliberal ideology that defines poverty as a problem of individual failing. To solve poverty, the poor must work harder, get educated, have fewer children, and act more responsibly....This rhetoric shifts poverty solutions away from collective, social efforts and onto the backs of poor women. (126)

But, again, is this really a fair characterization of Yunus's complete program? I don't think so. That some of the more emancipatory provisions of the Sixteen Decisions, particularly concerning the use of birth control (Decision 6) and the rejection of dowry (Decision 11), may not be taken seriously (or given only lip service) by individual male patriarchs does not imply that their intent is not genuinely subversive; it is. Indeed, were the Sixteen Decisions taken as seriously as I assume Yunus intends, the effect would be to lift the burden from individual women and their families and make the success of Grameen Bank loans a collective responsibility. Barker and Feiner might object that the Decisions are themselves a potential recipe for oppression, because they situate the success of an enterprise squarely on those who are engaged in it, and, as necessary conditions for securing microcredit, they are inherently coercive. Fair enough — but their objections simply underline a dilemma that confronts any endeavor to salvage capitalism by trying to shift its purposes toward human welfare: namely, that the effort to empower individual persons via economic programs inevitably makes them responsible for its success or failure. In other words, because individuals are the only possible sites of exchange, only individuals can be held responsible for it — regardless of other factors, be they religious, cultural, or environmental, that may play a role. Such is the ideological upshot of any neoliberal solution to poverty, and hence its inevitable conflict with the Sixteen Decisions.

The Grameen Bank is progressive in its vision of economic justice, however much it is challenged by an entrenched banking bureaucracy, competing heteropatriarchal institutions, or even its own stereotypes of the poor. Yunus's program may well be the best capitalism can do, and this may just be inadequate with respect to human welfare—not to mention environmental sustainability. But these are not its only challenges. Having found, on the one hand, a reinvigorated and often violent ally in the recent resurgence of religious fanaticism, heteropatriarchal privilege has begun to reassert itself through appeals to misogynistic and oppressive readings of the Koran and the Bible; some acts of terrorism, we might speculate, are as much a backlash against the liberation of women as they are an attack on the culture industry. On the other hand, global capitalism not only dwarfs projects like the Grameen Bank, it exploits patriarchal social institutions in the interest of guaranteeing pools of cheap labor as well as markets for products whose crassly opportunistic aims contribute to the reinforcement of gender stereotypes. As Yunus documents with respect to the response of the Bangladeshi ruling classes, the capitalist values that accompany the import of a Western-style work ethic can generate the conditions for backlash against the transformation of villagers into laborers, water supplies into refuse repositories, and people into debtors. It is hardly surprising that this resistance would include the reassertion of patriarchal prerogative against the appearance of what is often interpreted as Western licentiousness and vulgarity. Hence it is equally unsurprising that an aspect of this resistance would take the form of calls to return to a religiosity that repudiates the materialism associated with capitalist excess.

What is surprising, however, is that—backlash notwithstanding— religious fanaticism and global capitalism actually can make mutually profitable bedfellows. Both, after all, appeal to the same logic of domination that empowers human beings over nonhuman nature and men over women, Westernized peoples over indigenous ones. And both religious fanaticism and global capitalism benefit from the hierarchical and oppressive relationships that govern labor, production, and reproduction, whether the site of work done is within the patriarchal

CONTEMPORARY FEMINIST THEORY AND ACTIVISM

family or on the factory floor. Indeed, as religious fanaticism becomes a site for the consumption of weapons, petroleum, and private armies, it exemplifies a culture industry transformed by its new consumer, men empowered simultaneously by rigidly enforced religious prerogative and access to the enormous wealth generated by rising oil prices (not to mention the black markets for heroin). Global competition over the tools of religious war, moreover, will surely have a transformative effect upon the aspirations of religious patriarchs as their authority is enhanced through the control of the commodities that fuel—literally—the global market. As we shall see, however, hanging in the balance, as Yunus illustrates story after story, is not only human welfare, but quite possibly the capacity to support the life of the planet itself.

Chapter V

The Culture Industry, the Conceptual Economy of Difference, and the Allure of Religion: Feminist Discourses of Resistance

OPPORTUNISM AND THE COMMODIFICATION OF DIFFERENCE

A central aspect of my argument thus far has been that at the conceptual core of any capitalist enterprise, whether it be a Thailand clinic devoted to sex-reassignment surgery, an agency in India that caters to American couples seeking an inexpensive surrogate arrangement, or an arms dealer engaged in the politics of profit, is its opportunism. In order to be competitive, such an enterprise not only must seek out opportunities to create demand but must also be in a position to produce the products or services that satisfy that demand at the lowest possible cost. As we've seen, however, an enterprise that may be a boon for some may also be a source of the most debilitating oppression for others. Even in its most ostensibly humane instantiations, such as the microcredit programs of the Grameen Bank, the pressure to maximize profits at the expense of other values (moral, aesthetic, environmental, or familial) finds itself in conflict with the welfare of the people it may aim to serve, but of whom it cannot fail to take advantage. Because competition is necessary to the growth of any capitalist enterprise, it is unsurprising that a system of exchange that evolved from local trade to national corporations to global enterprises recognized by the United Nations as virtual nation-states exploits whatever divisions of labor are made available to it through existing institutions. What, then, determines these divisions? What exactly does the capitalist take advantage of?

In short, I think the answer to this question is "difference." Differences of sex, race, ability, sexual identity, and indigenous status—however stereotypically imagined—are ideal for capitalism in the sense that they're ready-made for determining wages, working conditions, and markets. Difference, in other words, provides the conceptual key to the commodification of labor because it supplies criteria on the basis of which to "justify" wages and working conditions, including those of the casualized "McJobs" that Alison Jaggar (1983) describes. Because it is presumed to be natural or inherent, difference serves both to "justify" a division of labor that consistently disadvantages women, non-white persons, and other groups, and to reinforce itself as an essential conceptual tool for successful capitalist enterprise. Difference thus defines what counts as commodifiable in terms of sex, ethnicity and other sociological factors.[1] Commodifiability is, however, a two-sided venture, since its appeal to difference (that is, "differences" exploitable as labor) determines who counts not only as maximally exploitable labor, but also as a maximally marketable audience. As we'll see, regardless of whether these are all the same people (and they're not), regardless of the relationship of difference to culture, difference functions as essential to the capitalist conceptual economy.

Having said this, however, difference also seems to be at odds with another key component of capitalism, namely, the demand for generality or sameness generated through standardizing the means of production (raw materials and equipment, for instance) and the globalizing of markets via, for example, the Internet. Simply put: mass production demands mass consumption of the same product or service, so there would seem to be little possibility for the accommodation of differences at the level of individuals. Difference determines levels of exploitability according to age-old divisions of sex, class, and

---

[1] Marx himself seems to make this assumption; see Lee (2002: 12–17) and Marx's *The German Ideology* (1981: 44).

so on, but differences in the talents, interests, or abilities of individuals can be accommodated only if they can be converted into either labor or commodity, that is, if they can be put to the service of mass production. If Marx is right, and our participation in the economy as wage-laborers and consumers estranges or alienates us from the creative activities or praxis in which we might otherwise be engaged, the individuality that may emerge and develop through such activities would itself seem to be in danger of being lost (Marx 1981: 47; 1964: 112–13). The greater likelihood, however, is that it will be co-opted. Imagine, for example, athletic talent—speed, agility, strength. It is certainly possible to develop these capacities within a culture whose primary objectives are to market them as desirable or attractive—as "cool." But given that they have been co-opted as a commodity for others—for the consumers of that "cool"—the motive for their development must itself undergo a fundamental transformation from being the praxis activity of an individual to being an activity whose value is set by the price it can command on a market for, say, sporting events. The capacities with which individuality distinguishes itself are thus only valuable when the desirability of their effects—speed, agility, strength—can be generalized to as many consumers as possible, when the difference that might distinguish the individual performer can be converted into the sameness demanded by mass marketing.

Difference, then, necessarily functions both as the conceptual instrument for determining the exploitable and as what must be promoted as the "cool" of a now purchasable individuality, *and* it must be able to be vanquished as the nemesis of mass marketing—lest it tempt some to (try to) opt out. The consequences of this transformation of individual differences into "difference" are, however, arguably devastating. From a socialist feminist point of view, the conversion of praxis-labor into wage-labor not only dehumanizes but depersonifies producers/consumers; that is, in the transformation of the capacity to produce creative work into factory-style wage labor, the worker not only effectively becomes equipment, but becomes fully substitutable equipment. The individuality of habits, tastes, and mannerisms are a distraction, not an asset. Hence the effect of "difference" is to replace, *as a matter of what we value*, human beings with "human beings," praxis with consumption, potential creativity with pre-made products.

Perhaps, then, the best strategy for challenging such a system is to raise to consciousness the conflict between the production of sameness and the desire for individuality, to lay bare the contradiction between being a worker/consumer and being a unique individual. This, however, is far easier said than done. After all, it would hardly be in the interest of the capitalist to encourage critical consciousness of such a contradiction. Her/his task is to make of culture an industry, to replace the desire for individual expression with one that requires the consumption of products to demonstrate "uniqueness"— a uniqueness defined not by an approach to life or a variety of artistic creation, but by the capacity to display and dispose of wealth.

According to Max Horkheimer and Theodor Adorno, authentic individuality—whatever this might mean—is naïve, if not inconceivable. In their view the primary product of capitalist enterprise is not a product as such, but rather a culture within which the consumption of products *imitates* praxis, and hence substitutes for it, dissolving the conflict—a culture that replaces the satisfaction of unique self-expression with material comfort and "coolness," however fleeting these might be. Soliciting the desires of individuals is thus tantamount to soliciting desires created through mass production *for* laborers *as* consumers (1972: 144–48). "The whole world," write Horkheimer and Adorno, "is made to pass through the filter of the culture industry" (126). "Individuality" remains an aspiration, but one now transformed into a purchasable good subject to competition with other demographically similar consumers; the aims, then, of this "individual" under construction are about what (and how much) can be bought, displayed, disposed of, and replaced. While "individuality" remains a driving reason to work harder and longer, this is not because it promises uniqueness, but because what it advertises is an *imitation* of itself taken as real.

What is more, given the culture industry's demand for "complete identification with generality," no one really believes the hype (154). Instead, individuality becomes a kind of performance of a well-entrenched self-deception about being an "individual," the concept itself compromised because the endeavor to realize it requires participation in an industry that replaces "the peculiarity of the self" with the "pseudo individuality" of the imitated and the popular:

In the culture industry the individual is an illusion not merely because of the standardization of the means of production. He is tolerated only so long as his complete identification with the generality is unquestioned. Pseudo individuality is rife: from the standardized jazz improvisation to the exceptional film star whose hair curls over her eye to demonstrate her originality. What is individual is not more than the generality's power to stamp the accidental detail so firmly that it is accepted as such. The defiant reserve or elegant appearance of the individual on show is mass produced…. The peculiarity of the self is a monopoly commodity determined by society; it is falsely represented as natural…. On the faces of private individuals and movie heroes put together according to the patterns on magazine covers vanishes a pretense in which no one now believes; the popularity of the hero models comes partly from a secret satisfaction that the effort to achieve individuation has at last been replaced by the effort to imitate, which is admittedly more breathless. (154–55)

Individuality is not then abandoned, but rather depersonified and "recommissioned" in the image of the supremely malleable consumer, that is, as "pseudo." However tempting it may be to cling to some notion of difference in terms of an original "peculiar" or distinct self, as something that could be recovered, this hope receives little encouragement from Horkheimer and Adorno. The desire for uniqueness evinced in the "defiant reserve" or the "hair curled over one eye" merely reproduces faux-difference. It intimates something more than differences accruing to sex or ethnicity, but is in no position to cash this intimation out in anything enduring like individuality. The reserve, the curl—or the waiflike thinness, or the muscle mass—are all accomplished through the consumption of products whose mass production appeals to the desires manufactured for every consumer within the relevant demographic, gender, age, and economic status. Whether what you're after is the conformity of the business suit or the apparent resistance to conformity signaled by, say, Goth piercings or visible tattooing is irrelevant to your status as a consumer. If Horkheimer and Adorno's analysis of the culture industry is correct, sameness can not only be marketed as difference, sameness just *is* "difference."

THE CONCEPTUAL ECONOMY OF DIFFERENCE AND THE PERFORMANCE OF GENDER

This economy of difference exploits desires created to be congruent with the division of labor. The desire to imitate a curl owes itself not in the first place to a yearning for individuality but, as feminist theorist Judith Butler might put it, to the performance of a specific incarnation of gender, one that can be gotten "wrong" and can therefore be punished (Butler 2003: 423). "Gender reality," writes Butler, "is performative, which means, quite simply, that it is real only to the extent that it is performed" (423). The gendered "self" may be performed *as* individualizing, but, if Horkheimer and Adorno (1972) are correct, it nonetheless signifies a stable referent in an economy dependent on its performance *as* gendered. While Butler doesn't trace this performance in terms of its status as a commodity in itself, her description nonetheless highlights its specifically gendered character:

> Genders then can be neither true nor false, neither real or apparent. And yet, one is compelled to live in a world in which genders constitute univocal signifiers, in which gender is stabilized, polarized, rendered discrete and intractable. In effect, gender is made to comply with a model of truth and falsity which not only contradicts its own performative fluidity, but serves a social policy of gender regulation and control. Performing one's gender wrong initiates a set of punishments both obvious and indirect, and performing it well provides the reassurance that there is an essentialism of gender identity after all. (423–24)

For Butler, gender epitomizes a variety of difference that is fixed according to a set of socially (i.e., patriarchally) mediated instructions or expectations, the violation of which results in punishment, namely, in the stifling of any capacity for less stereotypical expression or "fluidity" of gender performance. While any flirtation with individuality or praxis is perhaps only half-conscious in any case, repression in the form of punishment and reward for the "right" gender performance remains the order of the day. Implying neither originality nor individuality, the performance of gender enacts what feminist critical theorist Jennifer Eagan calls "unfreedom" (2006: 280–82); that is, it codifies social expectation designed to stabilize difference and to preclude the emergence of differences.

But what actually motivates the creation of social expectation? Horkheimer and Adorno (1972: 154-55) offer the important clue here. Demanding a "complete identification with generality," gender creates the desire for the commodities that facilitate its performance as a fixed, reliable division of labor and consumption. In this fashion, social expectation itself acts as a functionary of the culture industry; were we to query the advantage in its creation—that is, were we to query the purposes served by gender's oppressive regulation, the answer would invariably lead us back to the exchange made possible through it. Executed according to a socially policed script, gender as performance epitomizes capitalist opportunism precisely because it requires neither the true nor the false, the real nor the apparent. The conditions required of it are simply that it be convincing, that there be empowered beneficiaries, and thus that it be marketable. Like the curl, or the thinness, or the muscularity, those who are empowered are not necessarily those who fulfill these performances of pseudo-individuality. But it is indeed these beneficiaries whose marketing decisions effectively guarantee that no performance, whatever its gender or race or sexual identity, can fall outside the culture industry. And it is thus in this sense that reality is itself defined "simply" by/as exchange.

This reality is amply, if disturbingly, illustrated in feminist philosopher Susan Bordo's discussion of the diet and exercise industry in "Reading the Slender Body." Here, Bordo explores the predominantly Western preoccupation not merely with thinness, but with the tone, muscularity, and smoothness associated with slenderness, pointing out that while it might be tempting to focus attention only on the extreme cases (anorexia, bulimia), such a focus only obscures the extent to which slenderness itself functions to police and reproduce gender:

Of course, many of these behaviors are outside the norm [anorexia, bulimia], if only because of the financial resources they require. But pre-occupation with fat, diet and slenderness are not. Indeed, such preoccu-pation may function as one of the most powerful "normalizing" strategies of our century, ensuring the production of self-monitoring and self-disciplining "docile bodies," sensitive to any departure from social norms, and habituated to self-improvement and transformation in the service of these norms…. For women, who are subject to such controls more profoundly and, historically, more ubiquitously than men, the focus on "pathology"… diverts recognition from a central means of the reproduction of gender. (Bordo 1995: 468–69)

As a central means for the reproduction of gender, slenderness functions both as social expectation/norm and as a key component of a script internalized as value associated, unsurprisingly, with economic class, work ethic, discipline, or, as Bordo puts it, "the correct attitude": "[T]he well-muscled body has become a cultural icon; 'working out' is a glamorized and sexualized yuppie activity. No longer signifying lower-class status … the firm, developed body has become a symbol of the correct attitude; it means that one 'cares' about oneself and how one appears to others, suggesting willpower, energy, control over infantile impulse, the ability to 'make something' of oneself" (475). Literally embodied in the quest for slenderness, the "correct attitude" instantiates the ideal performance of gender for the culture industry. Facilitated as rigid discipline and achieved through the consumption of products and services perfectly suited to its reinforcement, the "attitude" epitomizes the "complete identification with generality," the habituated docility of the producer/consumer's self-control—including the implicit threat of punishment or social ostracism for those who fail to conform.

However, while Horkheimer and Adorno's account of the culture industry captures a vital element of its oppressive demand for conformity, it ultimately underestimates another of its key players, namely, failure, or rather, the guilt supplied by a "failure" defined in terms of the unachievable ideals pervasively reiterated in advertisements, for example. As Bordo shows, failure actually facilitates consumption and thus, although it effects a temporary appearance of instability (Bordo 1995: 171–73), it in fact operates to ensure an even greater degree of self-control. "On the one hand," she argues, "as 'producer selves,' we must be capable of sublimating, delaying, repressing desires for immediate gratification; we must cultivate the work ethic. On the other hand, as 'consumer selves' we serve the system through a boundless capacity to capitulate to desire and indulge in impulse; we must become creatures who hunger for constant and immediate satisfaction" (476). The guilt that follows capitulation to desire can only empower a system within which something as seemingly insignificant as a curl over one eye can wield so much influence. As Bordo remarks,

> Conditioned to lose control at the very sight of desirable products, we can only master ourselves through rigid defenses against them. The slender body codes the tantalizing ideal of a well-managed self in which all is "in order" despite the contradictions of consumer culture…. [M]any of us may find our lives vacillating between a daytime rigidly ruled by the "performance principle" while our nights and weekends capitulate to unconscious "letting go"…. In this way the central contradiction of the system inscribes itself on our bodies, and bulimia emerges as characteristic of modern personality construction…. (477)

In fact, Butler is correct, even "letting go" is part of a compulsory performance whose specifically gendered incarnation helps to maintain the distinction between a "wrong" performance and a right one.

Consider, for example, Paris Hilton, whose scripted public performance exemplifies not only the vacillation Bordo describes, but the "pretense in which no one believes" of an individuality long ago jettisoned in favor of the fashionable, the popular—the consumable. Vacillating between well-coifed, fashion-dictated, catwalk photo-ops and a weepy, somewhat (but not too much) disheveled release from jail, Hilton encodes and reinforces a gender performance that many, but not only, white Western girls seek to emulate. While Hilton's "letting go" appears to include fewer quarts of ice cream and more martinis, the operative "ideology," as Eagan puts it, following Adorno, is the same: "Ideology, for Adorno, is the false story about what reality is that becomes reiterated until it is accepted as truth…. [It] no longer functions explicitly in the form of propaganda, but has become embedded in social practices that have been reiterated and reenacted as social practice" (2006: 279).

The ideology of the "slender body" is one of these false stories. Embedded in practices like the self-starvation of anorexia nervosa or the binging and purging associated with bulimia, the quest for the slender body epitomizes the culture industry's paradox or "double bind" between our "producer selves" and our "consumer selves." As Bordo remarks,

> While bulimia embodies the unstable "double bind" of consumer capitalism, anorexia and obesity embody an attempted resolution of that "double bind." Anorexia could therefore be seen as an extreme development of the capacity for self-denial and the repression of desire...
> [while] obesity similarly points to an extreme capacity to capitulate to desire....Both are rooted in the same consumer-culture construction of desire as overwhelming and overtaking the self. Given that construction, total submission or rigid defense become the only possible postures. (1995: 477)

Given this construction of "self" and its implicit internalizing of its status as self-denying producer and self-indulgent consumer, no propaganda is needed to reiterate the value of slenderness as its "reality." Such a "self" is constructed by the double bind as "unfree": "The culture industry effectively eradicates freedom by prefiguring certain kinds of choices and in that sense limits the reality that we can receive" (Eagan 2006: 292).

In other words, although the slender-body industry advertises what appears to be a cornucopia of choices, because it precludes opting out of the economy of difference, it actually precludes even failure (of say, a diet or exercise program) from counting as anything other than a performance within "the story." Even failure, then, turns out to be an opportunity for consumption (of, say, laxatives or stomach stapling). Your options, in other words, are themselves wholly determined by the next opportunity for consumption. You can, for example, try a new diet product. Paris Hilton can "do rehab," you can blow your diet on a quart of Moosetracks ice cream, Hilton can violate parole—but these are no more genuinely free choices than is flipping that curl to the other side of your face, and it's not merely because every "choice" comes with a price tag, but because choosing is itself already encoded (prefigured) by difference, that is, by the construction of the gender-performing "self." This is not to say that choosing this nail polish or that hosiery might not be *experienced* as free; but since the experience is itself choreographed, not, as Yunus (2007) envisions, for human benefit, but by and for its profitability, it can be described as liberating only insofar as we define freedom as the freedom to consume. Indeed, even if this comprises only one definition of freedom, it is surely not what we're referring to when we speak of the emancipation of anyone whose life is permeated by oppression—however they might experience it.

The picture painted by the culture industry's seeming monopoly on human action is a dark one, especially for women and girls. According to Eagan, however, there is more to unfreedom, a "more" which offers an avenue for what critical theorists call "immanent critique"—really a variety of consciousness raising—from within a system, such as capitalist exchange, panned out in terms of its very real and often oppressive consequences. Following Adorno's lead, Eagan argues that the significance of unfreedom lies in the tangible suffering it produces and the potential for that suffering to expose the culture industry to an interrogation of its presuppositions. Solicited by the subjective experience of the material/physical individual, argues Eagan, "[s]uffering is a particular variety of unfreedom, and one that reveals our condition of unfreedom to us.... Ultimately, what saves us from the totalizing power of ideology is our own immediate and subjective experience. The experience of suffering...shakes us out of our own acceptance of the status quo" (2006: 282–83). Suffering is thus not merely a consequence of failure; rather, it is that experience of pain which—regardless of our association with success or failure—prods us to interrogate the purposes of our performance, that is, to see our performances as performances.

Eagan is not, of course, denying that suffering is itself constructed and interpreted within a context delimited by production and consumption (282–86, 295); anorexia and bulimia are, after all, both punished and rewarded even though both can produce death. Nor is she denying that much suffering (especially within the slender-body industry) is actively sought out as emblematic of the successful mastery of "self" (Bordo 1995: 483). What Eagan is suggesting is that the experience of suffering can serve to remind us that "my body" is not an abstraction, but rather "the site of someone's specific suffering" (285), namely mine, and from which I cannot easily escape. Suffering can shake us out of our autonomic acquiescence to the culture industry by reminding us that difference—however performed and encoded—is always embodied. Even if we experience it as something shameful, disgusting, or uncontrollable (Bordo 1995: 480–84), the experience of embodiment can serve to individuate us in a fashion that produces resistance.

Many feminist theorists have written on the significance of embodiment with respect to how gender is socially encoded as performance, expectation, or unfreedom. What Eagan contributes, however, is the opportunity to undertake as a distinctly contemporary project this discourse as one of resistance to the domination of the culture industry. Approached not only as an effort to raise consciousness about the profoundly harmful effects of capitalist exploitation on women's (and men's) bodies, but as an immanent critique of its systematic erasure of opportunities for praxis, and the suffering this produces, works such as Donna Haraway's "Manifesto for Cyborgs" (1990 [1985]) can be reread as a way of conceiving the performative subject within—but not compliant with—the strictures of global capitalism and its technologies of production. A return to Haraway's metaphor of the cyborg might then be useful:

> The cyborg is a creature in a postgender world.... In a sense, the cyborg has no origin story in the Western sense: a "final" irony, since the cyborg is also the awful apocalyptic telos [purpose/end] of the "West's" escalating dominations of abstract individuation, an ultimate self untied at last from all dependency....An origin story in the "Western," humanist sense depends on the myth of original unity, fullness, bliss, and terror....The cyborg skips the step of original unity, of identification with nature.... (1990 [1985]: 581–82)

As the crowning achievement of the technological mastery of capitalist enterprise, the cyborg represents both the ultimate expression of the economy of difference and its dissolution; after all, no such product-subject could become possible without the ideologies/stories that guarantee production and consumption. The cyborg is thus the product of the "correct attitude" both as work ethic and as aspiration; it epitomizes at once the complete alienation of self from the product of labor—without recognizable origin, it is not another "self"—and precisely the freedom that comes from being liberated from that origin in which difference and the division of labor are rooted.

The cyborg makes plain the opportunism that governs capitalist exchange in that its embodiment is entirely performative and can exist without gender or ethnicity—without exploitable difference. The cyborg has no connection to Enlightenment conceptions of inherent human dignity (however much the realization of such ideals excluded women); instead, it summarizes the value of (mass) production. It has no history in which to claim a stake. It has no roots in difference other than in whatever is required to produce it; given its patriarchal history, after all, gender offers the most advantageous means of production. Yet, and ironically, the cyborg is the ultimate aspiration of, as Bordo might put it, total self-mastery, and in this sense it embodies the same desires that propel the quest for the slender body. The epitome of the "correct attitude," the cyborg reveals our unfreedom through demonstrating—just by being possible—the extent to which the divisions of labor exploited in capitalism are the ultimately arbitrary products of a history that could have been otherwise, and to which the cyborg itself has no commitment. From this perspective, gender can be seen as nothing other than a vitally important technology (or technoscience) of (re)production.

The same story, then, that produces suffering for those most vulnerable to its compulsory performance can also, returning to Eagan, at least intimate the hope of liberation: with the production of the cyborg, the last vestige of the myth of difference, and hence the last (falsely obligated) debt owed on its behalf has been paid. As Haraway puts it, "[t]he cyborg is resolutely committed to partiality, irony, intimacy, and perversity," that is, to cultivating differences as resistance to difference (1990 [1985]: 582). However, she continues, "[t]he main trouble with cyborgs...is that they are the illegitimate offspring of militarism and patriarchal capitalism, not to mention state socialism. But illegitimate offspring are often exceedingly unfaithful to their origins. Their fathers, after all, are inessential" (582). For the cyborg, then,

[t]he home, workplace, market, public arena, and the body itself can all be dispersed and interfaced in nearly infinite polymorphous ways, with large consequences for women and others—consequences that are themselves very different for different people and make potent oppositional international movements difficult to imagine and essential for survival. One important route for reconstructing socialist feminist politics is through theory and practice addressed to the social relations of science and technology, including crucially the systems of myth and meanings structuring our imaginations. The cyborg is a kind of disassembled and reassembled postmodern collective and personal self. This is the self feminists must code. (595)

Legitimate or otherwise, to whatever extent the image of the cyborg can shake us up by compelling us to recognize that the slender-body stories (and their many analogues) have no other justification than the maintenance of the culture industry, it represents—albeit ironically—a kind of freedom. It is perhaps the freedom of satire: the kind of freedom irreverently performed by comedians such as Kathy Griffin, Jon Stewart, or Stephen Colbert, who turn on their head some of the absurdities of the culture industry by converting it into a tabloid consumable—still for sale, but complete with the joke that is on us. These are the cyborgs who know they are performing, as it were, in the cybernetic space of irony and satire.

The cyborg offers a totalizing metaphor both for the demand for complete generality and for the dissimulation of that totality into an indomitable profusion of differences. Having, after all, no other origin than the technology of mass production, the cyborg is not beholden to any single vision of the future's reiteration of the present, much less the past. Like the Internet, another techno-child of the culture industry, the cyborg represents both global citizenship and domination, the promise of freedom and, as the casualizing of labor demonstrates, its oppressive antithesis. As Fredric Jameson points out, "this whole global, yet American, postmodern culture is the internal and superstructural expression of a whole new wave of American military and economic domination throughout the world; in this sense, as throughout class history, the underside of the culture is blood, torture, death and terror" (1991: 5). What feminist critique makes equally clear is that this underside is divided not only by class but by the exploitations of sex, a fact made especially clear, for example, in the profoundly male-dominated American economic and military involvement in Iraq.

Still, for all of its drawbacks, few doubt that the economic position for a sizable number of Western/Northern women is better in the present than in the past, that globalization can mean access, opportunity, and communication; this too is reflected in the image of the cyborg. Hence we must ask an obvious question: Why, given the considerable opportunity made available through the feminist critique for challenging the marriage of capitalism and patriarchy, for confronting its "love child" in the culture industry, hasn't the feminist movement been more globally successful? Given decades of excellent analyses like those of Jaggar and her descendants, why haven't we seen more and more substantial change? Where's the revolution? The answer to this question is, of course, no more one-size-fits-all than the specific conditions women face, but one source I think we must look to is the re-emergence of religious fundamentalism, especially in its extreme and profoundly patriarchal manifestations, and with respect to its own complex, nuanced, often antagonistic, but deeply interwoven relationship with and within the culture industry.

A CONTENTIOUS THREE-PARTY MARRIAGE: PATRIARCHY, CAPITALISM, AND RELIGIOUS FUNDAMENTALISM

Among the most disturbing phenomena of recent years, at least for those of us whose politics tend to the left of center, has been the re-emergence of fundamentalist, sometimes fanatical, strains within mainstream religious traditions such as Christianity, Judaism, and Islam. Indeed, while it's not my aim here to comment at any length on the US involvement in Iraq, what does seem clear is a country that endured a secular—however brutally administered—government under Saddam Hussein is now endangered by sectarian religious violence. What is perhaps less clear—though the prospects are certainly ominous given the influence of, for example, the Taliban— is what the status of women will be in a postwar, and post–civil-war Iraq, but there is good reason to think it will be diminished under any government or regime dominated by either Sunni or Shiite leaders. Of course similar criticism has been leveled at many of the more conservative denominations of Christianity (say, the Southern Baptist Convention); disputes about the ordination of women pastors remains standard fare on the religion pages of newspapers both in the United States and in Europe, and anyone who has read Margaret Atwood's *The Handmaid's Tale* (or has seen the film version) comes away with at least an idea of what a patriarchal Christian dictatorship might look like.

My point is that it's not exactly news that religion—Christianity, Islam, and Judaism included—often supports (and is supported by) heteropatriarchal institutions both inside and outside the church, mosque, or synagogue. The feminist critique of the relationship between patriarchy and religion reaches back at least as far as Gerda

Lerner's *The Creation of Patriarchy* (1986), as well as to the biting (and highly contentious) analyses of Mary Daly.[2] Also, feminist accounts such as Margaret Denike's "political economy of the concept of evil" answer important questions concerning the origins of the sexual division of labor, its own conceptual economy of difference rooted in a religious iconography that depicts women as (the source of) evil, particularly with respect to sins like gluttony, sexual perversion, and, as Denike chronicles in rich detail, witchcraft (2003: 25–29). "The sexualized demonology born of the doctrine of the Fall," writes Denike, "and elaborated through Christian asceticism, speaks of a deep ambivalence toward femininity and female sexuality. It ensures that, on the one hand, *woman* was to remain the weaker, feeble *other* sex—an embodied passivity, prone to deception and seduction and that, on the other, she represented a destructive force and malevolent power; in consorting with the devil, woman became dangerous enough to pose a perpetual threat to the world, and especially to man" (23–24; emphasis in original). This notion of demonology explains not only how a profoundly unequal sexual division of labor is influenced historically by Christian religious tradition, but also how male control of women's bodies—depicted as "evil incarnate" —and thus women's (re)productive labor, came to be "justified" as a virtual necessity of men's survival (24–25).

Unsurprisingly, much feminist analysis of religion is influenced by Marx's critique of what he claimed to be the mutually exploitive and mutually advantageous relationship between religion and capitalism, between "speculative or abstract thought" and the socially manipulable elements of the economy. As Amy Newman remarks, "Marx was the first to articulate clearly the idea that criticism of speculative or abstract thought—the God's eye view—was an essential prerequisite for social criticism and that 'criticism of religion is the premise of all criticism'" (1994: 18). Marx held this view for a number of reasons, not the least of which is that the concept of the immaterial soul stands in stark contrast to his materialist concept of species being

---

2   In addition to Lerner (1986) and Daly (1975), see Hoagland and Frye, eds. (2000) for a full survey of the feminist critique of religion. Also see the special issue of *Hypatia* (Fall 1994) on the feminist philosophy of religion.

(Marx 1981: 44). His principal criticism of religion, however, is rooted in the advantage it supplies to the capitalist, and hence the role it plays in the exploitation and consequent alienation of the worker: "[T]he more the worker externalizes himself in his work, the more powerful becomes the alien, objective world that he creates opposite himself, the poorer he becomes himself in his inner life and the less he can call his own. It is just the same in religion. The more man puts into God, the less he retains in himself" (quoted in McLellan 1972: 78–79).

Indeed, religion provides a malleable worker who, always in need of opportunities for redemption, not only is ready to commit to a work ethic perfectly suited to the labor required by mass production, but also stands in absolute need of whatever wage it affords. Bordo's description of the bulimic whose "letting go" must be met by reinforced resolve provides an apt illustration of "sin" transformed by socially mediated guilt into the work of atonement, and of how religion—like diet pills—can offer a redemptive opiate, but at the cost, following Eagan, of considerable suffering (Bordo 1995: 477; Eagan 2006: 485–86). Given Denike's (2003) illustration, moreover, of the association of women and bodily indulgence, it's hardly surprising that, again, we would see women effectively internalizing the Inquisition as the self-mortifying gender performance of the anorexic. Add to this union of capitalism and religion heteropatriarchal institutions like the family, within which the sexual division of labor supplies to the male head of household a (re)productive/ domestic worker whose relationship is an analogue of worker to capitalist (Lee 2002: 34–37), and you have all the essential ingredients of global capitalism's casualized and feminized labor; you have, in short, a three-way, male-privileged marriage of religion, capitalism, and patriarchy.

This story seems straightforward. But if Newman is correct, appearances can be deceiving. In fact, it's neither as obvious nor as universally explanatory as it seems. Following Butler, Newman argues that although feminists (especially socialist feminists) have tended to follow Marx's monolithic view that all religion amounts to "a logical category representing the opposite of rational or critical self-consciousness," such discourse in fact "mimics the strategy of the oppressor" (Christianity) in reverse. In other words, it merely repeats in reverse the tendency to universalize as well as Westernize, about which many feminists are otherwise rightly critical (Newman 1994: 20).[3] "Although feminists have criticized the universalizing tendencies of traditional scholarship in other respects," argues Newman, "few hesitate to make these same moves when it comes to the subject matter of religion" (20); this tendency to identify the enemy as singular in form can, however, seriously hamper and distort feminist analyses of the causes of oppression:

> [a]lthough feminist theorists have criticized the privatization of gender relations in Marxist and neo-Marxist critical theories on the grounds that privatization has the effect of excluding women from public moral and political decision making... they have not questioned the privatization of religion in Western social and political theories. Failure to criticize this aspect of Marx' theory of religion allows religion to be seen as irrelevant to moral and political considerations and to the formation of ethical subjects, and, conversely, it allows religious beliefs and practices to remain exempt from moral accountability. In addition, it contributes to certain common misunderstandings concerning the relationship between religion and power in non-Western cultural traditions. (Newman 1994: 29–30)

Within the conceptual economy of difference, women's domestic and reproductive labor is privatized in the sense that, relegated to the home, it comes to be regarded as exempt from public scrutiny; privatizing labor thus has the effect of excluding women from public discourse and representation. Similarly, to whatever extent a theory of religion is developed as one-size-fits-all, it tends to preclude any specific analyses of particular religious practices or beliefs; such practices and beliefs become "exempt from moral accountability" because they are already effectively "privatized," if not simply dismissed, by the universal theory.

Exemption can, however, prevent us from gaining a clear view of the status of women not merely within patriarchal institutions, but also within one of the most powerful of these, namely, religion. In

---

[3] For a fuller account of Judith Butler's relevant argument on this issue, see her *Gender Trouble* (1990: 13 ff.).

addition, it can prevent us from seeing that while good arguments can be made that each of the mainstream religions is essentially heteropatriarchal, none is merely so (or in the same fashion), and each in fact offers something that, even in its most restrictive fundamentalist incarnations, some women actively embrace, practice, and promote. Exemption from scrutiny can also obscure our understanding of religion's relationship with and within the culture industry, a relationship that I suggest is not only essential to the existence of religion, but simultaneously antagonistic and mutually reinforcing. If Jaggar is correct with respect to the casualization and feminization of labor, then the global capitalism represented in the culture industry is inextricably linked to the reinforcement of women's commodification as domestic and reproductive laborers. At the same time, however, if Horkheimer, Adorno, and Bordo are right, values promoted by the culture industry—avarice, waste, conspicuous display, self-interest—offer an ideal foil against which to promote religious virtues such as self-sacrifice, modesty, and piety. A consequence, in other words, of global capitalism's opportunism—its taking advantage of existing divisions of labor supplied in part by religious institutions—is that it provides reinforcement to the heteropatriarchal values strongly advocated by fundamentalists; yet at the same time, because the premises of capitalist enterprise involve values inimical to those espoused by most religious traditions (especially proscriptions against avarice and greed), it provides an enemy against which to formulate pietistic diatribes, and in some cases even terrorist assaults.

The attack on the World Trade Center (WTC) offers a case in point. However mediated by technologies made available through capitalist exchange, however dependent on communication devices associated as readily with Hollywood starlets as with suicide bombers, however telling it is that the bombers were all male, the attack on the WTC was, among other things, an attack on capitalist values and a wholesale rejection of what Horkheimer and Adorno perceptively identify as the ultimate void produced by the culture industry:

> The less the culture industry has to promise, the less it can offer a meaningful explanation of life, and the emptier is the ideology it disseminates....Value judgments are taken either as advertising or as empty talk. Accordingly ideology has been made vague and non-committal and thus

neither clearer nor weaker. Its very vagueness...acts as an instrument of domination. It becomes a vigorous and prearranged promulgation of the status quo. *The culture industry tends to make itself the embodiment of authoritative pronouncements, and thus the irrefutable prophet of the prevailing order.* (1972: 147; my emphasis)

While there may be no adequate justification for the WTC attack, it is not difficult to imagine the attraction of a religious tradition's "explanation of life" in the face of the alienating and economically oppressive conditions of the "McJobs"; that such labor is also feminized may provide a clue to explaining some women's attraction to these traditions. To whatever extent the culture industry is perceived from within a religious tradition as morally vacuous, irresolute, or as encouraging avarice and envy, it is quite plausible to imagine religion as a positive, purposeful alternative, one that is readily available regardless of economic class, and hence likely to be perceived as an opportunity by those whose access to other choices—art, music, culture—is limited or negligible.

Religion can, of course, offer a number of tools for creating a meaningful way of organizing daily life, as Saba Mahmood observes in her work *Politics of Piety: The Islamic Revival and the Feminist Subject* (2005: 44). Mahmood's description of reasons offered by Islamic women for participating in the Women's Mosque or Piety movement in Egypt reiterates important aspects of Horkheimer and Adorno's analysis, and it provides a context for explaining women's motives for embracing apparently oppressive religious traditions:

According to participants, the women's mosque movement emerged in response to the perception that religious knowledge, as a means for organizing daily life, had become increasingly marginalized under modern structures of secular governance. Many of the mosque participants criticized what they considered to be an increasingly prevalent form of religiosity in Egypt, one that accords Islam the status of an abstract system of belief that has no direct bearing on how one lives, on what one actually does in the course of the day...."[W]esternization" (*tagharrub*) is understood to have reduced Islamic knowledge (both as a mode of thought and as a set of principles) to the status of "custom and folklore." (2005: 44)

Beyond merely criticizing the "westernizing" or reduction of Islam to "custom and folklore," these women embrace something in Islam that, for them, cannot be replaced through other means, namely, a way of "organizing daily life" governed by a variety of knowledge and a set of accompanying principles. Contrary to a Marxist account, Mahmood shows that guilt is neither the only nor even the main consequence (or motive) of religiosity, at least for some women in Islam. Indeed, the piety movement both reinforces and challenges the place of women in Islam, especially with respect to the daily practices associated with religious observance. For example,

> [e]ven though women's participation in the field of da'wa ["activities that urge fellow Muslims to greater piety" (201)] has grown in recent years, it is important to realize that this participation is structured by certain limits. Foremost among these is the condition that women, while encouraged to carry out da'wa among other women, are not allowed to do so among men. This is consistent with prohibitions forbidding women to deliver the Friday sermon or to guide men in the performance of collective prayer.... The reasoning behind these restrictions is two-fold. First is the general belief that since the Quran makes men the guardians of women, the latter should not serve in significant positions of leadership over men. Second is the prevailing notion that a woman's voice can nullify an act of worship because it is capable of provoking sexual feelings in men—though it must be noted that this view is not shared across all Muslim societies.... (Mahmood 2005: 65–66)

The picture that Mahmood paints of women's participation in da'wa illustrates why, according to her, it may be that "[t]he vexing relationship between feminism and religion is perhaps most manifest in discussions of Islam" (1). She argues that "[t]his is due in part to the historically contentious relationship that Islamic societies have had with what has come to be called 'the West,' but also due to the challenges that contemporary Islamist movements pose to secular liberal politics of which feminism has been an integral (if critical) part" (1).

From a feminist point of view, the limitations imposed upon women wishing to participate in da'wa indicate the extent to which Islam is premised on oppressive patriarchal assumptions; for socialist feminists, the desire to participate exemplifies what Marx called false consciousness, i.e., being mistakenly conscious about what are one's true interests (including what may be in one's best interests). As Mahmood effectively shows, however, false consciousness offers at best a distorted picture of women's participation in Islam, and it fails to query the specific activities involved in women's participation in da'wa, especially with respect to the order and purpose it provides to daily domestic life. In short, such explanations offer too little concerning holding Islam morally accountable with respect to the status it accords women. Nevertheless, Mahmood asks, "[w]hy would such a large number of women across the Muslim world actively support a movement that seems inimical to their 'own interests and agendas,' especially at a historical moment when these women appear to have more emancipatory possibilities available to them?" (2).

Part of the answer to this question involves the specific ways in which some Muslim women participate in Islamic practice. Mahmood, for example, describes an Islamic teacher:

> Hajja Faiza has also become known in the mosque circles for some controversial practices, which she has been able to continue to uphold despite being publicly criticized for them. Key among these is her practice of leading women in the performance of collective prayer in mosques, even when there is a male imam available to perform the task. While three of four schools of Islamic law...allow a woman to lead other women in the performance of the obligatory prayer ritual, the common custom in Egypt is that if a man is present who is capable of leading the prayers, then women defer to him, especially when in a mosque where a male imam is always present. (86–87)

While it's tempting to interpret Hajja Faiza's prayer practice as an example of feminist resistance to patriarchal authority in the sense that it appears to subvert and thereby undermine it, this interpretation assumes intentions and beliefs that the participants may not have. That is, although resistance is certainly appropriate to describe the actions of women who have already embraced feminist arguments concerning oppression and emancipation, it may not be appropriate to a context where such arguments may or may not be embraced, where the participating women may or may not see themselves as oppressed, and where the purposes of an action, in this case leading a prayer, are very different. In seeking out Hajja Faiza—whose adherence to Islamic text is reputed to be rigorous—these women seek a deeper religious connection, not a justification for the rejection of Islam (Mahmood 2005: 83–85). It is difficult to imagine the same sorts of intentions playing out in a Western context. Devoutly fundamentalist Christian women may very well reject the trappings of the culture industry, and they may well seek a deeper connection to God, but since they are the direct beneficiaries of a movement whose history in the West is a long one, steeped in Western notions of autonomy and self-interest, the context of their participation in Christian churches is a significantly different one.

Hajja Faiza's leading of prayer is, however, not non-subversive either; in that its performance does challenge the prevailing practice in Egypt, and it is experienced by the women she leads as especially meaningful because *she* leads it. Is it explanatorily useful to refer to her actions as feminist? Only, I suggest, in the sense that it can help us to gain perspective about the reasons these women give for rejecting the westernizing of Islam, for incorporating Islamic religious values into daily life, and for what, in light of recent events like the advent of the women's mosque movement, being Muslim may come to mean in the present century for its female adherents. Feminist or otherwise, what the Women's Mosque movement certainly demonstrates is that it makes little sense to treat the relationship between religion and capitalism as if religion were merely a supplier of labor, a variation of heteropatriarchy (Newman 1994: 15–16), or an inflexible monolith incapable of adapting to contemporary conditions. Indeed, as a last example concerning female circumcision will illustrate, the relationship between capitalism, religion, and how we conceive of the relationship between women and freedom is a profoundly fraught one:

> During one of her lessons, for example, Hajja Faiza was asked about female circumcision (khtan), a practice that is quite common in Egypt and that has come under increasing criticism for being either un-Islamic or injurious to the woman's health and sexuality. Hajja Faiza did not condone or condemn the practice in her answer. Instead she reasoned that the hadith [prophetic tradition] on which the practice of circumcision is

based is actually da'if (weak), a classificatory term in hadith literature that refers to a prophetic tradition of dubious authority.... [S]he argued that it was an optional practice. (Mahmood 2005: 85–86)

Hajja Faiza goes on to recommend that any woman contemplating the procedure consult a physician.

However much we might be tempted simply to condemn female circumcision as a piece of brutal medieval misogyny, what Hajja Faiza's counsel illustrates is the importance of women's decision making—even in a context that may systematically discourage it. On the one hand, by neither condoning nor condemning it, Hajja Faiza would seem to accord primary decision making to the woman considering the procedure, and we might rightly see this as a feminist moment in her teaching; on the other hand, by not condemning it, she lends credence to the view that such practices are morally and medically defensible. As bioethicist Loretta Kopelman shows, however, free choices are not the norm for this procedure (2006: 484–96). In fact, a substantial number of Muslim women and girls are subjected to circumcision in Egypt, Kenya, the United States, and elsewhere without their consent (or are too young to consent)—and this too is a serious issue, especially in a context where tradition fosters, if not a false, at least a faulty consciousness of what might best serve a young woman's (or girl's) interests. Poor economic circumstances encourage fathers to arrange to have the procedure performed on their daughters at younger and younger ages in exchange for higher "bride prices" (Kopelman 2006: 484), and, at least in Kenya among the Masai, female circumcision is associated with a range of oppressive practices such as the denial of education to girls for fear that they might choose to leave their communities or their arranged marriages (484–85). Lastly, as Kopelman details at length, the dangers to health and life posed by female circumcision are especially grave where the economic circumstances are impoverished and access to physicians, anesthetics, and antibiotics is scarce (487–90).

However much Hajja Faiza's view of female circumcision and Kopelman's differ, what is most striking about each account is that, from a socialist feminist perspective, they are linked in several ways. First, Hajja Faiza's reference to seeking the care of a physician and Kopelman's graphic description of the impoverished circumstances under which the procedure is often performed both intimate the role that economic class plays in this practice. As Mitter (1997) shows, those who are most vulnerable to the casualization of labor are also most vulnerable to other forms of oppression, so it would not be surprising to discover that many of the women and girls to whom Kopelman refers are also those who fit the demographic that Mitter (and Jagger [2002]) describe. Being in a position to consult a physician, after all, is as much a privilege for the citizens of developing nations such as Kenya (and to some extent Egypt) as it is for over 48 million uninsured Americans.

Second, the connection that Kopelman suggests between "marriageability" (reflected in the "bride price"), the younger ages of arranged-marriage brides, and female circumcision illustrates the economic motives embedded in this religious practice. That a higher price might be expected for the arrangement of marriage to a circumcised twelve-year-old girl speaks poignantly to the opportunism at the core of a capitalist venture—but it has very little to say about freedom of decision making. The point, of course, is that extracting the commodification of female sexuality from female circumcision is as impossible as isolating the motives for engaging in a particular religious practice from those that govern other forms of exchange. Like the Indian mother who signs on to become a surrogate mother for an affluent American couple in order to be able to educate the children she has already had (without access to health care), the young woman whose father has arranged her marriage to an older man may have a choice in the sense that she could—in theory—decline the offer; but in both cases the certain consequences of rejecting such "offers" effectively ensure compliance—and it is pretty hard to call this a free choice.

Third, female circumcision is as entrenched in the dynamics of the globalized culture industry as is any practice capable of converting a value into a price, or a practice into a product. Indeed, at least some of the people who advocate it have as much access to the Internet, and hence to knowledge about the procedure, its adherents, and its variations, as anyone on the planet. To whatever extent the value of a woman is reflected either in the bride price or in the willingness to pay a physician to perform the procedure, she functions as an exchangeable good; if the procedure does not come with some promise of economic gain, it seems highly unlikely that—especially given the risks—it would continue. To insist, then, that female circumcision is either solely a religious practice, or that its value lies exclusively in exchange, or that it is primarily a reflection of heteropatriarchy distorts any endeavor to hold its advocates, as Newman (1994: 29-30) puts it, morally accountable.

No simple account like this will do. Some might argue that being a religious practice exempts female circumcision from additional moral scrutiny or that it would be found defensible if its advocates were held morally accountable—at least on their own religious grounds. But insofar as religious teachers like Hajja Faiza hold that the practice should be regarded as optional, and that its grounds are of "dubious authority," it seems clear that at least some regard female circumcision neither as exempt from scrutiny nor as obviously defensible. It is, then, simultaneously ironic and fitting that the practice is associated with marriageability, beauty, purity, and modesty, for this both ensures that a woman (or girl) is a more marketable product and distinguishes her religious devotion from the crass self-interest associated with capitalism. Indeed, the very values that are repudiated in the rejection of the Western face of the culture industry and reflected in continuing a practice like female circumcision are themselves embraced in its practice. After all, it is precisely because its association with beauty makes a bride more marketable that female circumcision makes her more marriageable, and it is precisely because she is more marriageable that the practice instantiates her both as a symbol of the rejection of the culture industry and as its unwitting advertisement—particularly to men seeking a wife that will cement their religious and economic authority.

Newman's cautionary account is thus well borne out in the development of these complex relationships. Jettisoning the Marxist view that all religious critique can be modeled after that leveled at the relationship between Christianity and capitalism opens the door to precisely the questions anyone committed to advancing the cause of women's emancipation would surely want to ask. Why? Because, from Newman's perspective, no institution, belief system, or practice should be exempted from questions concerning its participation in human welfare or, more specifically, in oppression, exploitation, or unfreedom. What, for example, is the relationship between the commodification of women's sexuality or capacity for reproduction and the specifically religious practices associated with marriageability? Can useful comparisons be drawn between primarily Western phenomena like anorexia and bulimia and non-Western practices like female circumcision? How has the relationship between capitalism and contemporary forms of Christianity evolved with respect to the commodification of women as, for instance, brides, mothers, or casualized workers? However unobvious the comparison, female circumcision is comparable in some ways to in vitro fertilization; both, for instance, are reproductive technologies. While IVF is more directly tethered to the production of babies, female circumcision is intended to produce a marriageable bride who is made ready by the procedure for motherhood. Both support traditional religious proscriptions of women's proper place, and both identify the value of a woman in terms of her capacity to produce offspring.

Perhaps a more challenging comparison can be made between female circumcision and sex-reassignment surgery. Some readers might regard this comparison as odious, but here, too, the materialist method we adopted early on offers a clue. While the former can be done "low tech" and the second requires highly sophisticated surgical tools and expertise, both not only involve similar areas of the body, but may also in some cases be the same procedure (for female-to-male transsexuals, for example). What distinguishes the cases would then seem to be the goals—but not really, or at least not necessarily. After all, while the goal of female circumcision is marriageability, built into this is a conception of "being a real woman" that the procedure is alleged to accomplish. But isn't this what many transsexuals hope for with respect to reassignment surgery? And aren't some transsexuals also hoping that by becoming their "real" selves they will be more likely to receive proposals of marriage? Although the transsexual opts for reassignment in the face of potentially overwhelming bigotry, that bigotry is itself a reflection of what many—including the transsexual—think it means to be a "real woman" or a "real man." Furthermore, many transsexuals report with deep conviction that they did not have a choice about the procedure, that they simply are members of the "opposite" sex "trapped" in the "wrong" bodies, and hence that they are coerced into the procedure by their own true identities.

Similarly, although the context may be very different in the case of female circumcision, the fact that it includes a coercive element that produces unfreedom remains its most significant feature. While the transsexual may experience pressure originating from "within" and, as Kopelman (2006) illustrates, the pressure confronted by many Islamic women originates in parents, community, and the demand for religious piety, both make decisions under duress. Still, one might object that because the consequences of sex-reassignment surgery are profound satisfaction and a sense of peace with oneself, it could hardly be more different than what women who have been subjected to female circumcision are likely to experience. But this inference, I suggest, trades on stereotype. As Newman (1994) and Mahmood (2005) show, the relationship between women and the practices of religion cannot merely be relegated to the annals of oppression, so it seems folly to assume that female circumcision always produces unhappiness—or that sex reassignment always produces satisfaction.

Instead, the real difference between sex reassignment and female circumcision has to be understood within the conceptual economy of difference and its endless variation within the global culture industry. Were sex reassignment covered by standard health insurance policies in the United States, Bangkok would not likely be the sex-reassignment capital of the world; if female circumcision did not elevate the price of a potential bride, it's unlikely that it would retain the allure it does. Both are coded as sexually exploitable in the economy of difference, and both are vulnerable to the possible deflation of their value or even the collapse of their markets. Here, however, the similarities end, in that the transsexual and the subject of female circumcision occupy radically different situations with respect to the economic, social, and political power they can command. However vulnerable to violence and harassment the transsexual might be, and however much bigotry invades her/his private life, she/he still has the option of passing in a way that the woman or girl who is subject to circumcision does not. I am not suggesting that passing has anything morally defensible to recommend it; but what little respite is available to the transsexual is not available in the case of circumcision. She may have no escape hatch. My aim in pointing out this difference is neither, of course, to make a competition of oppressive conditions, nor to suggest that the situation for female circumcision is hopeless, but rather to illustrate the extent to which each represents a very different point of departure as a potential site of resistance within this economy.

The transsexual may save for years—even decades—to be able to afford her/his transitional procedure, and because access to the procedure is essentially determined by its expense, he/she retains an element of control as the prospective consumer. He/she could spend the money on something else (however she/he may feel about it) and hence remains defined as a fully enfranchised participant in the culture industry. But this cannot be said of at least some of the women—or any of the girls—who undergo female circumcision: they are not likely to be the ones undertaking the monetary transaction that may determine the disposition of their bodies; they are not the consumers, but rather the consumables. They are a part of the culture industry, but only insofar as they can be "made" to be a more lucrative commodity exchangeable for higher-value goods. Perhaps, of course, the transsexual could be said to treat her/his body as a consumable or a commodity in the sense that a "new" body is effectively purchased through a surgical procedure much like a "new" body is purchased via, say, gastric bypass. But since the transsexual has the choice to spend the money otherwise, she/he is still in a position to make decisions about whether to conceive her/his body in this way. The woman or girl coerced into female circumcision, however, occupies no such position and may well be a witness to the bargaining that takes place to secure her bride price—especially if she comes from a family whose economic means are meager. She cannot spend the money otherwise; it is not hers to control even if her body is represented in its value. The participation of such a woman or girl in the culture industry is coerced not necessarily by any desires she might claim as her own, but by the material conditions of her family in a fashion not altogether unlike that confronted by victims of the international sex trade.[4]

---

[4] The international sex trade is a profoundly important topic worthy of far more attention than I have space for here. Suffice it to say that a book entitled "*Seven Global Issues*" would not do justice to this wrenching example of the dark belly of capitalist exchange—but still, I'd argue, a fully fledged participant in the culture industry.

Yet, while it's tempting to imagine such a woman's experience as oppressive—and I don't doubt that it often is—Mahmood's and Newman's more nuanced accounts should serve as a reminder of the dangers of universalizing too broadly around what counts as liberating (finally getting to have the sex-reassignment surgery), and what counts as imprisoning (entering an arranged marriage). Both the transsexual and the circumcised woman can be fruitfully considered as a site of resistance to oppression; however, particularly where experience is infused and informed by powerful institutions like religion, I think our analyses must include as a feature of such sites, of their construction and articulation, the voices of the people who occupy them. This is what analyses like Mahmood's offer. Feminist theorizing has come a long way on this score, and it is perhaps a tired criticism of the movement that emancipation has tended to be modeled after that of Western women's longings, say, to leave the suburbs. But in the face of some very real challenges—especially those raised by the resurgence of religious fundamentalism—the temptation to return to such universalizing as a way to condemn the Taliban, for example, is surely palpable. It's in resisting this temptation, however, that I think we may yet discover the most precious asset of the movement, namely, the voices of those who are empowered or disempowered by global markets. Perhaps, as we will explore in the next chapter, a discourse of resistance is not so much a single or unified platform; maybe there is no one manifesto. Perhaps it's something more like the chorus of stories whose telling—especially where the telling involves risk—doesn't merely raise consciousness, but elicits a conscience exemplified by a more global sensibility that is attuned not merely to marketplaces, but to the voices of those who are more likely to be its commodities than its consumers. This, of course, is an old feminist idea. But perhaps it is time to reignite it in a context whose technologies—like the Internet—need not be the sole domain of the culture industry, but could be appropriated one story at a time toward a feminist activism grounded in the collective recognition that what binds us all are the consequences of global capitalism's logic of domination. These consequences, I will argue, connect us as surely—as viscerally—as does our dependence on soil, water, and air.

Chapter VI

Religious Fundamentalism, Terrorism, and the "New" Anti-Feminism

FEMINIST RESPONSES TO RELIGIOUSLY MOTIVATED
TERRORISM AND OPPRESSION — AND THEIR
DETRACTORS

Among the most striking of the apparent contradictions of the early twenty-first century is that of the undeniable economic, political, and social progress made by women in the face of an all too often violent and fanatical resurgence of religious fundamentalism — especially Christian and Islamic. Whichever is the focus of our analysis, the Christian Identity Movement or the Taliban, religiously motivated domestic terrorists like Scott Roeder,[1] or internationally known terrorists like Osama bin Laden, the aim of these acts of violence is not merely to carry out some, often very narrowly conceived, notion of God's will, but to provoke terror in the interest of witnessing a world remade according to "His" "true" image. Not unlike poverty, starvation, environmental degradation, and war, the effects of this resurgence

---

[1] Scott Roeder is, as of this writing, arrested but not yet convicted of the murder of Dr. George Tiller while Tiller was attending church. Tiller was one of the last three providers of late-term abortions in the United States and had been a target of the pro-life movement for many years. A long-standing member of the far right wing of the American pro-life movement's "Operation Rescue," Roeder's personal history offers a particularly disturbing story of religiously motivated domestic terrorism.

have been disproportionately borne by women and girls. The aims of religious terrorism are not, however, adequately explained solely by reference to the heteropatriarchal logic of domination advocated by true believers; rather, as feminist Rosalind Petchesky and others argue, a fuller and more acute understanding of this resurgence calls for analysis of the economic and political conditions, interests, and potentially lucrative gains that provide the material motives both to the sponsors of terrorism and to its recruits.

Petchesky (2002) argues that "the conditions in which transnational terrorism thrives, gains recruits, and lays claim to moral legitimacy include many for which the US and its corporate, financial interests are directly responsible, even if they don't for a minute excuse the [September 11] attacks" (366). But what are these conditions? In what way could US corporate interests be responsible for them such that the World Trade Center would become a target? What can convert ordinary believers into suicide bombers? Faithful servants into violent fanatics? For Petchesky, the answer lies at least in part in the same expansion of western values (the culture industry) and global capitalism explored by Alison Jaggar and Chandra Mohanty; what better way to produce recruits for terrorism than a casualization of labor that gives rise not only to destitution but to boredom and restlessness. As Petchesky is quick to point out, however, Western-style expansion need not be accompanied by stereotypically Western-looking faces. Consider Osama bin Laden: however much it appears that he's motivated primarily by a wholesale rejection of Western values as an affront to his faith, a deeper examination reveals that the exchange value represented in access to oil reserves, control of territory, and amassing of arms may be as much—if not more—a motive than religious fervor. Petchesky refers to bin Laden as "the legendary Arabic counterpart to the Godfather" (364); if she's right, terrorists may have more in common with their alleged corporate nemeses than meets the eye, and terrorism might be better understood as a kind of shock theater than as a form of payback.[2]

The evidence of the role played by both economic conditions and the prospect of economic gain is, argues Petchesky, made starkly clear

---

[2] For more on the use of shock as an instrument of free-market aggression, see Klein (2007).

in the status and welfare of women and girls who, under the Taliban for example, have suffered immensely while Taliban warlords gain greater and greater economic power over entire regions of Afghanistan and Pakistan.[3] Petchesky's approach, however, has its critics. Daphne Patai and Phyllis Chesler, for example, argue that feminists—especially feminists in the academy—not only unjustly impugn Western "free-market" values in connection to religious terrorism, but also, in the name of "tolerance" or "diversity," turn a blind eye to the plight of their Muslim sisters. Chesler claims that "[f]eminists have been taught to feel ashamed of America [by their feminist professors] and guilty for the alleged 'crimes' America has committed against people both here and in other countries. This is another reason that many feminists forgive the gross misogyny abroad" (2005: 194). For Chesler, in other words, an approach like Petchesky's, one that takes political and economic conditions into consideration along with religious zealotry, strikes at the wrong target—American involvement in the Middle East—and in so doing discounts the real issue, namely, the strictly religious oppression of women in Islam.

If Chesler is right, the implications for the contemporary feminist movement are devastating. How could a movement whose aim is to emancipate women from all forms of oppression and exploitation miss so obvious a threat? How could we possibly ignore the Taliban? The question, of course, is whether Chesler *is* right. One response is that arguments like Chesler's are more polemic than they are substance—and this may be true, but substantive content is not always the only reason for confronting a particular line of reasoning. In other words, it's not necessarily the sophistication of an argument that demands a response; some arguments demand address in virtue of the persuasive power they appear to exercise over, say, a particular political constituency, in this case religious conservatives in the United States. Arguments like Chesler's have had, I suggest, a significant effect on how feminists are currently perceived, and on how feminism in the Western, and especially American, media is portrayed. As my

---

[3] See, for example, Sanjay Suri, "Afghanistan: 'Taliban Taking Over,'" *Inter Press Service*, <http://ipsnews.net/news.asp?idnews=34595>, and Barnett Rubin, "The Debate over US Policy," *Frontline*, <http://www.pbs.org/wgbh/pages/frontline/taliban/pakistan/uspolicy.html>, among many other documented publications.

students sometimes put it, "feminism" has become the new F-word; my argument is that if this is so, it is in no small measure due to the influence of arguments like Chesler's and Patai's. If the aim of feminist theory is, at least in significant part, progressive action, then we do ourselves little good by turning away from politically charged polemics. Indeed, I think we need to do more to understand where these arguments come from, and more to counter them in our public activism.

I propose, therefore, to translate Chesler's view in a maximally charitable fashion in terms of the many questions it raises: should feminists treat religious oppression as historically, conceptually, and otherwise distinct from economic and political oppression? Is it unfair to include any or all of these factors in analyses of the bombing of the World Trade Center? The brutality of the Taliban? The murder of reproductive services providers? Is criticism leveled at American corporations tantamount, as Chesler claims, to being made to feel guilty for being an American? Is the criticism that Jaggar, Mohanty, and others level against global capitalism the same thing as accusing "America" of committing crimes? Are their critiques supported by evidence? If so, does it imply that feminists are likely to ignore—or even "forgive"—the misogyny of, for example, the Taliban by virtue of their claimed resistance to Western "free-market" values? In short, are Western feminists guilty of condoning religious oppression—so long as it occurs in the name of opposing capitalism?

I think the answer to this last and crucial question is a demonstrable "no." Although many feminists have not embraced the military response advocated by Chesler (2005) and Patai (as discussed in Glazov 2007), this in no way means that they've conceded to the Taliban or to any other form of religious oppression. Patai, however, explicitly denies that the feminist critique of oppression within denominations of fundamentalist Christianity can be fairly compared to oppression within Islam: "The closest I've seen to criticism of radical Islam is a 'plague on both your houses' attitude, which pretends that fundamentalist Christians are every bit as dangerous to the world as Islamic fundamentalists, and that 'the West' manifests precisely the same problems as Muslim countries. This is sheer fantasy, but a very popular one at the moment." Elsewhere, she argues that it is "preposterous" and "myopic" to compare Islamic-sponsored terrorism with, for example, the Christian Inquisition of the Middle Ages; yet Patai insists that the feminist critique amounts to little more, and that such comparisons fail to acknowledge that Islam may itself "evolve" to be more like contemporary Christianity and Judaism (Patai 2006).

Such claims, however, not only reiterate the view that Western feminists have ignored the plight of their Islamic contemporaries; they also promote a particular interpretation of religious tradition, namely, that Judeo-Christianity (presumably including its fundamentalist incarnations) represents an "evolved" form of faith, and, by comparison, Islam a primitive one. This, of course, demands its own extensive argument, and Patai does claim that she shares her "friend's" "distaste for all types of religious fundamentalism" (2006). But this disclaimer doesn't prevent Patai from holding "radical Islam" almost exclusively responsible for contemporary expressions of misogyny, homophobia, anti-Semitism, and anti-democratic sentiments:

> I am astonished that so many academics on the supposedly progressive side simply do not admit that everything they value (including cultural diversity, gay rights, women's empowerment, the freedom to express their own ideas) is literally intolerable to radical Islam, and that millions of people today adhere to this view of Islam and loudly proclaim their hatred of the West and all it stands for. The silence of most American feminists is particularly appalling, and I can only imagine that they are caught in their own ideological schemata, which somehow blinds them to the necessity of protesting oppression when it is perpetrated by non-Anglo, non-White people. (Patai 2006)

On the one hand, Patai insists that Western feminists have failed in their responsibility to critique and condemn the oppression of women in "radical Islam"; on the other, she insists that they have criticized fundamentalist forms of Christianity as much or more than they have Islam. In other words, according to Patai, Western feminists both have and have not ignored the plight of women under fundamentalist Islam—but resort to "sheer fantasy" if they subject fundamentalist Christianity to the same critique. Clearly Patai can't have this both ways, and this isn't because fundamentalist forms of Christianity ought or ought not to be compared to fundamentalist forms of Islam, but simply because her claims are inconsistent: even if she's right, Patai must believe that feminists have subjected "radical Islam" to criticism—or it would make no sense to compare this criticism as failed to their critique of Christianity. She tacitly acknowledges, moreover, that "cultural diversity, gay rights, and women's empowerment" are values worth pursuing. Hence it seems doubly inconsistent that she ignores the fact that these remain perennial issues in the "contemporary" Christianity she endorses.

In her implicit, but clear, insistence that the West stands for equality and freedom, Patai must also ignore an enormous body of work which, while not accusing "America" of being "criminal," nonetheless does not hold the United States, its allies, its multinational interests, its institutions, or its military to be above criticism in the effort to understand the conditions that produce the potential for terrorism. Should we reject the notion that religious extremism *alone* can produce the kind of hatred that motivates terrorists like Osama bin Laden? Oppression on the scale of the Taliban? Yes, in fact I think we must if what we claim to be doing is scholarship—as opposed to the promotion of ideology. As Petchesky remarks,

> Nor, however, do I believe that we should succumb to the temptation of casting our current dilemma in the simplistic Manichean terms of cosmic Good vs. Evil. Currently this comes in two opposed but mirror-image versions: the narrative, advanced not only by the terrorists...but also by many on the left in the US...that blames US imperialism and economic hegemony for the "chickens coming home to roost"; versus the patriotic, right-wing version that casts US democracy and freedom as the innocent target of Islamic madness. Both these stories erase all the complexities that we must try to factor into a different, more inclusive ethical and political vision. (2002: 358)

It is important to emphasize that Petchesky holds some "stories" of both the political left and the right responsible for oversimplifying the complexities of terrorism. Moreover, she points out, no analysis could appear as anything other than distorted if it did not account for the key roles played by the masculinism and racism of both US policy and Islamic extremism (363–65).

Chesler and Patai, however, appear to endorse one of these stories—the "Islamic madness" version—while simultaneously demonizing those who dare to consider whether any of these other factors may play a role as mere shills for the left. But is this fair? Analyses like Jaggar's (1983) and Mohanty's (2003) are "left-leaning" in the sense that they argue for a socialist feminism that includes a critique of capitalism. But what neither Patai nor Chesler shows—or even tries to show— is that the arguments for such a critique are wrong, misguided, and lacking in evidence. Instead, what they effectively offer is the claim that any view other than the "madness" view of Islam is unpatriotic. This is not scholarship; it is ideology. It aims to shut down any discussion that impugns US policy or compares fundamentalist Christianity with fundamentalist Islam. And it is important in that it helps to explain why terms such as "feminism," "liberal," "left," and "environmentalism" have become terms of derision in much mainstream media and public discourse.

It is not the case that Patai, for example, engages the work of feminists like Jaggar and Mohanty and finds it wanting; she offers no specific criticism of arguments that criticize global capitalism at all. Still, the prospect that the charges she levels at Western feminists are made out of ignorance is unlikely; her academic credentials are more than impressive. These considerations lead me then to conclude the following: the charge of Western feminist indifference is not inspired by concern for the welfare of women, but instead is motivated by an ideological agenda which, by pitting the "wrong" religion, "radical Islam," against the "right" one (or at least the one whose oppression and violence is "sheer fantasy" compared to Islam), Christianity, promotes the realization of goals that are ultimately more nationalist and corporatist than religious. And this—regardless of the scholarly substance of such a view—is something to which we must pay more acute attention if we are to be activists and not "just" theorists. "We [in the US] are the headquarters of the corporate and financial megaempires that dominate global capitalism and influence the policies of the international financial institutions," writes Petchesky (2002: 359). But "[w]ealth is also a driving force behind the Al Qaeda network, whose principals are mainly the beneficiaries of upper-middle class or elite financing and education" (359). If Petchesky is right, the war on terrorism is not primarily a war over human rights, religious freedom, or women's welfare; it's far more complex than this despite the polemics to the contrary. It *is*, however, a war over who, and under what conditions, will control access to the resources upon which the realization of ideologies—political, religious, or economic—depends.

THE "NEW" ANTI-FEMINISM: NATIONALISM, TERRORISM, AND RELIGIOUS FANATICISM

Casting themselves as the "real" feminists who defend the emancipation of women from the misogyny of Islam, critics like Chesler and Patai promote "Western values" which, on the surface, appear to be democratic; they speak, for example, of the importance of women's free choices. But what a closer read suggests is that in this context "freedom" refers less to freedom to engage the political process or to be equally represented as citizens, and more to the freedom to become a consumer in the globalized free market.

Critic Christina Hoff Sommers also plays an important role in these dynamics—especially given her high-profile media attention. In her "Case Against Ratifying the United Nations Convention on the Elimination of All Forms of Discrimination Against Women," Sommers (2002) writes that "[f]or the past decade, moderate feminist academics like myself, and a growing number of dissidents scholars such as...Daphne Patai ...[among others] have been hard at work correcting the misinformation, *challenging the naïve hostility to the free market system*, and calling for an end to the male-bashing rhetoric that is standard fare at most of our colleges and universities" (my emphasis). In Sommers's view, the challenge that feminists pose to the free-market system is "naïve" because it refuses to sanction the assumption that such a system is largely if not universally beneficial. The difficulty is that on the overwhelming evidence and analyses of theorists like Jaggar (1983), Mitter (1997), and Yunus (2007), this assumption is false. Moreover, it is at least reasonable to ask whether calling for an end to institutions that systematically privilege men is "male-bashing." Yet she casts herself and Patai as "moderate feminists" who *as such* oppose the UN convention to eliminate discrimination against women.

Chesler defends a similar position in "A Radical Feminist Comes Out for Bush," where she insists that the values of Western nations such as the United States stand in stark contrast to the religious misogyny of Islam: "The West (capitalism, colonialism, imperialism) did not cause the oppression of women under Islam in Afghanistan. On the contrary. Afghan Islam defended its 'honor'-bound mistreatment of women and manfully resisted all western inroads" (2004). The problem with Chesler's argument here is that few—if any— feminist scholars argue that capitalism, colonialism, or oppression *causes* oppression; indeed, Petchesky (2002) argues for a far more complex and nuanced relationship between Western consumer values and the economic ambitions of terrorists. What one-dimensional "Islam as madness" claims like Chesler's encourage, however, is demonizing as anti-American feminists engaged in the critique of global capitalism in *any* of its instantiations, the effect of which is to stifle public discourse about these issues. But this is simply fear-mongering, and however much we as theorists and philosophers might thus be tempted to dismiss it, I think we fail to challenge such a rhetoric at our peril. This is not because it is false that feminists claim that capitalism causes oppression; it is because the women and men we want to reach are not themselves necessarily immune to the manipulation contained in the shrill rhetoric of being an "America-hater," or that of characterizing feminists as male-bashers. But we must reach them if it is real and enduring change we are after.

The fact that terrorists such as Osama bin Laden may have economic as well as religious aspirations cannot be accommodated by Chesler's view, for in that case it would not be possible to cast Western free-market values as the Good in opposition to the Evil of "radical Islam." In an interview with Bernard Chapin, Chesler claims that

I believe that a feminist can also be a patriot and believe in God and in the reality of a just war. She can also be a Zionist and a capitalist. These views are not the views of the feminist professoriate. However, genuine, bona fide feminists are currently working in the Bush administration against the trafficking in women and children. I honor such work. I have not changed my mind about a woman's right to economic or reproductive freedom but I do not demonize those who may disagree with me on these and other points. I believe that western civilization is under both cultural and military siege and that we must fight to survive. We must forge alliances with each other against jihad, no matter who we may vote for and no matter what ideological flag we may happen to salute. (2006)

Many feminists, of course, do believe in a god, are patriots, and do argue for "the reality of a just war." In fact, no one doubts this, so what could Chesler's motive for stating the obvious be other than to mischaracterize certain feminists as anti-American, atheistic, and anti-Semitic? So labeling the "feminist professoriate," however, does accomplish the creation of an enemy — in this case, Western feminists as the enemy of Islamic (and, via opposition to the UN convention, all) women by virtue of being the enemy of those "Western values" best situated to "liberate" women from "radical Islam," namely, pro-"free-market" values. The "real" feminists are, as Chesler puts it, radicals who voted for Bush.

I am not suggesting that feminists ought not to vote for conservatives; what I am suggesting is that views like Chesler's evince no real interest in the welfare of women. In fact, they use feminists (or "feminists") as a foil to advance "free-market" nationalism; hence it is no surprise that anything falling short of wholesale condemnation of Islam will be characterized as "anti-American" (and anti-Semitic). Yet few feminist scholars would be likely to sign onto the wholesale denunciation of any religious tradition without careful historical, cultural, economic, and political analysis — particularly given the criticism from within that tradition of its own extreme variations, for example the Taliban. But this position knows no special monopoly among feminists; this is the difference between performing scholarship and sponsoring propaganda, between confronting a complex social reality that doesn't divide neatly into good versus evil and demonizing an "other" in order to ensure the uninterrupted dissemination of a worldview. Petchesky remarks that while she "does not see terrorist networks and global capitalism as equivalent," she "does see some striking and disturbing parallels between them" (2002: 358). She goes on to argue that feminists may be in one of the best positions to make this "double critique," by virtue of their own rich tradition of analyses of oppression: "Whether in the United Nations or national settings, we have been challenging the gender-biased and racialized dimensions of *both* neoliberal capitalism and various fundamentalisms for years, trying to steer a path between their double menace" (p. 358; emphasis in original). This double critique helps to make sense of why the September 11 bombers chose the World Trade Center; and this is not, as Petchesky points out, because radical

Muslims "hate our way of life," or simply because "our [capitalist] chickens have come home to roost," but because conditions rightly critiqued and exposed as oppressive know no single religious, social, economic, or cultural tradition.

It is in precisely this more analytical light, however, that the anti-feminist strategy is instructive: If the charge of feminism's failure can be made to stick, it creates a kind of "queen's fork" in that it effectively undermines both the feminist movement and Islam—both cast as versions of "evil"—all at once. An essential aspect of any feminist critique of the complex relationship between religious oppression and the advance of global capitalism involves understanding how views such as Chesler's and Patai's sanction what amounts to mendacity in the service of advancing its agenda. Mendacity, moreover, is not too strong a characterization of such views because, as Petchesky shows, feminist critique of religious oppression is not only rich, complex, and contentious, but also as accessible as is feminist theory and activism generally. Feminist theorists and critics are not hiding in closets. Understanding this strain of anti-feminism is important because a worldview that sanctions the propagandizing of falsehood in order to discredit what it perceives to be a threat is as potentially oppressive as the worldview it demonizes, if not ultimately more so. "[L]ike high-tech militarism," writes Petchesky, "terrorist low-tech militarism is also based on an illusion—that millions of believers will rise up, obey the *fatwah*, and defeat the infidel. It's an illusion because it grossly underestimates the most powerful weapon in global capitalism's arsenal... infinite Nikes and CDs" (2002: 363)—in other words, the commodities that Chesler and others identify with freedom.

Conservative political pundit David Horowitz (2007) may capture this worldview best when he refers to the "Islamofascists," a term intended to solicit both comparison with the Nazi regime and the unthinking but fear mongering assumption that Islam just is "radical" and "extremist" (terms co-opted in the service of soliciting an image of evil).[4] As feminist scholar Barbara Ehrenreich (2007), writing for

---

[4] In Horowitz's (2007) promotion of Islamofascism Awareness Week (IFAW), he attacks "leftist" academics who adopt much the same strategy as I do here. See also my various responses to Horowitz: <http://www.freeexchangeoncampus. org/index.php?option=com_content&task=view&id=491>, March 14; <http:// www.dailykos.com/storyonly/2007/3/14/95719/5903>, March 14; and <http:// philosleft.blogspot.com>, February 15.

The Nation, argues, however, the image it conjures is intended to solicit much more than anti-Islamic sentiment; indeed, she suggests, it evokes a "veritable witches' brew of Cheney-style anti-jihadism mixed with old-fashioned, right-wing, anti-feminism and a sour dash of anti-semitism." According to Horowitz, Ehrenreich continues, "feminists and particularly the women's studies professors among them, have developed a masochistic fondness for Islamic fundamentalists." Consider Kay Hymowitz's "The Sisters They Ignore":

> Every year on March 8, feminists across the world celebrate International Women's Day. As it happens, the holiday was first proclaimed in the early 20th century by the Socialist International—making it the perfect symbol of a movement that, it has become increasingly clear in the past four years of the war on terror, is more dedicated to leftist, utopian politics than to women's rights. For many years before September 11, 2001—and much to their credit—Western feminists tried to rouse a sleeping world to the plight of women in increasingly radical Islamic countries. In the US, it was the Feminist Majority that pressured president Bill Clinton to impose sanctions against the woman-hating Taliban regime.... But in the months after the attacks on New York and Washington... feminists went uncharacteristically mum. Here was the perfect opportunity to convince a stubborn public that remained ambivalent about feminism... yet in the communiques from feminist offices the phrase "Islamic extremists" was barely uttered. Why the relative silence on a subject that would seem to epitomize feminist concerns? Because in the eyes of the sisterhood, worse than stoning women for adultery or forbidding girls to go to school are the policies of white men such as George W. Bush. It was only a mark against those men if they committed themselves to spreading democracy. ...feminism has long been entwined with anti-Western, anti-nationalist and especially anti-American feeling. Radical feminists, especially those who congregate in the universities, view everyone in the Islamic world as victims of Western imperialism, exempt from all judgment. (2005)

Hymowitz simultaneously congratulates pre-September 11 feminists for "[rousing] a sleeping world" to the lives of women under the Taliban and discredits the movement for its socialist associations. She chastises feminists both for not being feminist enough and, in this case, for not using the preferred terminology of the Bush Administration's "Islamic Extremists" to condemn the Taliban; this, indeed, constitutes "silence" in Hymowitz's view. She singles out "radical" academic feminists for particular opprobrium as "anti-Western, anti-nationalist and especially anti-American," reinforcing the link between feminism and a socialist orientation identified for all practical purposes with "the enemy."

What Hymowitz does not address, however, is why the same "socialist" pre-September 11 feminists were concerned with the lives of women under the Taliban, but post-September 11 feminists were not, as she claims. She implies that this may be because earlier feminists found Bill Clinton's approach to religious extremism more attractive than George W. Bush's; that may well be the case. But if so, it would likely have been because Clinton was thought to be more sensitive to feminist issues generally—for instance, support for reproductive rights, closing the wage gap, making daycare for working women more accessible—or emancipating women living under the Taliban. What Hymowitz doesn't ask, in other words, is why many feminists might have opposed Bush's response to the rise of a fundamentalist version of Islam—a question that in no way denies the oppressive violence meted out by the Taliban, but asks, "What is the response most likely to succeed in the emancipation of women from the brutality of the Taliban?" and "Who constitutes the 'we' whose response to the Taliban ought to be taken most seriously?" In castigating what she characterizes as feminist "silence," and then insinuating that this "silence" is somehow connected to the movement's presumed socialist/leftist commitments, Hymowitz effectively identifies feminists with the evil, oppressive, anti-democratic war against which her own worldview—tacitly promoted via her endorsement of Bush—prevails as good, liberating, and democratic.

The issue is not whether the particular ideology Hymowitz tacitly endorses is itself "good" or "bad"; the issue is that her strategy is to discredit feminists in the interest of endorsing a narrowly tailored "pro-American" worldview. The real value of the Taliban to Hymowitz is that of a weapon to utilize against American feminists; but this hardly speaks to the liberation, much less the welfare, of the women who live under the Taliban. It might be tempting simply to dismiss her for over-generalizing, or for failing to offer supportive evidence. Patai, however, makes a similar claim in an interview with Jamie Glazov (2007):

As far as I can tell, there is not a great deal of teaching of a critical kind going on in women's studies programs about Islamic fundamentalism and the particular dangers it represents, or about how Sharia operates in countries where it is enforced. It's been more than ten years since I parted company from the women's studies program at my own university, out of dismay at its narrow politics and lack of intellectual seriousness. But I still follow the field and read what academic feminists say and how they define their programs, and I participate in discussions on the Women's Studies E-mail List (WMST-L). I can tell you that identity politics continue to prevail, and this means that everyone is supercautious about which groups may be criticized, which not, and who is entitled to make criticisms. Third world "Others" are usually treated as a protected category, while the increasingly mythical White Patriarchy is constantly blamed for everything these feminists do not like about the world. This is why Islamic fundamentalism is not criticized while home-grown evangelicals certainly are.

The characterization of feminists as "supercautious about which groups may be criticized" hardly describes Petchesky, whose analysis of the appropriation of religious symbolism sheds valuable light on the dynamics of what Patai derisively refers to as the "Third world 'Others'" and the "mythical White Patriarchy":

As many others have commented, the "clash of religions" or "clash of cultures" interpretation of the current scenario is utterly specious. What we have instead is an appropriation of religious symbolism and discourse for predominantly political purposes, and to justify permanent war and violence. So bin Laden declares a jihad, or holy war, against the US, its civilians as well as its soldiers; and Bush declares a crusade against the terrorists and all who harbor or support them. Bin Laden declares himself the "servant of Allah fighting for the sake of the religion of Allah"… while Bush declares Washington the promoter of "infinite justice" and predicts certain victory because "God is not neutral." But we have to question the authenticity of this religious discourse on both sides, however sincere its proponents. A "Statement of Scholars of the Islamic Religion," circulated after the attacks [on the World Trade Center] firmly denounces terrorism…as contrary to *Sharia* law. And Bush's adoption of this apocalyptic discourse can only be seen as substituting a conservative, right-wing form of justification for the neoliberal internationalist discourse that conservatives reject.... [I]t is worth quoting the always wise Eduardo Galeano ... [:] "In the struggle of Good against Evil, it's always the people who get killed." (2002: 361)

Unlike Patai, Petchesky offers a pass to neither bin Laden nor the Bush administration, but shows instead the extent to which both utilize the language or symbolism of religion to "justify permanent war and violence." In a similar vein, I made the following observation in a piece for *Free Exchange on Campus*:

In her interview with [Jamie] Glazov, Patai asks: "Do these students not understand that radical Muslims are serious? Have they failed to notice that these Islamists act on their beliefs and kill those who do not agree with them? And that their targets include political dissenters, Jews, Christians, other Muslims, homosexuals, writers, filmmakers, women who are thought to have transgressed, apostates, critics, infidels of all kinds—the list goes on and on." Patai criticizes what she perceives as a failure particularly of Women's Studies academics to interrogate Islamic religious fanaticism, but she fails to ask the same questions about fanatical Christianity: "Do these students not understand that these Christian ideologues act on their beliefs and have killed those who don't agree with them? That their targets include political dissenters, Jews, Muslims, other Christians, homosexuals, writers, filmmakers, women, apostates, and infidels of all kinds?" It's not like we have to go back to the Inquisition or the Boxer Wars to find these examples. [Pundit Ann] Coulter's promotion of the forced conversion of Muslims to Christianity and her stunning remarks about how Christians are perfected Jews is cut of the same cloth as the Jihadist's "striving in the way of God." As [Joe] Bageant puts it in *Deer Hunting with Jesus*, "The push toward theocracy and the infiltration of mainstream Protestantism by religious extremists was one of the biggest underreported political stories of the second half of the twentieth century" (p. 168). Right on, Bageant; how could Patai miss this? She's not living in the outback. She lives in Massachusetts—and has access to books and the Internet. (Lee 2007)

Patai, of course, denies that fundamentalist Christianity promotes any comparable religious theology or represents a comparable threat, and the burden belongs to feminist theorists (among others) to show that this comparison can be legitimately made. But consider again Petchesky's astute analysis: bin Laden declares that he's a servant of Allah; President Bush invokes similar religious symbolism to refer to "infinite justice" because "God is not neutral" (2002). Ann Coulter (2001) claims, as if it fell well within the bounds of ordinary reason, that the 9/11 terrorist attack is the responsibility of a "fanatical murderous cult," and, clearly assuming that this includes all Muslims, argues that the appropriate response is to "invade their [Islamic] countries, kill their leaders and convert them to Christianity."[5] We do not need to reach back into the Middle Ages to find confirmation for these examples, and much more needs to be shown to make the case for comparing Christian and Islamic extremisms. But if Joe Bageant (2007) is right that religious extremism in America is among the most important stories of the late twentieth century, it seems at least plausible to suggest that rhetoric like that of the "new" anti-feminists may contribute to this underreporting, at least in that it promotes a "Good vs. Evil" worldview, where Muslims play only the latter role.

Therefore, feminist columnist Katha Pollitt's observation that she ought to have reviewed Chesler's *The Death of Feminism* when it first appeared is most apposite:

In a way I was right [for not reviewing the book]. The book tanked. But its argument has taken on a life of its own. That selfish Western feminists have abandoned Muslim women has become a truism on the right. Well, with Iraq a shambles and Afghanistan on its way to becoming a Taliban-friendly narco-state, these can't be happy days for the proponents of gunpoint liberation. You can see how it would go in the offices of The Weekly Standard: Hmmm ... maybe invading countries and killing a lot of innocent people isn't the way to get women out of those burqas? (2007)

---

5 The relevant part of Coulter's article reads as follows: "Airports scrupulously apply the same laughably ineffective airport harassment to Suzy Chapstick as to Muslim hijackers. It is preposterous to assume every passenger is a potential crazed homicidal maniac. We know who the homicidal maniacs are. They are the ones cheering and dancing right now. We should invade their countries, kill their leaders and convert them to Christianity. We weren't punctilious about locating and punishing only Hitler and his top officers. We carpet-bombed German cities; we killed civilians. That's war. And this is war."

Feminists cannot afford to ignore this "truism." The recent murder of George Tiller as he attended church is, I think, rightly characterized as an instance of domestic terrorism, in this case from the Christian right. Islam holds no more a monopoly on terror than does Christianity on moral rectitude. The mutually antagonistic *and* mutually support-ive relationship between the emergence of religious fundamentalism and its well financed proponents suggests a global conflict less over the tenets of faith and more about the marketable rights to lucrative commodities like petroleum, or access to ports, or even "rights" to trade in the black market's heroin, body parts, or sex-trafficked chil-dren. It is this connection, I suggest, that the anti-feminists aim to obscure in the interest of liberating Muslim women to become, like their Western sisters, workers and consumers. Hence it is hardly sur-prising that they would resort to labeling feminists who are critical of the culture industry as "anti-American." But such a strategy also presupposes that it is acceptable to identify America not with its democratic ideals, but rather with its power to dominate global mar-kets. The central question, therefore, is this: What is the relationship between this emergent social/cultural phenomenon called "religious fundamentalism" and the growth (and crises) of global capitalism? Who benefits? Who pays?

THE FEMINIST RESPONSE TO RELIGIOUS OPPRESSION AND THE "VERTIGO OF SECULARIZATION"

Contrary to the caricatures tendered by the anti-feminists, the fem-inist response to the oppression and even violence of some religious fundamentalisms is philosophically sophisticated and politically diverse. It is neither monolithic nor insensitive to the economic, social, and political context in which religion plays a role; neither does it privilege any particular religious faith, as if faith alone could provide an incontestable standard of moral and/or political judg-ment. Philosopher Maria Pia Lara exemplifies this tradition in schol-arship in her 2003 article "In and Out of Terror: The Vertigo of Secularization," where she argues that

> the terrorist attacks on the World Trade Center (WTC) must be under-stood as part of the radical expression of the vertigo of secularization [that is]...a historical reaction that we humans repeatedly feel when

societies seek to find political orders with legitimate grounding as separated from the sphere of religion.... [Hannah] Arendt captured a perfect image of this "vertigo": "Nothing perhaps distinguishes modern masses as radically from those of previous centuries as the loss of faith in the Last Judgment: the worst lost their fear and the best lost their hope." (184)

For Lara, in other words, the transition from religious to secularly grounded institutions is accompanied by the experience of a loss of moorings—a sense of vertigo—in that, while such institutions may promise an end to the injustice and inequalities perpetuated by religion, they also help to erode the vital certitude and consequent stability that religion provides its believers.

Philosopher Fredric Jameson offers a similar diagnosis concerning what he calls the "cultural logic of late capitalism" (i.e., the culture industry), when he remarks that "this whole global, yet American, postmodern culture is the internal and superstructural expression of a whole new wave of American military and economic domination throughout the world; in this sense...the underside of culture is blood, torture, death, and terror" (1999: 5). Moreover, although Jameson penned these words two years before September 11, 2001, and does not specifically identify "blood, torture, death, and terror" as the result of the loss of religious or transcendent moorings in the wake of global capitalism, it is clear that the World Trade Center bombings exemplify the righteous anger and consequent rejection of what are perceived to be the corrupted values of the "infidel," in this case, the secular societies associated with the West or "America." What, we might ask, better describes this "underside of culture" than the religious traditions compromised and displaced, as Petchesky might put it, by the "false gods" of Pepsi, Nike, and Exxon? What could produce so violent a reaction other than a challenge to the very moorings of human life and salvation? In this case, however, challenge is also temptation; that is, the experience of vertigo is the consequence not merely of "American military and economic domination," but also of the material and political desires that accompany the expansion of the culture industry, desires that are inconsistent with a "transcendent order of things."

Lara argues that secularization describes "the demise of a transcendent order of things from which to derive standards and criteria for

establishing all kinds of truths" (2003: 185). Add to this disenchantment the erosion of values encouraged by global communication,
immigration, and trade, "and no possibility exists of preventing religious views to remain uncontaminated" (185). "Disenchantment has
become widespread in our global era," she writes, "but not because
societies can aspire to live in idyllic closure, but rather, because the
pressures of modernity provide concepts that express [in Robert Bellah's
words] 'the doubts and demands that were already just below the surface of consciousness'" (185). Vertigo is thus not simply the product
of coercion or confrontation with Western market values; it is also the
consummation of "doubts and demands" already percolating within
the minds of the faithful facilitated through, for instance, movies, television, and the Internet. Jameson remarks similarly that "[t]he technology of contemporary society is therefore mesmerizing and
fascinating not so much in its own right but because it seems to offer
some privileged representational shorthand for grasping a network of
power and control even more difficult for our minds and imaginations to grasp" (1999: 37–38). Certainly neither bin Laden nor the
Taliban are exempt from this "fascination," despite the vertigo it pre-
cipitates—a vertigo that surely aids in recruiting young men whose
own conditions (and the envy and/or resentment they may inspire) may
make them easy to enlist. Experienced as a precipitous loss of value *and*
an exhilarating liberty, it's no wonder, argues Lara, that violence aimed
at the perceived causes of that vertigo might be among the consequences (2003: 185), and this despite the fact, as Petchesky remarks,
that "[w]ealth is also a driving force behind the Al Qaeda network,
whose principals [including bin Laden] are mainly the beneficiaries
of upper-middle class or elite financing and education" (2002: 359).

There is irony here in that perhaps only religion can provide the
necessary counterweight against which the culture industry can really
strive; yet there is no fundamentalism that can prevail against global
capitalism without adopting its technologies of communication, without mastering its "representational shorthand." Note, moreover, the
striking contrast between Lara's argument and those of Chesler and
Patai: whereas the latter argue for a view of "Islamofascism" in which
Islam is depicted as primitive, anti-Western, and essentially fascistic,
Lara paints a far richer, more nuanced picture in which "[b]in Laden
emerges as a warrior-prophet whose aim is to reenchant the world":

He uses weapons and narratives [broadcast through global news media] to craft his story carefully and define his view with a symbolic construction of good and evil. He...recreates a world where all the symbols of the Muslim past are brought back to justify his view of jihad. He portrays Muslim history as a continually linear saga of humiliations....These are described not as historical failures of the Muslim peoples but as how they became victims of the West and of its "Satanic" forces. (2003: 186)

Bin Laden, in other words, drafts precisely the narrative most likely—especially given its global availability via news networks and the Internet—to be effective in recruiting followers; he offers them a world within which the disaffected and displaced victims of the corrupt West get to share in the wealth produced by jihad. That this wealth may not be available in this world but must await the next is only further inducement towards suicidal martyrdom since the sacrifice required to defeat forces of "Satanic" proportion promises reward in afterlife (Winters 1997).

While it might be tempting to read Lara's description of bin Laden as consistent with Chesler's and Patai's condemnation of him as an "Islamofascist," this would be misguided. Bin Laden's objectives are as much political and economic as they are religious; in other words, although they may be fascistic, this is not because his motives are exclusively or even primarily religious, but because they're politically authoritarian and, consistent with a capitalist worldview, opportunistic:

This kind of narrative is *useful* for various purposes. The first is to capture the interest and unconditionality of all the disenchanted young men who have lost hope about the promises of modernity.... The second purpose is to ensure that the influence of the West is seen by these young men as a false promise: After all, all of their life experiences have been related to poverty and to tyranny.... Third, this all-encompassing narrative renders these disaffected young men incapable of questioning their authoritarian regimes under which they live in their own political terms. It is much easier to blame others for all of the problems they have experienced. Fourth, this type of narrative is something that has always been *a useful tool* for those authoritarian regimes that foster anger toward the West as an easy way to disguise their own failures. (Lara 2003: 186; my emphasis)

Like Petchesky, Lara neither exempts the West from responsibility in the production of the conditions that may make young men vulnerable to bin Laden or to the Taliban, nor does she excuse terrorism. Instead, Lara offers a set of reasons that explain why bin Laden's warrior narrative is so attractive to disaffected young male Muslims—and how he can exploit their conditions to his own ends. However much a caricature, Western values are indispensable to bin Laden as the foil against which he can construct his narrative of the evil West and thereby recruit willing soldiers to his crusade, soldiers who effectively function as commodities whose exchange value is cashed out in the suicidal labor they are willing to perform on the promise of an other-worldly reward. Far from being primitive or anti-Western, bin Laden actually epitomizes Western-style advertising: just as commercials sell not merely products but desirable lifestyles, he too "sells" a lifestyle created after a mythic past that calls out for justice, tethered to an equally mythic future replete with the material rewards of afterlife. That the photographs of martyrs are commonly displayed on billboards along with their names, family connections, and a description of their bravery in death is hardly surprising; located in poor and/or war-torn neighborhoods ripe for recruiting, such photographs sell the cause of jihad even more effectively—and commodify its martyrs (Winters 1997).

Offering the promise of social status (especially in self-sacrifice) distinguished by masculine bravery, righteousness, and ultimate reward, bin Laden's warrior narrative sells what many disaffected and economically destitute young Muslims desire, but to which they have little access—a purpose that re-enchants their place in the world and insures their transcendent identity as men. Hence it is unsurprising that essential to this narrative is the depiction of women as that against which masculine self-possession must prevail, as representations of temptation and of evil itself:

The political is definitively erased when an arbitrary system destroys the civil rights of its citizens, who ultimately become outlaws in their own country. This applies especially to women, who become stateless and homeless. Women became another key component in this new totalitarianism when they began to be portrayed as the embodiment of evil. Women represented all the possible temptations that Satan whispers to Muslim men. (Lara 2003: 188)

At once resistant to the evil that "woman" represents *and* acting on behalf of women's protection from Western corruption, the warrior of bin Laden's narrative is constructed not merely as a profoundly oppressive enforcer of the patriarchal constraints of fundamentalist Islam, but as a symbol of an authoritarian worldview that can justify the suspension of civil liberties, the closing of schools, the imposition of the veil, and terrorism against a West depicted as promoting licentiousness and immorality — especially women's. Hence, it would be short sighted to assign this worldview solely to religious motives:

> Politically speaking, authoritarian regimes need to prevent collective discussion of their political institutions, corruption, and their failure to build a society that respects...human rights. Their citizens' lack of experience in building democratic institutions in the past makes them believe that it is not through the Western promises of modernity that they will find the way out of their fears and needs, but rather, only through the magical power of religion. This constitutes the new reenchantment.... (Lara 2003: 187–88)

Religion, in other words, serves as the instrument with which bin Laden (and the Taliban) erects his authoritarian political regime, not because he's not a true believer, but because, as a self-proclaimed servant of a god, he can claim the "magic" with which to impose law — and curtail dissent — in the interest of a political *and* religious vision of society (187–88).

That the control of women forms an essential element of this authoritarian rule is hardly surprising. As Lara points out,

> [t]he vertigo of secularization assumes an unprecedented new shape when confronted with a patriarchal tradition that has remained almost uncontested in the Muslim world until the last century. Global media, education, and movies have brought new ideals for women in the Muslim world. Muslim men fear this influence the most. The link between Satan and women is crucial. The internal wars over how to cope with new-born expectations from women in Muslim societies and the lack of possibilities to fulfill their needs under the most rigid interpretation of Islamic law are reflected in the hardening of fundamentalist strategies against any aspiration by women. If women feel entitled to the same rights as men there will be no possibility of a world reenchant-

ment.... In constructing a new way in which women were treated as less than humans, the Taliban created a new kind of Apartheid. (189)

Quite contrary to the charges leveled by nationalist anti-feminists, Lara does not mince words with respect to her view of the Taliban's dehumanizing treatment of women; instead of simply condemning Islam, however, she seeks to grasp how its fundamentalist—and profoundly misogynist—incarnations are facilitated by the secularizing opportunities presented by media, education, etc. This is not "blaming" the West; much less is it "America hating." It is an attempt to comprehend the vertigo induced by the loss of foundations and the panoply of reactions—some violent—produced by the globalizing culture industry. The "crucial" link forged between "Satan" and "woman" is not, then, adequately explained by reference to crude and monolithic notions like "Islamofascism." As Lara puts it: "[t]he vertigo of secularization only shows how we humans struggle to live without an idea of a final judgment" (192). To whatever extent women's aspirations represent the West's secularizing influence, they necessarily represent this loss of judgment; women thus epitomize the vertigo from which only the jihad waged by men can redeem them. Without women, in other words, there would be insufficient peril against which the transcendent concept of judgment (and its rewards) could be restored, and therefore insufficient criteria for justifying the use of terror to achieve these ends.

MASCULINISM, MISOGYNY, CLASS, AND RACE AT THE INTERSECTION OF POLITICS, GLOBAL CAPITALISM, AND RELIGION

"Masculinism and misogyny take many forms, not always the most visible," writes Petchesky (2002: 364), and are often enough concealed by the rhetoric of "rescuing" but to ends that have little if anything to do with forwarding the rights of women and girls:

Global capitalist masculinism is alive and well but concealed in its Eurocentric, racist guise of "rescuing" downtrodden Afghan women. Feminists around the world, who have tried for so long to call attention to the plight of women and girls in Afghanistan, cannot feel consoled by the prospect of US warplanes and US backed Guerrilla chiefs coming to "save our Afghan sisters." Meanwhile, the US will send single mothers who signed up for the National Guard when welfare ended to fight and die in its holy war.... (364)

No doubt Chesler and Patai would find such a comparison odious, but is it not precisely the notion of "rescue" that characterizes the position they advocate, and the one they claim feminists have failed to adopt? Isn't it military action they endorse as the best vehicle for this mission? If, however, Afghan women are unlikely to feel consoled by "the prospect of US warplanes," this is surely in part because such a response illustrates the extent to which the "US media overlook the activism and self-determination of groups like RAWA [the Revolutionary Association of Women in Afghanistan]," whose specific aims are to promote the human rights of women and girls (Petchesky 2002: 364).[6] It is clear that Chesler and Patai are party to these media, but at the peril of their positions. In epitomizing *both* the vertigo of secularization and a positive response to oppression under the Taliban, RAWA effectively rejects the rescue narrative and its attendant militarism.

Consider, for example, RAWA's 100th Anniversary Statement for International Women's Day, 8 March 2008:

[6] For additional context concerning the roots of organizations like RAWA, please see the Sima Wali story: see "The Woman in Exile returns: The Sima Wali Story," <http://www.grailwerk.com/woman-in-exile-returns. htm>. The following is a short summary taken from that site:

> The Story: After 24 years in exile, Sima Wali returned to the Afghan capital of Kabul in October of 2002 to help rebuild her shattered nation. "I am apprehensive and I know that I'll be devastated," Wali tells us as the aging 727 Ariana Afghan Airlines plane descends over the blasted suburbs of Kabul. "But I'm also hopeful that I will be able to help those who are returning to Afghanistan, especially the women—to rebuild a devastated country and the lives of the Afghan people." Just looking out the window of what was once a vibrant city should be enough to cause despair. But Wali has become inured to the sight of ruined societies and the toll the process has taken on women. As president of Refugee Women in Development, Wali transformed herself from victim to advocate as she worked for decades to empower uprooted women to participate in their own economic and social development. So keen is her understanding that she attended the UN Peace Talks on Afghanistan in Bonn representing the former king of Afghanistan, Zahir Shah.

> Also see RAWA's website at <http://www.rawa.org/index.php>, Refugee Women in Development: <http://www.un.org/events/women/2002/ wali.htm>.

After the US and allies invaded Afghanistan around seven years ago, they misleadingly claimed of bringing peace and democracy and liberating Afghan women from the bleeding fetters of the Taliban. But in reality Afghan women are still burning voraciously in the inferno of fundamentalism. Women are exchanged with dogs, girls are gang-raped, men in the Jehadi-dominated society kill their wives viciously and violently, burn them by throwing hot water, cut off their nose and toes, innocent women are stoned to death.... But the mafia government of Mr. Karzai is tirelessly trying to conciliate with the criminals and award medals to those who should be prosecuted for their crimes and lootings.... The true nature of the US "war on terror" drama has been exposed today and we witness that they are killing thousands of our innocent people under the name of "fighting terrorists" while on the other hand they are busy in dealing with the barbaric fascist Taliban trying to gloss some of them as "moderates" in order to share power with them. These treacherous acts of demagogy have revealed it once again to our people and to the world that the US government and its allies were just pursuing their strategic, economic and political gains in Afghanistan and pushing our people to increasing destitution and disasters. Installing the "Northern Alliance" brutal warlords on power and changing Afghanistan into the center of the world drug mafia, have been the first and foremost objectives of their wrong policies.[7]

The issue here is not so much whether RAWA offers an objective account of the causes of the brutality meted out against Afghan women; it is whether RAWA can be accommodated within a view, like Chesler's or Patai's, of what a feminist response to this brutality should look like. It cannot. In fact, RAWA offers a radically different kind of response, and this is not merely because Chesler and Patai would reject the claim that the US government effectively condones brutality by putting military, economic, and political interests before the welfare of women and girls; it is because RAWA refuses to treat women solely as victims in need of rescue. RAWA's response demonstrates the extent to which the anti-feminist rhetoric depends on an essentially heteropatriarchal view of women as victims. By treating women as moral actors capable of conceiving and acting on their

---

[7] See <http://www.rawa.org/events/mar8-2008_e.htm>.

own judgment, RAWA transforms Muslim women from being the objects of oppression into agents engaged in meaningful resistance. RAWA epitomizes the vertigo of secularization, but not because its members necessarily reject any or all of the tenets of Islam. Instead, in their demand that Afghan women be treated as fully human beings, they become agents of change interested in determining their *own* political conditions and economic options, which may conform neither to any particular interpretation of Islam nor to a Western vision of freedom as the freedom to consume.

Imagine Chesler's and Patai's likely response to Saba Mahmood's account of the Women's Mosque movement and its impetus in a modernizing Muslim world:

> Contrary to expectations fostered by developments in European history, public education and urbanization have not led to a decline in religious observance in the Muslim world. Instead, the state-mandated system of secular education [in Egypt] has served as an impetus for popular interest in various kinds of Islamic knowledges and forms of virtuous conduct.... Modern Muslim citizens, raised in a culture of mass media and public literacy, have become increasingly well-versed in doctrinal arguments and theological concepts that were hitherto confined to the domain of religious specialists. This has fostered a market for reprints of old classical texts.... Furthermore, the advent of televisual and aural media has helped make many religious concepts...available even to unlettered Muslims.... (2005: 79)

However much we may identify mass media and public education with the fostering of Western ideals such as equal access and expanded literacy, it is the ways in which these ideals have been adapted to a specifically Islamic context that challenges how we conceive of the emancipation of women. In the women's mosque movement, for instance, expanded literacy, combined with access to new images of women's lives made available through the media, has created the conditions for a resurgence of interpretation of Islamic texts—especially those alleged to bear on women's virtue, place, and choices. Consider again Hajja Faiza, who offers lessons in the Quran, including a compilation of the prophet Mohammed's sayings called the *Garden of the Pious*, to women at an upper-middle-class mosque in Egypt:

By laying out the range of views among jurists on a particular topic, she trains her audience in a mode of interpretive practice that foregrounds the importance of individual choice and the right of the Muslim to exercise that choice.... [However,] neither the field of choices nor the agents who exercise these choices simply reproduce the assumptions of the liberal humanist's tradition. As such, choice is understood not to be an expression of one's will but something one exercises in following the prescribed path to becoming a better Muslim. (Mahmood 2005: 85)

On the one hand, Hajja Faiza's approach to empowering women departs significantly from RAWA; in fact, "[s]he seldom, if ever, makes any comments about political events in Egypt or elsewhere, and has become even more careful since the government increased its scrutiny and surveillance of mosque lessons post-1996" (Mahmood 2005: 84). But on the other, by emphasizing the agent's capacity for choice—and the obligation of others to respect it—Faiza presents a formidable challenge to masculinist oppression and its denial of choice to women within Islam. Her devotion to the scholarly inter-pretation of Islamic texts also challenges a humanist tradition for which the exercise of reason is strictly secular; yet at the same time, she doesn't close the door to a reading of the Quran that is consis-tent with the Taliban's. While the government surveillance of mosque lessons is no doubt aimed at preventing terrorism, it too is both liberating and oppressive: liberating in that the prevention of terrorism and the securing of public safety are worthy goals, oppres-sive in that surveillance inevitably comes with a chilling effect for engaging in discourse about what counts as virtuous human action.

As mentioned in Chapter V above, Hajja Faiza epitomizes these conflicts in the practice of "leading women in the performance of collective prayer in mosques, even when there is a male imam [teacher] to perform the task" (Mahmood 2005: 87). While several schools of Islamic law permit the practice, one does not, and the common custom is to defer to the male alternative. Accused of "unwarranted innovation" (87), Faiza insists that because there is no firm agreement among scholars about the practice, she is not in violation of Islamic law. But, as Mahmood points out, what is impor-tant about Faiza's strategy of justifying a practice by locating it "within the space of disagreement among Muslim jurists" (88) is that she does not appeal, at least directly, to women's equality, reason, or rights:

> It is precisely her knowledge of authoritative sources that enables Hajja Faiza to challenge the widespread Egyptian practice of deferring leadership of prayer to men; a *daiya* [religious teacher] with less command of such sources would not be able to accomplish such a task.... In the absence of religious institutions that train women in the scholarly Islamic arguments, it is within the institutional space of *dawa* [instruction to greater piety]...that women have come to acquire the requisite knowledge and create the conditions for their exercise of religious authority. (89)

It is, in other words, within the context of instruction to piety—to becoming a better Muslim—that women can become agents of their own decision making. Hajja Faiza's authority, moreover, derives directly from her own knowledge of the relevant religious texts, a knowledge equal to men's, and thus on its own is a challenge to male authority. However, practices like Faiza's leading of women in prayer would be condemned not only by the Taliban, but also by Chesler and Patai who, in their indiscriminate damning of "Islamofascism" fail to appreciate the possibility that women could choose ways of life both meaningful and agential within an Islamic tradition—just as some women do within a Christian (or Jewish or Hindu) tradition. We might ask the thorny question whether genuine decision making for women is possible within the confines of any of the currently growing religious fundamentalisms—Islamic, Christian, or otherwise. Hajja Faiza clearly thinks that it is, at least within some interpretations of Islam, but this merely restates the question whether religious fundamentalisms are essentially masculinist in ways that preclude women's active agency. The concept of "fundamentalism" may not resonate any more than "feminist" does with either Faiza's experience or that of her pupils. Nonetheless, however much it may be the case that empowering her listeners toward a more virtuous life is fundamental, in Faiza's view, to being a good Muslim, it is clear that this virtuous life does not entail Taliban-style domination. By leading women in prayer in the face of serious criticism, Faiza does exemplify at least some of feminism's most basic aspirations. Is it possible to be feminist and religiously devout? Is Hajja Faiza a subversive? A hypocrite? A progressive interpreter? Consider recent US Republican vice-presidential candidate Sarah Palin, committed fundamentalist Christian, former governor of Alaska, mother of five, and grand-mother. In her first speech standing next to presidential candidate John McCain, Palin insisted that her candidacy was another break in the "glass ceiling" with respect to wages and workplace equality for women. Although she didn't use the word "feminist," her very appearance on the American political stage, following on the heels of Hillary Clinton's attempt to secure her party's nomination for president, implies progress for the feminist movement.

But are Palin's political aspirations consistent with her religious beliefs? Does this matter? Should it? Hajja Faiza is careful to steer clear of making (publicly accessible) political claims, but she cannot fail to know that her position of authority, her leading women in prayer, and her appearance on the Egyptian Islamic religious stage have implications for women's political status that are profoundly inconsistent with at least one religiously, politically, and economically powerful incarnation of Islam, the Taliban's. Indeed, Faiza likely avoids politics precisely because it would jeopardize her mission to serve Muslim women; only by avoiding political comment can she be in a position to accomplish her goal—instruction in virtue as a Muslim. Nonetheless, however much Faiza may avoid direct commentary, her actions include an inescapably political dimension in that they challenge the status quo for prayer. This affects not only women's religious lives, but also their cultural, social, and political status. Going to hear Hajja Faiza's instruction, and remaining for prayer, *is* a political act as much as it is a religious one.

The women who attend Faiza's lessons may be motivated by primarily religious aims, but so too are many of Palin's supporters. However, the context is different in some important ways. Whereas Egypt's response to the vertigo of secularization includes democratizing access to religious texts, and its consequent broadening of opportunity for their interpretation (albeit amidst the repressive surveillance of the state's response to terrorism), Americans remain deeply divided over the meaning of the Establishment Clause's separation of church and state. Whereas Faiza personifies secularization in the sense that her instruction in religious virtue takes advantage of Egypt's liberalized access to religious texts, Palin epitomizes vertigo in that among her primary motives for entering public life included the reintroduction of specifically religious values into public policy-making. David Brody (2008) of the Christian Broadcasting Network (CBN), for example, is positively effusive about Palin's signing of a "Christian Heritage Week" Proclamation:

> Here's a "ca-ching" moment for Evangelicals. John McCain's new vice-presidential running mate signed a proclamation back in October of 2007 which emphasized the Christian heritage of America.... You can read the proclamation that she signed below: WHEREAS, the celebration of Christian Heritage Week, October 21–27, 2007, reminds Alaskans of the role Christianity has played in our rich heritage. Many truly great men and women of America, giants in the structuring of American history, were Christians of caliber and integrity who did not hesitate to express their faith.... NOW, THEREFORE, I, Sarah Palin, Governor of the State of Alaska, do hereby proclaim October 21–27, 2007, as Alaska's 9th Annual Christian Heritage Week in Alaska, and encourage all citizens to celebrate this week.... I'm telling you folks. The Evangelical base is revved up about this pick. A McCain campaign source told me that there is so much excitement from the Evangelical community about this pick that it's making their heads spin....

Whether Brody represents Palin's own religious sentiments accurately, and whether Christian Heritage Week is more about the politics of the Christian right than it is about Palin's personal views are fair questions. But consider her stated view of the role of religion with respect to the business of the state. After accepting the vice-presidential nomination, Palin was asked whether religious leaders should endorse political candidates. She responded that "[f]aith is very important to so many of us here in America, and I would never support any government effort to stifle our freedom of religion or freedom of expression or freedom of speech" (Pew Forum 2008). On one level, Palin is exactly right: the Establishment Clause protects just such liberties. On another, however, she doesn't really answer the question whether religious figures should support political candidates. Palin's position on the role of religion in public life is made clearer in a *Chicago Tribune* piece where Manya Brachear (2008) reports that Palin "has called on people to pray for the cooperation necessary to build a natural gas pipeline across Alaska, labeled the US mission in Iraq a 'task that is from God' and argued that students should be taught the creation account from Genesis in public schools." Brachear goes on to quote Palin: "'I can do my job there in developing our natural resources and doing things like getting the roads paved and making sure our troopers have their cop cars and their uniforms and their guns, and making sure our public schools are funded,' she said in June to ministry students at her former church. 'But really, all of that stuff doesn't do any good if the people of Alaska's heart isn't right with God.'"

It is this last quotation that signals something important about Palin's view of the relationship between church and state. That the people of Alaska's "heart" should be "right with God," and that doing good is somehow dependent on this, implies that for Palin the work of the state must cohere with the apparent intentions of the creator. Her pastor, Tim McGraw, reinforces this interpretation, "I believe Sarah would not live in a fragmented world.... The idea that Sarah would take this huge influence of the worldview that really only the Bible and the relationship with Jesus opens up ... and suddenly marginalize it and put it over on the shelf somewhere and live apart from it—that would be entirely inconsistent" (quoted in Brachear 2008). But is Palin's apparent belief that God directs and justifies her actions as governor really different from what Taliban leaders believe? I don't think so. While the method of imposition may be very different, the goal is largely the same: getting it "right with God."

But Palin also epitomizes the nationalist/capitalist "feminist" advocated by Chesler and Patai in the sense that although she embodies in practice a number of feminist values (political empowerment, for example), she does so specifically in the context of advocating for gas pipeline construction across Alaska. Moreover, since she ran as a vice-presidential candidate on the Republican Party ticket of John McCain, we can safely assume that she shares at least in broad outline her party's view of the "war on terrorism." Despite the fact that Hajja Faiza would not likely take a stand on terrorism in any explicitly political arena, both raise similar challenges to contemporary feminism in that both represent—albeit in different ways—the embrace of religious traditions arguably in conflict with their agency as women, *and* both effect this agency at least in part for the sake of

empowering women. Yet here the comparison ends: however carefully she treads the line between her public position as a teacher of
virtue and her place as a Muslim woman, Faiza clearly does not seek
a life for Islamic women comparable to life under the Taliban; the
fact that women can take advantage of her instruction at all qualifies
as an act of resistance to Taliban brutality. Palin offers us a very different metaphor. No doubt, First Amendment guarantees make
avenues for imposing Christian fundamentalism far more difficult in
the United States than in a nation like Afghanistan torn by decades
of war and civil unrest. But—unlike Faiza—Palin is not only
embraced by Christian fundamentalists; her credentials as a political
candidate are coterminous with her credentials as a fundamentalist.
Whereas Faiza actively interrogates the place of women in Islam by
encouraging women to become decision makers, Palin identifies as
virtuous only those women who conform to the religious ideology
of her fundamentalist base, explicitly excluding, for instance, lesbians
and pro-choice advocates.

Palin's support for constitutional amendments such as Pennsylvania's
Senate Bill 1250 (and Alaska's 1998 analogue), her endorsement of
the denial of benefits to same-sex partners (Hopkins 2006), and her
active support for Wasilla Bible Church's sponsorship of the so-called
"pray away the gay" movement all suggest that, given the opportunity, she would seek to make her vision of "getting it right with
God" enforceable policy. Palin also favors overturning the 1973
Supreme Court decision *Roe v. Wade*, which recognizes a woman's
right to abortion up to the end of the first trimester of pregnancy,
and she opposes access to legal abortion even in cases of rape and
incest. Palin also opposes funding for stem-cell research, supports the
teaching of creationism in publicly funded high schools (Yardley
2008), and she applauds the use of faith-based materials in home
schooling (Palin 2006).[8]

Palin, of course, has the right to any of these beliefs under the
Constitution. But this is not at issue. Rather, the issues are whether

---

[8] Additional sources for this paragraph are as follows: "Pray Away the Gay Movement": <http://www.msnbc.msn.com/id/26567170>; *Roe v. Wade: Anchorage
Daily News*, 2006 gubernatorial candidate profile, Oct 22., 2006; abortion: Alaska
2006 Governor Debate, Associated Press coverage of public television debate
Nov. 3, 2006; stem-cell research: <http://www.boston.com/news>, Aug. 30, 2008.

positions held on specifically religious grounds and consistently identified as contrary to the interests and welfare of women can be maintained without hypocrisy against the condemnation of other similar positions, for example, the Taliban's, and whether in holding these positions it is reasonable to think of oneself as a feminist. I think the answers to both of these questions is "no." Certainly we want to hold, both in theory and in practice, that feminism is a big tent able to accommodate a wide array of views and points of departure. But if we insist that what counts as a feminist includes at a minimum leaving to women decisions about the fundamental dispositions of their own bodies, particularly concerning sexuality, marriage, and reproduction, then Palin can no more count herself among feminists than can the Taliban. Palin's politics, at both the state and the national level, personify the fundamentalist's response to the vertigo of secularization; in this respect, she has more in common with bin Laden's vision of re-enchantment than she does with Hajja Faiza's scholarly instruction. Ironically, however, there can also be no doubt that Palin's political success is anathema to the Taliban's dehumanizing view of women; in this respect, Palin epitomizes the Western feminist dream of a self-possessed activist woman, and particularly insofar as she is a mother as well as a governor.

According to Andrea Mrozek, Palin not only exposes a narrow and exclusivist ideology at the heart of feminists who would reject her conservative credentials, but in embracing the pro-life, pro-defense, pro-gun, pro–free-market politics of the West, she represents the face of the "new feminism":

> She's unqualified. Anti-woman. A "right-wing man in a skirt and fetching up-do." Feminists went apoplectic when Alaska Governor Sarah Palin was chosen as Senator John McCain's running mate. The same feminists who keep saying we must have more women in politics suddenly changed their minds. We need more women—just not that kind of woman.... How did we manage to get here?... Today, few are sure what feminism is. If all it means is the right of women to self-determination and to equal opportunity then virtually no one stands against it. That battle has already been won.... North American feminists should be working to extend the fundamental freedoms they enjoy to parts of the globe where such freedoms are absent. But instead, they pitch a

package of partisan political beliefs at home. Their palette is left-wing and non-negotiable—especially the part about unrestricted access to, and, ideally, public funding for, abortion.... But the "choice" label is not something every woman wants.... In this very polarized context, it's not surprising that only the very strongest of conservative and pro-life female politicians would rise to the top. It takes a lot of guts not only to stand up to the kind of sisterly abuse described above, but also to compete effectively in a traditionally male-dominated field. To those untainted by ideology, Sarah Palin is gritty determination personified. To establishment feminists, however, she's a disaster.... Why? Two words: family values. She has five kids...and she's pro-life, even in cases of rape and incest. That she also insists on having the rewarding career that feminists wish they had themselves is just too much. It's driving her feminist opponents around the bend.... (2008)

Like Chesler and Patai, Mrozek claims that the feminist movement has become ideologically rigid, particularly with respect to the pro-life politics of fundamentalist Christian women. Palin is a "disaster" to "establishment feminists" because her "family values" are inconsistent with an all-too-narrow view of feminist autonomy. On the assumption that these are women who would otherwise identify with the emancipatory goals of the feminist movement (itself in need of some scrutiny), it is precisely these for whom Palin stands as a kind of lightning rod of reform. But in her September 2008 interview with ABC news reporter Charles Gibson, Palin conflates what she calls her "personal feelings" about abortion rights and what she thinks ought to be codified as law:

GIBSON: In the time I have left, I want to talk about some social issues.
PALIN: OK.
GIBSON: Roe v. Wade, do you think it should be reversed?
PALIN: I think it should and I think that states should be able to decide that issue.... I am pro-life. I do respect other people's opinion on this, also, and I think that a culture of life is best for America.... What I want to do, when elected vice president, with John McCain, hopefully, be able to reach out and work with those who are on the other side of this issue, because I know that we can all agree on the need for and the desire for fewer abortions in America and greater support for adoption, for other

alternatives that women can and should be empowered to embrace, to allow that culture of life. That's my personal opinion on this, Charlie.

GIBSON: John McCain would allow abortion in cases of rape and incest. Do you believe in it only in the case where the life of the mother is in danger?

PALIN: That is my personal opinion.

GIBSON: Would you change and accept it in rape and incest?

PALIN: My personal opinion is that abortion [should be] allowed if the life of the mother is endangered. Please understand me on this. I do understand McCain's position on this. I do understand others who are very passionate about this issue who have a differing.[9]

On the one hand, Palin insists that it is her *personal* opinion that abortion should only be allowed in cases where the mother's life is in danger, but not in cases of rape or incest. Personal opinions, however, are perfectly consistent with maintaining the right to abortion: to state a personal opinion is to stipulate what one would personally do under particular circumstances, but it is not to stipulate what others ought necessarily to do, much less what the law demands. In other words, Palin is claiming that she would not have an abortion under circumstances of rape or incest, but only were her life in danger, and since what the current law provides for is precisely this personal moral choice, Palin's decision is covered.

On the other hand, she speaks directly to what she thinks should be "allowed," and she calls for overturning Roe v. Wade. This reasoning is faulty in that it assumes that, given the choice, most women would choose abortion. Not only is there no evidence to support this assumption, but many women—including Palin—choose otherwise. Palin acknowledges that others, including presidential candidate John McCain, have differing views, but in calling for the outlawing of abortion in all cases except to save the life of the mother, she would in fact deny the very choice to other women that she reserves to herself, namely, that one's "personal opinion" about the disposition of one's own body with respect to the reproduction of offspring can be realized in practice. Note that I am not taking any position here on the rightness or wrongness of abortion *per se*. What I am suggesting

---

[9]   Accessed at <http://abcnews.go.com/Politics/Vote2008> on September 14, 2008.

is that Palin's position on abortion is not only dictated by her religious predisposition—something to which she has every right *for her own case*—but is also premised on the notion that since it ought to be every woman's "choice" to reject abortion except to save their own life, it is acceptable—even requisite—that this "ought" should become law. What is implied by her remarks is that none but the morally destitute who fail to recognize that abortion is an "atrocity" would make any other decision; hence the criminalizing of abortion effectively protects women from themselves (and presumably from some women's incapacity to make the "right" decision) by denying them the right to make immoral choices.

But this "new feminism" is simply hypocrisy. Contrary to Mrozek's claim that feminists are ideologically rigid because they won't brook the notion that one could be a feminist and be opposed to abortion, what feminists in fact oppose in Palin is the hypocrisy evinced by a political candidate who would utilize the success she owes at least in part to the sacrifices made by countless women whose feminist activism paved the way for her choices in order to deny a fundamental human right to future women, namely, the right to choose whether or not to have children. It is worth noting, too, that in encouraging women to seek the opinion of a physician before they make a decision about female circumcision, Hajja Faiza effectively puts decision making in the hands of individual women, and while abortion isn't female circumcision, both are not only intimately bound up with a woman's reproductive rights, but also subject to heteropatriarchal religious proscription for the same reasons: "There are people who support female circumcision...on the basis that it is good for the psychological health of the woman, and that it is prudent to follow even a weak hadith [religious law] since there is wisdom...in it. *It is up to you which opinion you want to choose*, but make sure that you consult a medical doctor before doing it" (quoted in Mahmood 2005: 86; my emphasis). The difference, then, is that what Faiza seeks to empower—decision making—Palin seeks to criminalize.

Physician Rahul K. Parikh puts this point succinctly in the context of Palin's recent birth of a Down's syndrome child, Trig:

We could ask, given that Palin had no doubts about seeing her pregnancy through, why she bothered to take a genetic test [to determine

Down's syndrome]. Why not, as you might expect a woman in her position and with her outspoken beliefs to do, decline any testing or counseling? Of course, it seems very reasonable to want to know about the health of your baby and to have time to prepare (emotionally and otherwise) for a baby that may have a genetic disorder. But that doesn't negate the fact that by having a blood test, Palin was given a choice about what to do....And what she has chosen to do is fantastic. The love that she and her family have for Trig was clear in her speech at the Republican National Convention. It was inspirational to see a mother in a position of political power stand up for a child with special needs. But Palin was given a choice whether to have that child, something, if she had her way as a lawmaker, she wouldn't give others. According to legal experts, should Roe v. Wade be overturned, some states could outlaw abortion for Down syndrome or other birth defects, and women wouldn't have Palin's choice. (Parikh 2008)

And that, of course, is just the point: the fact that one might be a feminist, a Christian, an opponent of abortion for oneself is consistent with the core emancipatory beliefs of the feminist movement. Palin, facilitated by her economic stability, her access to health insurance, her supportive family, and the feminist movement, got to make a "fantastic" choice. But it is inconsistent with the very spirit of that movement that the same choices should be denied to others. Of course, we would all likely agree that creating the conditions for fewer abortions, more accessible adoptions, and more supportive social arrangements for child care are in every child's interest, but Palin's claim that women should be "empowered" only to make the decisions supported by her religious fundamentalism is plainly doublespeak, and in this respect is no different than the Taliban's insistence that Islamic women are "free" only when they are protected from Western influence and their own evil impulses.

Unlike Palin, Faiza assumes that women are capable moral agents who can make up their own minds. Like her Western feminist counterparts, Faiza is neither decrying nor supporting a controversial practice; she is advocating choice. The ultimate point is no more about Faiza than it is about Palin: it's about the very real danger that religious fundamentalism poses to the future of any movement that seeks to emancipate women from this kind of oppression. This danger has, it turns out, fairly little to do with the actual beliefs—however masculinist, racist, anti-Semitic, or otherwise oppressive—particular to any faith, but it has everything to do with the imposition of unfreedom through political, military or economic channels. And it has everything to do with the appropriation of a language whose essential claim to the freedom of choice is in danger of being lost to those who deny the most basic of human rights, namely, the disposition of one's own reproductive life. My view is that, however dressed in the garb of feminism, the arguments of Chesler, Patai, Sommers, Horowitz, Hymowitz, Mrozek, and others must be rejected by contemporary feminists, not because there exists some litmus test like being pro-choice to determine who gets to count, but because they stand in stark contrast with the recognition of the most fundamental of human rights. If we do not demand that women be treated as capable decision makers, the language of emancipation is meaningless. Perhaps it goes too far to suggest that the politics of religious fundamentalism foreshadows a world like that of Margaret Atwood's famous 1986 novel, *The Handmaid's Tale*:

> In the world of the near future, who will control women's bodies? Offred is a Handmaid in the Republic of Gilead. She may leave the home of the Commander and his wife once a day to walk to food markets whose signs are now pictures instead of words because women are no longer allowed to read. She must lie on her back once a month and pray that the Commander makes her pregnant, because in an age of declining births, Offred and the other Handmaids are only valued if their ovaries are viable. Offred can remember the days before, when she lived and made love with her husband Luke; when she played with and protected her daughter; when she had a job, money of her own, and access to knowledge. But all of that is gone now.... (1)

But once the choice of control over the disposition of one's own body is precluded on religious grounds enforceable by law, how far have we to go before such stories become a potential reality? Not far at all. As RAWA documents so clearly, we're already there.

Chapter VII

Ecological Feminism: A Critical Praxis for the Future as Now

FROM CENTEREDNESS TO CHAUVINISM: RELIGIOUS FUNDAMENTALISM AND ENVIRONMENTAL DESTRUCTION

In August 2008 Alaska Governor Sarah Palin "issued a last-minute statement of opposition to a ballot measure that would have provided added protections for salmon from potential contamination from mining, an action seen as crucial to its defeat" (Yardley 2008). Earlier that same month she "filed a lawsuit in US District Court for the District of Columbia seeking to overturn Interior Secretary Dirk Kempthorne's decision to list the polar bear as threatened under the Endangered Species Act" (Palin 2008). Palin's reasoning in both cases stems directly from her commitment to a "resource-first philosophy" that squarely locates human interest, especially economic and commercial interests, at the center of state policy making and implementation (Palin 2006). A strong advocate for oil and natural-gas exploration in Alaska, Palin has argued vigorously for opening the Alaskan National Wildlife Refuge (ANWR) to drilling:

[W]e're trying to convince the rest of the nation to open ANWR, but we can't even get our own Pt. Thomson, which is right on the edge of ANWR, developed! We are ready for that gas to be tapped so we can fill a natural gas pipeline. I promise to vigorously defend Alaska's rights, as resource owners, to develop and receive appropriate value for our resources. (Palin 2007)

A governor whose popularity derived in part from her devoted pursuit of oil and natural-gas revenues, Palin typifies the view that non-human animals and the environment as a whole exist to be resources for human use and consumption. There are, of course, many ways to interpret this "to be," not all of them at odds with animal welfare or environmental stability. But finding a balance did not appear to be among the concerns of the former Alaska governor. Faced with the possible extinction of an entire species of animal and its consequences for the Arctic ecology that depends on it, Palin opted neither to protect polar bears nor even to regulate the oil/gas industry, but instead sued the US federal government on state's rights and "resource owners" grounds.[1]

The issue, however, is not Sarah Palin herself; it's what she represents: a worldview within which value is assigned not merely according to human interests, but according to a set of interests designed to bring to fruition the religious and political aims of what has now come to be called "the base." In fact, closer scrutiny of this worldview brings to light the fact that while human material interests provide the superficial justification for activities such as drilling in ANWR, the real justification lies elsewhere: Palin's support for drilling instantiates her faith in one variety of the logic of domination, that is, in a hierarchical order of value through which God's purposes and intentions are made manifest. To pray, as Palin does, for a pipeline, and to believe that its construction is a manifestation of God's will, as Palin appears to believe (Schweitzer 2008), is not just about material interests; it's about interests better described as otherworldly. The fact that she has ignited the enthusiasm of millions of adherents to "the base" is not first and foremost about environmental exploitation—even though the consequences for affected ecosystems are just as devastating (if not more so). No, in this worldview it is also about salvation —regardless of the consequences for human or nonhuman nature.

---

[1] If the polar bear example is unconvincing, consider pundit Walter Brasch's characterization of Palin's response to the pardon, and then slaughter, of Thanksgiving Day turkeys (Brasch 2008). For further critique see Cuomo, Eisner, and Hinkel (2008).

Such an outlook is tethered not to this world, but to the world promised as the reward for bearing the burdens of salvation. From this point of view, folks who evince significant environmental concerns are at least shortsighted—perhaps even inclined to sin in the form of excessive worldliness. In short, for Palin and her base, nonhuman nature exists for human use, and as an opportunity to demonstrate faith in God's intentions. Following out God's instructions to "subdue the earth" thus constitutes an act of committed devotion (Genesis 1.26) which, while it may not prescribe, for example, animal cruelty, also does not proscribe aerial wolf hunting. "Warped," however, is what *Huffington Post* writer Jeff Schweitzer calls it:

> Governor Palin is a tsunami of environmental destruction, a direct consequence of her warped religious view of the world. Palin subscribes to the notion that God put resources here on Earth for man's exploitation, as described in Genesis. She believes God is not only on her side, but supports her specific environmental and energy policies. Concerning a proposed $30 billion gas pipeline in Alaska, she actually said, "I think God's will has to be done in unifying people and companies to get that gas line built, so pray for that." God takes time out from Darfur, terrorism, disease, hunger and suffering to make sure Palin gets her pipeline.... Her answer to our energy needs, with God's approval: drill baby drill.... Renaissance scholar Lynn White famously wrote in 1967, "We shall continue to have a worsening ecologic crisis until we reject the Christian axiom that nature has no reason for existence save to serve man." Now 40 years later, Palin proves him right again. (Schweitzer 2008)

Harsh words—but what they underscore is a Christian anti-naturalism within which nonhuman nature not only is valued in terms of use, but is simultaneously devalued as transient, as fleeting epiphenomena of no ultimate consequence in the quest for salvation.

Religious anti-naturalism is not merely human-centered; it's chauvinistic. Such a worldview does not merely privilege human interests over nonhuman ones (rightly or wrongly); it systematically delegitimates interests that cannot be readily subordinated to a "logic" within which value is determined not only by interest, but also by the human capacity to alter and dominate the environment in accord with that interest. The fact that Sarah Palin can treat Beluga whales, polar bears, moose, and wolves (not to mention trees, brush, and other flora and fauna) as obstacles in the path to revenue production testifies to the authority with which she can elevate market interests above the stability or welfare of nonhuman nature. But her authority derives not from the market alone; it derives from "the base." That is, it derives from that worldview whose consistent practice is substantially responsible for the environmental erosion we now face. And, as we will see, such a worldview can underwrite many forms of oppression—including Palin's own.

ENVIRONMENTAL CHAUVINISM: THE GENDERED, HETEROSEXUALIZED, AND RACIALIZED LOGIC OF COMMODIFICATION

Nowhere is the history of human chauvinism more comprehensively well documented than in philosopher Frederic Bender's *The Culture of Extinction* (2003). Bender shows the extent to which Christian anti-naturalism is appropriated and put to the service of transforming non-human nature into a resource for the capitalist production of material wealth. In conjunction with the emergence of the modern nation-state and the rise of industrial capitalism in the sixteenth to eighteenth centuries, anti-naturalism takes on the distinctively "resource first" characteristics that distinguish human-centeredness from human chauvinism. Indeed, the difference between the former and the latter is simply the difference between a worldview in which human interests are prioritized and one in which that priority is believed to derive either from supernatural authority or the nation-state, or both (Bender 2003: 214–29). Competition between church and state serves to advance the logic of domination in that both have a stake in legitimating their sovereignty over human life; nonhuman nature and animals are thus equally subsumed to use-value on both worldviews. "Modernism," argues Bender, "legitimates Earth's complete subordination to human purposes... and delegitimates criticism of Earth's devastation as irrational or regressive" (210). "Christianity," he goes on, "in particular, [in] Lynn White's words, 'bears a huge burden of guilt,' since modernity grew out of medieval Christendom and several novel Christian ideas and practices" (210). Among these are ideas appropriated from Aristotle, who claims that since nature makes nothing in vain, its plants and animals must exist for human use (211).

Further buttressed, then, by the Christian imperative to distinguish the heavenly from the worldly, God from mortal human beings, human beings from nonhuman nature, the soul from the body, and men from women, a Christianized Aristotle is ready-made for the conversion of the worldly, the nonhuman, women, and other human beings into the labor and resources of industrialization.[2] Captured in perhaps its most basic form, Karen Warren puts this version of the logic of domination this way:

(A1) Humans do, and plants do not, have the capacity to...change the community in which they live.

(A2) Whatever has the capacity to...change the community in which it lives is morally superior to whatever lacks this capacity. .

(A3) Thus, humans are morally superior to plants and rocks.

(A4) For any X and Y, if X is morally superior to Y, then X is morally justified in subordinating Y.

(A5) Thus, humans are morally justified in subordinating plants and rocks. (2002 [1990]: 236)

Absent from this formulation are nonhuman animals, sentient and otherwise, particularly important among them the ones that may have some capacity to change their "communities" (chimpanzees and gorillas, for example). Absent, too, is any mention of the logic's historical, political, economic, or religious roots. Such missing pieces, however, make Warren's formulation so apt an illustration of the operating presuppositions espoused by Palin and the "base." If, according to that worldview, building a gas pipeline through Alaska's North Slope is merely a realization of God's will, it hardly matters how we arrived at this juncture or whether there exist morally relevant distinctions to be drawn between plants and nonhuman animals. Building the pipeline demonstrates our capacity to "change our community." Whether salmon and polar bears are resources or obstacles depends on what human interests are to be served by any given revenue-producing enterprise. As Palin puts it, salmon may create a revenue resource, and polar-bear protection thwart one, but where

---

[2] See, for example, Bender's account of emergent capitalism and the Christianizing of Aristotle via the medieval theologians Albertus Magnus and Thomas Aquinas (210–14).

salmon protection is in the way of mining, and polar bears create an opportunity for, say, ecotourism, a change in our behavior toward them would hardly constitute any breach of the logic. According to it, after all, the issues are always the same: Who are the intended beneficiaries of a decision? How are institutions created and maintained to ensure that these beneficiaries remain the same?

In her sweeping *The Death of Nature* (1980), Carolyn Merchant provides further insight into the historical connection between a "resource first" philosophy and its religious rationale: "Mechanism, which superseded the organic framework [of the ancients], was based on the logic that knowledge of the world could be certain and consistent, and that the laws of nature were imposed on creation by God" (102). As she documents in rich detail, such laws not only confirm the subordination of nature to human interests, just as human interests are subordinate to God's will (and the planets to God's celestial mechanics), but they also confirm an order of value and social place for human beings. Warren situates this order of value within the logic:

> A logic of domination is not just a logical structure. It also involves a substantive value system, since an ethical premise is needed to permit or sanction the "just" subordination of that which is subordinate. This justification typically is given on grounds of some alleged characteristic (e.g., rationality) which the dominant (e.g., men) have and the subordinate (e.g., women) lack. (2002 [1990]: 236)

As Merchant shows, such "ethical premises" are themselves rooted in the maintenance of social class and religious dogma, so it is unsurprising that the logic serves to "justify" the subordination of women on largely the same grounds that it justifies the domination of nonhuman nature:

> Symbolically associated with unruly nature was the dark side of woman. Although the Renaissance Platonic lover had embodied her with true beauty and the good, and the Virgin Mary had been worshipped as the mother of the Savior, women were also seen as closer to nature than men, subordinate in the social hierarchy to the men of their class, and imbued with far greater sexual passion. The upheavals of the reformation and the witch trials of the sixteenth century heightened these perceptions. Like wild chaotic nature, women needed to be subdued and kept in their place. (132)

Ecological feminist philosopher Lori Gruen spells out even more specifically the connection between the logic of domination, religious faith, and women's status:

> Droughts, storms, and other natural conditions led to the devastation of crops [in early agricultural communities], which in turn caused much suffering. Thus, nature was simultaneously the source of great fear and that which provided the means of survival. Woman, likened to the earth for her ability to bring forth life, was also feared. With the increased risks and uncertainties of the farming life came an intensified desire to dominate. This domination of both natural forces and women was often sought through "divine intervention." In order to enlist the help from the "gods," various rituals were devised. By removing themselves from the natural activities of daily life, men believed they would be in closer touch with the "supernatural" powers that would protect them from nature. In religious mythology, if not in actual practice, women often served as symbols for the uncontrollable and harmful and thus were sacrificed in order to purify the community and appease the gods. Animals too were sacrificed.... Religious belief can thus be seen as a particularly pernicious construction of women and animals as "others" to be used. (1993: 63–64)

At one level, it is hard to imagine Palin signing on to the view of women's status implied by this history; she has occupied high political office, and she claims (sometimes) to be a feminist. Moreover, Palin would surely deny any association of women with nature that could justify symbolic sacrifice—much less burning at the stake. But at another level, her opposition to virtually all abortions, for example, suggests that she does not regard women as moral agents fully adequate to the task of determining the disposition of their own bodies (including herself).

Criminalizing abortion is certainly one way of keeping women subordinated to religious proscription. But it then seems at least peculiar that although Palin's position on abortion is consistent with her "resource first" view of nonhuman nature insofar as it coheres with her religious worldview, it is inconsistent with her former position as governor, especially if, as Warren points out, the subordination of women is grounded on a lack of *rationality*. Put differently, Palin's political authority and popularity with her own religiously self-defined base do not cohere with the view of either women or nature advocated by her or her supporters since, as Merchant shows, the latter is premised on a logic of domination that has no place for women empowered to make, for example, high-level political decisions—even if those decisions ultimately disempower women.

What accounts for this inconsistency? My view is that nothing does—other than the expediency that favors a woman in cases where a particular political and economic agenda may be more effectively carried out by one (for example, as vice-presidential nominee on a ticket otherwise disfavored by female voters). What is important here, in other words, is that whereas expediency may sometimes favor a woman in a position more typically filled by a man, it nonetheless works to reinforce a logic which, in "justifying" the domination of nonhuman nature and women, legitimates a social order in which every attribute of human and nonhuman being is assigned a place according to that logic. Palin supplies one particularly rich metaphor for these mercenary dynamics, and in so doing she displays a chauvinism that cannot be delineated solely in terms of its implications for nonhuman nature. A fully comprehensive understanding of these dynamics must in fact include gender, sexual identity, and race among its axes of analysis.[3] If we are, in other words, to comprehend how a human contribution to climate change, species extinction, deforestation, and desertification has become possible, we must come to understand the ways in which human chauvinism is itself gendered, sexed, and racialized. It is no accident that Palin is not a woman of African (or Asian, or Middle Eastern, or Native American) descent, not gay, not unmarried, not childless, not Islamic, Hindu, Buddhist, or Wiccan, and not vegetarian or vegan. Indeed, for whatever lip-service we might offer to the claim that, for example, any born or naturalized citizen could become president, she could not be or embrace any of these, and remain (at least ostensibly) electible. Just as the logic of domination defines reason such that the instrumental

---

[3] We could also include here axes of explanation devoted to ableism and ageism; I have not done so only because these are beyond the scope of my present concern. But much of what I have to say about racism, sexism, and heterosexism has application to these equally pernicious and chauvinistic forms of bigotry.

valuation and consequent domination of some human beings by others is "justified" as the discoverable order of nature, so too does it define how human beings ought to behave toward nonhuman nature as, for instance, a resource bestowed by God for use by his faithful servants. "Resource first" does not refer, then, merely to pipelines, Northern slopes, salmon, or polar bears, but to whatever sustains the priorities of those whom the logic authorizes as rational.

In her essay "Standing on Solid Ground: A Materialist Ecological Feminism," Gwyn Kirk argues for a socialist feminist reading of the causes of environmental deterioration, and she explicitly identifies the conversion of instrumental value into commodity value as its primary culprit: "Ecological feminists and women environmental activists need to understand and challenge the source of environmental devastation: the unsustainable priorities, values, and living standards of industrialized countries based on highly militarized, capitalist economies" (1997: 346). What we need to understand, in other words, is how a logic that advertises itself as a rational interpretation of our place in the world can so effectively create the conditions for a future uninhabitable by anything other than viruses and bacteria. However much "the base" may hold with the late pastor Jerry Falwell that "[i]t is God's planet—and he's taking care of it. And I don't believe that anything we do will raise or lower the [earth's] temperature one point" (Falwell 2007), the evidence is unmistakably on the side of a very human contribution to global climate change, deforestation, pollution, species extinction, and so on (United States 2009). But what can explain such wholesale denial of fact? Falwell, again, offers a clue: "The whole global warming thing is created to destroy America's free enterprise system and our economic stability" (Falwell 2007). In other words, global warming is a myth created by those who would dare to question the authority of God, whose planet is intended for free enterprise; to question the stability of the environment amounts, therefore, to blasphemy.

The problem, of course, is that it doesn't. Instead, Falwell's claim epitomizes what Kirk calls the "logic of capitalist accumulation" (1997: 349). By imputing directly to God intentions associated with the commodification of nonhuman nature, Falwell not only authorizes Palin's "resource first" approach to the environment, but actively encourages capitalist expansion regardless of the consequences. Global in her scope, Kirk argues that the foreseeable products of this view are economies "based on production for profit, not needs." Now, Falwell might have responded that Kirk's is a false dichotomy, that God's "taking care" will fulfill needs as well as turn a profit; again, however, the evidence is not on his side. As Kirk points out, by the mid-1980s more than a billion people lacked access to clean drinking water, at least 40,000 children were dying daily from disease borne by contaminated water, and even in the America Falwell thought to be the promised land (Wolfe 2007), "children's health is compromised by environmental factors such as lead in paints... [and] air pollution" (Kirk 1997: 345). The toll taken by environmental destruction is as global as its markets, the economies based on these markets as demonstrably wasteful, trash and pollution producing, and derelict with respect to land and buildings as they are exploitive of their labor, particularly that of cultural minorities, women, and children (350). Under such conditions, Kirk argues, "the role of governments is to maintain political and economic conditions favorable to profit making through laws, regulations, tax breaks, and other incentives" (350).

Regardless of Falwell's stalwart support of this "logic of accumulation" or Palin's faithful incarnation of it, the maintenance of such conditions would not be possible without the defining roles played by sexuality, gender, and race. Informed by each of these axes, human chauvinism produces particular patterns of environmental destruction, nonhuman animal exploitation and cruelty, and social injustice. It is the task, I think, of an ecologically inspired feminism to identify these patterns, spell out their place in the logic, and dispel the illusion of their naturalness or divine sanction. The "who," "where," and "how" of the commodification of nonhuman nature is made not merely visible but also predictable via such an approach, precisely because its foci are not the axes alone, but also the patterns of domination and subordination that connect them and render those who are identified as subordinate particularly vulnerable. A careful analysis of these patterns can show the extent to which sexuality, race, and gender define not only a logic of domination, but also a logic of accumulation and exploitation; what informs such a pattern is not merely what or who is defined as superior as opposed to inferior, but whose interests are served in such an arrangement—and by what means.

Contrary, however, to the view among some feminists and non-feminists alike that virtually all human interests are justly described as chauvinistic, or that we ought to concern ourselves primarily or even solely with the effects of these patterns for nonhuman nature, human-centeredness has, I suggest, a vital role to play in imagining an environmentally livable future—for human and nonhuman beings alike. Given the intimacy of the connections among the axes that inform the logic of domination, the failure to see how it informs each axis will likely result in the failure to address any of them adequately—including those most relevant to environmental activists.[4] It is in understanding the full range of dynamics that produce such patterns that we stand the best chance of contributing to the production of new ones—of institutionalizing new practices—that lead toward a more sustainable as well as more just future. If we fail to attend to the consequences of these patterns for human beings, we will find our activism short-sighted and ultimately wanting, precisely because we will be unprepared to target the "who," "where," and "how" of specific environmental issues. Human-centeredness need not be chauvinistic: as we will see, a careful look at how human-centeredness has become heterosexualized, racialized, and gendered illustrates in what chauvinism consists; but it also demonstrates that just as we can agitate for change in the institutions that sustain heterosexism, racism, and sexism, so too can we agitate for change in the ways we have institutionalized the exploitation of nonhuman nature. In fact, if there's to be a livable future, we *must*.

PATTERNS OF DOMINATION: ANTHROPOMORPHIZING, ANIMALIZING, ERASURE

Social justice, concern for nonhuman animal welfare, and achieving environmental sustainability are, then, inseparably connected projects. While the inclusion of human interests and welfare need not be cast as chauvinistic, it has become so in the hands of those whom, as Bender (2003) shows, chauvinism most benefits. That these beneficiaries include those who have long been the foci of feminist analyses

---

[4] I make the case for this position at some length in Lee (2005, 2006, 2008, and 2009).

of exploitation and oppression is hardly surprising, but, as Merchant (1980) and Warren (2002 [1990]) demonstrate, human chauvinism cannot be adequately understood solely in terms of human action, but rather must be understood in terms of factors—gender, sexual identity, race—which define one's status as beneficiary or commodity, empowered or vulnerable, user or resource. I have recently argued, for example, that in the course of anthropomorphizing nonhuman animals and things, we also heterosexualize them:

> The heterosexualizing of nonhuman nature...is not merely *a* function of anthropomorphizing, but a *basic* function, that is, a function without which we would experience nonhuman nature in substantially different ways. What we discover, in fact, is that such linguistic practices are not only gendered, but that they serve to naturalize and thereby normalize a heterosexist view of the nonhuman world which then reinforces asymmetrical divisions of status and power reflected in institutions like church, family, and the military. "Basic," then, does not imply "determined" or "inevitable," but rather "naturalized" in that what is reflected in our linguistic practices—in anthropomorphizing especially—are the specific ways in which human beings have institutionalized relationships of prerogative and power. (Lee 2009: 42)

To say that anthropomorphizing is a "linguistic practice" is to point out that it is a specific sort of *language use*:

> To anthropomorphize is to treat nonhuman entities or systems as if they exhibited distinctively human qualities. Disney movies may be the quintessential example. Dancing penguins, talking cars, and singing flowers entertain us because they *are* us—*as* penguins, cars, and flowers. Regardless whether the object of our anthropomorphizing is a living or a nonliving thing, an animated character from *Happy Feet* or a nonhuman animal from *March of the Penguins*, what we attribute to them are qualities we recognize in ourselves, for example, fear, desire, envy, empathy, temptation, sadness, joy, and so on.... We speak usefully of bee "dances," "vicious" viruses, "industrious" ants, and the "desires" of flowers to warm themselves in the sun—to say nothing of the human qualities we attribute to our dogs and cats. (42; emphasis added)

Consider, for example, a use of anthropomorphizing language to conduct field research in cognitive ethology (the study of nonhuman animal intelligence and cognition):

> Mitani and Waters found that the number of males in the [chimpanzee] group, not the presence of estrous females, best predicted active hunting. Males also shared meat more with one another than with any female, and they did so reciprocally: *give me some of yours and I'll give you some of mine.* Those males who routinely shared the spoils also formed partnerships in other arenas; they groomed one another more often and aided one another in fights. Chimpanzee hunting is not about using scarce and valuable resources to attract females, Mitani says it's about using this resource to form and build alliances with other males. (Small 2001: 26; my emphasis)

"Whatever the actual cognitive capacities of our nearest primate relatives," I argue, "Mitani and Waters' use of anthropomorphizing language helps shed light on the behavior of hunting males" (Lee 2009: 43).

However, while anthropomorphizing chimpanzee behavior is useful, the *way* in which Mitani and Waters employ such language is equally as revealing:

> Consider the chimpanzees. There may be more to what *appears* explanatorily useful in this passage than what may in fact *be* so in that what seems to shed light on male chimpanzee behavior depends on our assumptions about relationships among them. It depends, that is, on what beliefs we think they ought to have. But what we discover when we examine the passage more closely is that what governs how we ascribe beliefs to the chimpanzees are *our* beliefs about what *human* relationships ought to be like, in this case, composed of "ladies," presumably gentlemen, and *heterosexual.* If, in other words, we find Mitani and Waters' explanation useful, it may be because we identify with the presuppositions reflected in the article's title, "Sigma Chi Chimpy: Forget the Ladies— For Chimps, Hunting is About Fraternity." (Lee 2009: 43–44)

This use of anthropomorphizing language is, in other words, also heterosexualizing in that part of what makes this explanation useful is that it conforms to what we are already socialized to expect in *human* behavior:

[W]e gender and heterosexualize in the very course of assigning human characteristics to nonhuman animals and things precisely because these are the characteristics we implicitly regard as the most basic and "normal" in human beings. Taken for granted, these are the qualities we expect to experience in our observations and interactions with nonhuman beings, hence it's hardly surprising that we do. [The] relevance [of how we use language] to environmental philosophy is clear: anthropomorphizing does not occur in an historical vacuum, but within very rich and specific social and political contexts.... (Lee 2009: 44)

The use of heterosexualizing language informs a pattern in the way we conceive of nonhuman animals in much the same way that referring to "Mother" nature as female informs a pattern in the way we conceive of women. We expect to experience attraction, desire, and even friendship as heterosexual, and then predict that we will discover the same in others—even, as in this case, nonhuman others. We expect to find women's behavior irrational or "untamed," and as with anthropomorphizing we find much in the language to support this stereotype. As Gruen observes: "[t]he categories 'woman' and 'animal' serve the same symbolic function in patriarchal society. Their construction as dominated, submissive, 'other,' in theoretical discourse ...has sustained human male dominance. The role of women and animals in postindustrial society is to serve/be served up; women and animals are the used" (1993: 61).

It is somewhat ironic that a linguistic practice as scientifically useful as anthropomorphizing could contribute to a construction of women and nonhuman animals as the "used." But the symbolic function of this construction pervades the way in which we conceive of what it means to be male or female all the way down to the most fundamental of natural processes. It is hard, for example, to imagine, a more transparent instance of this symbolic function than the extent to which we gender and heterosexualize sexual conception. "Take the egg and the sperm," remarks feminist theorist Emily Martin, citing standard course texts in reproductive biology:

'It is remarkable how "femininely" the egg behaves and how "masculinely" the sperm. The egg is seen as large and passive. It does not move or journey, but passively "is transported," "is swept," or even "drifts" along the fallopian tube. In utter contrast, sperm are small, "streamlined," and invariably active. They "deliver" their genes to the egg, "activate the developmental program of the egg," and have a velocity that is often remarked upon. Their tails are "strong" and efficiently powered. Together with the forces of ejaculation, they can "propel the semen into the deepest recesses of the vagina." (1999: 181–82)

Patterned after stereotypical heterosexual romances, the relationship depicted in this textbook not only exemplifies the logic of domination, but underscores the extent to which *otherness* and *opposition* play a role in maintaining it; the lethargic egg, cast as female, is assailed by the forceful sperm, cast as male. The passage, moreover, isn't just a human-centered way of illustrating conception; it is chauvinistic precisely because it casts a natural phenomenon—the union of egg and sperm—in terms of human relationships naturalized as a union of unequal opposites, not merely as male and female, but as feminine and masculine.

Feminist animal-welfare theorist Carol Adams reveals a similar pattern with respect to the language of race. She argues that "the concept of the beast functions to justify perceiving some people as other and disempowering them":

The marker of attributed beastliness, of less-than-humanness, exists to constitute whiteness as well as human maleness. One cannot discuss the idea that some people are situated between man and beast without acknowledging the way that white supremacist beliefs depicted people of color in general and African-Americans in specific: as not (white) man and (almost) beast…. As [Zuleyma] Halpin points out, "Even when groups labeled 'inferior' are not explicitly equated with women, they are often compared to animals, usually in ways designed to make them appear more animal than human" (using white males as the prototype of humanity). (1995: 73)

"Otherness," in other words, functions to "constitute" and empower whiteness and maleness by defining such qualities in opposition to non-whiteness and femaleness. But even more important is the fact that otherness is so entrenched in the language, that even when no explicit comparison with femaleness is made, the inequality of

women's status as "other" can be assumed because the same comparison can be drawn with nonhuman animals—the pattern is already
available for the assignment of place.

Note, too, that it does not matter whether we are anthropomorphizing nonhuman animal behavior or, as Adams points out, "animalizing" it. We anthropomorphize when we attribute human characteristics to nonhuman animals, and in so doing elevate their status, and
we animalize when we attribute "animal" or "beastly" characteristics
to human beings, but in so doing devalue their status. Both presuppose the superiority of human beings. While the elevation of status
occurs as more or less incidental in the former case (and appears to
have little bearing on our treatment of nonhuman animals), devaluation is the specific purpose of the latter. "Euro-American human
maleness," remarks Adams, "used the 'less-than-human' definitions to
demarcate racial as well as sexual differences, to institutionalize
racism as well as sexism" (1995: 73). Consider, for example, the recent
case of the Barack Obama Sock Monkey Puppet:

> A toy being sold over the internet by a Utah couple is causing an uproar
> from supporters of democratic presidential candidate Barack Obama. It's
> a sock monkey wearing a suit with a lapel pin for Obama. Supporters of
> Obama have been filling online forums and blogs with angry words over
> what they see as the degrading depiction of a black man as a monkey.
> Such portrayals are a throw back to the days of "Jim Crow" laws in south-
> ern states. The depictions were designed to make one man appear infe-
> rior, less than human, for no other reason than the color of his skin.
> From different blogs, one writer puts it simply: "The 'Sock Obama' is dis-
> gusting." Others say its makers are racists. With such a reaction, it is ironic
> that the toy was being marketed to Obama supporters. The sales pitch on
> the website reads: "We don't get enough of him at his public speaking
> events. Now you can have your very own TheSockObama™ 24/7! Fall
> in love with your chosen candidate all over again." (Hunsaker 2008)

It *is* ironic that the Obama Sock Monkey was marketed to Obama
supporters, since it is precisely in comparing him to a monkey that
the racism of the "toy" is realized. And while it should be acknowledged that a Joe Biden monkey is also available on the website, this
hardly accounts for the claimed "naivete" on the part of either toy's

creators. However much the "white" sock monkey might seem to blunt the animalizing message of the Obama option, it can't: the history of animalizing black men specifically *as* monkeys is simply too long, and too entrenched a part of the culture:

> The Sock Obama is the creation of David and Elizabeth Lawson of West Jordan. They say they are shocked by the anger. In responding to a handful of the emails that are filling their inbox, they wrote: "We at TheSockObama Co. are saddened that some individuals have chosen to misinterpret our plush toy. It is not, nor has it ever been, our objective to hurt, dismay or anger anyone. We guess there is an element of naiveté on our part, in that we don't think in terms of myths, fables, fairy tales and folklore. In earnest folks, we're so sorry we offended anybody." So far, few web commentators are buying their plea of "naiveté," especially since the Lawsons have said nothing about stopping the sale of their Sock Obama. (Hunsaker 2008)

It's hard to imagine that the Lawsons have no idea of the "myths, fables, fairy tales, and folklore" that perpetuate the racism implicit in the Obama sock monkey. The toy does not, moreover, merely signify racist images of African American men; it capitalizes on them. This is a toy *for sale* on the Internet ($29.99), and despite the sincerity of the Lawsons' apologies, it's still for sale—as post-election "memorabilia."[5] And despite the fact that the toy appears to be marketed to adults, the fact that it is modeled on the sock monkey traditionally popular with (and marketed to the parents of) small children is particularly troubling, since among the most pernicious features of racism is its durability in adults who've been exposed to it as youngsters.

Chief among these "myths" and "fables," and perhaps even more unsettling, are the sexualizing—and heterosexualizing—images of black men and women captured in the animalized (especially with reference to monkeys and apes) pornographic language of so-called African sexual "rapaciousness." This is not to say that sock monkeys evoke these images directly, but they do evoke a history rife with comparisons of stereotypical images of monkeys or apes and persons of color, comparisons that lurk just beneath the sock monkey's surface. As Adams explains,

---

[5] See TheSockObama website at <http://www.thesockobama.com>.

By viewing African-Americans as black beasts, Euro-American men created two pornographic scenarios, one about rapacious black men, and
one about lascivious black women available to anyone, man or beast.
Both concepts interacted with the notion of white women as pure, virginal and sexless.... Black men were seen as beasts sexually threatening
white womanhood, a white womanhood defined to aggrandize the
sense of white manhood. Black women were seen as sexed, as not able
to be violated because they would enjoy anything—including sex with
animals.... Indeed, Winthrop Jordan concludes that "[t]he sexual union
of apes and Negroes was always conceived as involving *female Negroes* and
male apes." (1995: 74; emphasis in original)

It is against this historical backdrop that denials of the racism implicit
in the Obama Sock Monkey are exposed not merely as naïve, but as
willfully ignorant. And this is not because the sock monkey itself
conveys a sexualized message, but because its creators cannot fail to
have an idea of what will sell, namely, a tradition of racism premised,
as Adams shows, on the animalizing of black men. But note too that,
according to the logic of domination, by the same token that black
men and women are animalized, sexualized, and heterosexualized,
white persons are humanized, heterosexualized, and situated as superior to black men, black women, and nonhuman animals and nature.
As male, men—black or white—are implicitly situated as superior to
women—black or white. Nonetheless, white women—as white—
are situated as superior to black men as black. Both black and white
women, however, are vulnerable to commodification insofar as black
women as black and female are the (sexualized) property of white
men, and white women as female are the (desexualized) property of
white men. Black men, however, fare little better in this logic in that
not only are they likely to be sexualized as black and as "animal," they
are also likely to be sexualized as predatory—a "justification" for
especially violent forms of oppression—and they are as likely to be
commodified as black, *and* as "animal" in the form of beasts of burden, as are their black female counterparts, despite the fact that, as
male, they are superior to black women as women.

The point, of course, is that human chauvinism is demonstrably
not generic, but rather relies on the maintenance of social institutions
whose privileges and prerogatives are defined according to a logic

that evokes patterns of comparison and identity between specific (however conventional) categories of human being and equally specific images of nonhuman animals and nature, patterns that establish not only otherness, but commodifiability as well. However much (or little) the sexualized and racist content of these images is more indirectly than directly available in the sock monkey, we should not read this as an invitation to ignore the monkey's contribution to maintaining the status quo, even if this is what the Lawsons are counting on us to do. Consider an anonymous blogger who writes that he finds it funny

> that none of the media furies are comparing this instance [of comparison of Obama to a monkey] to the many images I've seen in past years of George W. Bush depicted as a monkey. I guess it is OK to show a white man in America as a monkey. When you do the same to a black man different standards are applied. Makes perfect sense if you are a mentally retarded person I suppose.[6]

What this blogger fails to comprehend is that it's not that "different standards are applied," it's that while comparing Bush to a monkey evokes either smug amusement or disdain, it does not evoke the devaluing of his essential humanity—much less fear or dread. It threatens neither his place in the logic nor his prerogative to respond. In fact, Bush is in exactly the position to respond that Obama isn't (even as president).

Consider, for example, the racially tinged rhetoric of some conservative pundits over Obama's response to the July 2009 arrest by white Cambridge, Massachusetts, officer Sgt. James Crowley of black Harvard professor Henry Louis Gates, Jr., for disorderly conduct when Gates expressed anger at the officer's apparent assumption that he was breaking into what turned out to be his own house. Obama remarked of the incident that the police officers "acted stupidly," but later backtracked to some extent, remarking that the incident was "a sign of how race remains a factor in society," (Seelye 2009). Responding to Obama, however, conservative radio talk-show host Rush Limbaugh remarked that "[l]ast week we saw white firefighters under

---

6   Posted on <http://willtoexist.com> on May 14, 2008.

assault by agents of Barack Obama and Sonia Sotomayor [then-Supreme Court candidate and now appointee].... Now, white policemen are under assault from the East Room of the White House, by the president of the United States after admitting he had no—he didn't know all the facts, what went on in there" (Kleefeld 2009; emphasis in original). Or consider Glenn Beck's remark that what Obama's comment demonstrated was that "Obama had exposed himself...as a guy who has a deep-seated hatred for white people" (Weisbrot 2009). Would President Bush have generated the same charged criticism had he remarked that the police "acted stupidly"? (Would Bush have made the remark at all?) Would he have felt pressured in the wake of these remarks to backtrack to a somewhat softer claim about race as a "factor" in American society? This seems at least unlikely. As Weisbrot perceptively argues,

the fact that President Obama had to backtrack from his remarks says more about certain institutional aspects of racism in the United States than it does about individual attitudes among the electorate or among police officers.... [A]lthough individual attitudes obviously matter and are influenced by deep historical factors such as slavery and segregation, the persistence of such prejudices over time can be substantially strengthened by certain political institutions and strategies. As the Gates case illustrates, in today's context this means the Republican party and the right-wing media—which overlap considerably.... The National Republican Senatorial Committee distributed an online petition asking whether "it's appropriate for our nation's Commander in Chief to stand before a national audience and criticize the men and women in law enforcement who put their lives on the line every day.... Obama was being generous to Crowley; a better description would have been "acted maliciously." Even if we accept Crowley's own police report as a completely accurate version of events, there was no excuse for putting Professor Gates in handcuffs and dragging him down to the police station.

One might object, of course, that the fact that Obama—an African American man—was elected president mitigates against the charge that such examples illustrate the persistence of racism. Indeed, Weisbrot himself acknowledges that race was likely only one factor for Southern voters who voted for McCain in the 2008 elections, since many would not have voted for a Democrat in any case. However, to the extent that Weisbrot, like Adams, is correct that racism is not merely about individual attitudes, but also about institutionalized practices, it's hardly surprising that the Gates incident generated the specifically racially charged condemnation of the President that it did. Put simply: calling Obama racist for having dared to bring attention to institutionalized racism is itself demonstrably racist. It's at least arguable, moreover, that, contrary to the charge that the "Commander in Chief" overstepped his place in criticizing "men and women in law enforcement," Obama had—and in fact executed—a responsibility to bring attention to the incident in the interest of raising awareness about the extent to which race is, indeed, a factor in American justice, a position for which he is particularly qualified as a black president.

To return, then, once more to the sock monkey: as Crowley's response to Gates illustrates, the default assumption is that black men are violent, and that, as such, they are more like animals than people. Yelling at an officer warrants arrest and booking on disorderly conduct if you are a black man, even in your own home, and even if yelling is not a crime. Thus institutionalized, otherwise innocuous things—like sock monkeys—become pervaded with meaning determined by the racialized dynamics that make it marketable. When white men are compared to monkeys, they look stupid; when black men are compared to monkeys, they look stupid *and menacing*. Had President Bush claimed that the Cambridge police acted stupidly, he might have been criticized as having misspoken; when Obama makes the remark he "has a deep-seated hatred for white people." In the hands of pundits like Limbaugh and Beck, the Gates incident is not merely an opportunity to promote the Republican Party, it's an opportunity—under the guise of touting "our men and women in law enforcement"—to reinforce white supremacy.

To put it in terms of the linguistic practices that propel these social institutions into the future: words have histories. "Cracker" is a nasty epithet, but it does not and cannot have the meaning and force of "nigger"; just as "prick" might be mean-spirited, it cannot contain the force and implicit threat conveyed by "cunt." While Bush could be ridiculed, he could not be animalized. Why? Because in the absence of a history that lends content to this specifically racist (and/or sexist) use of the language, the notion that Bush really is bestial and sexually rapacious makes little sense at least in a context where his sexual forays would count, for example, as rape. In other words, insofar as black women are historically depicted as willing sexual partners, white men cannot be said to commit rape against them. As is well borne out by the fact that white men do, on average, less jail time for committing acts of sexual assault against black women, the language of sexual assault doesn't apply with anything like equal representation. Similarly, black men coded as "animal" are commonly regarded as having committed what counts as rape even with willing white women, the latter being coded as "pure" or "virginal." To the same extent, then, that language codes for race, it also codes for sex and for the intersection of race and sex as these are hierarchically represented in the logic of domination. For example, although black women are animalized, their place in the logic as female—and therefore as inferior to black men—locates them solely as the objects of sexual (and other forms of) exploitation by men—black and white:

> [s]uch representations [of black females with male apes] excused as well as invited sexual exploitation by white men. These representations still animate white racism today, from the fact that "men who assault black women are the least likely to do jail time," to the continuing strength of the image of the black male rapist of white women (in fact this is statistically the least likely rape situation). (Adams 1995: 74)

In addition, men and women—both black and white—are not only sexualized but also heterosexualized, and (as we have seen previously) this binarism is crucial to maintaining the logic with respect to inferiority and otherness: black men are not located in the logic as *sexually* threatening to white men, but as a potential danger to white women, and gay men—black or white—are stereotypically ridiculed as effeminate, that is, *as* women. Black women are located as fully exploitable by men—black or white—and hence as both hypersexualized and asexual: although the ape with which she is imagined to copulate is depicted as male, it matters less than the fact that he is an ape. White women, on the other hand, epitomize heterosexuality in a different way in that they are depicted in opposition to black men and women as in need of (white male) protection from black men, but not from black women.

In her *Black Sexual Politics* (2005), Patricia Hill Collins argues for a similarly "intersectional" approach to theorizing racism, sexism, and heterosexism (10–12). Like Adams, Collins insists that we are unlikely to comprehend the complexities of contemporary social injustice without understanding its historical underpinnings:

> In the United States, for example, slaveowning relied upon an ideology of black sexual deviance to regulate and exploit enslaved Africans. Because Black feminist analyses pay more attention to women's sexuality, they too identify how the sexual exploitation of women has been a basic ingredient of racism.... [However,] because much of the literature assumes that sexuality means heterosexuality, it ignores how racism and *hetero*sexism influence each other. (87–88)

Collins is critical of analyses of racism—feminist or otherwise— which attend to the sexist dimensions of slavery-ideologies but ignore their heterosexist aspects. A fully intersectional approach, she argues, takes every dimension of oppression and exploitation into consideration. Like Adams, Collins recognizes the extent to which ideologies like those employed to justify slavery appeal to images of nonhuman animals to legitimate their case:

> [Black] men allegedly possessed the wildness attributed to Blacks as a race, but they carried the additional characteristic of being prone to violence. This combination...made Black men inherently unsuitable for work until they were trained by White men and placed under their discipline and control. To explain these relations, White elites created the controlling image of the buck. Unlike images of African natives who roam their wild homelands like beasts untamed by civilization...the representation of the buck described a human animal that had achieved partial domestication through slavery.... Because the vast majority of enslaved African women and men did agricultural labor, these controlling images of the mule, jezebel, breeder woman, and buck justified Black economic exploitation. (56–57)

However, while Collins contributes an important insight concerning slavery conceived as a form of domestication, she assumes without argument that the nonhuman animals with which black men's strength and capacity for labor are compared really are, for example, "promiscuous," or without intellect—acceptably exploitable. She fails, in other words, to interrogate that axis of domination crucial to a full understanding of racism, namely, the ways in which we conceive nonhuman animals in order to animalize human beings in that fashion most favorable to preserving the racist status quo. By this omission, she effectively reinforces the view that the commodification of nonhuman animals is just—an implication that undermines the very intersectional approach she advocates. If, after all, it *is* offensive and demeaning to be compared to nonhuman animals, it must be because they are inferior in value to human beings. Maybe so, but without an argument for this claim, Collins's view can itself be held up as an example of chauvinism.

In the context of slavery, the injustice of the prison system, and in other forms of contemporary bigotry, Collins is, of course, right: comparing African men to bucks *is* offensive and demeaning. But it is so precisely because of the chauvinistic ways in which we conceive of nonhuman animals as other, in opposition to characteristics conceived of as properly human. Both challenging the logic of domination and reinforcing it simultaneously, she rightly rejects casting black men as other compared to human beings, but then reincarnates the very pattern of comparison she rejects by casting people as *not*-animals:

> Linking African people and animals was crucial to Western views of Black promiscuity. Genital sexual intercourse or, more colloquially, the act of "fucking," characterized animal sexuality. Animals are promiscuous because they lack intellect, culture, and civilization. Animals do not have erotic lives; they merely "fuck" and reproduce. Certainly animals could be slaughtered, sold and domesticated as pets because within capitalist political economies, animals were commodities that were owned as private property. As the history of animal breeding suggests, the sexual promiscuity of horses, cattle, chickens, pigs, dogs, and other domesticated animals could be profitable for their owners. (2005: 100)

What is troubling here is not that Collins is actively endorsing the slaughter of nonhuman animals; she's not. It's not even that she necessarily believes that nonhuman animals do or don't have intellectual, emotional, or erotic lives. What's troubling is that by making the comparison of African men and women to nonhuman animals solely about its consequences for human beings (African or otherwise), Collins effectively condones the view that exploitation is bad because it's bad for us, but this creates another "other": this "bad" is not bad for any nonhuman "them."

In condoning this image, then, of an opposing and defining "other," Collins unwittingly reproduces the conceptual conditions for "justifying" other forms of oppression; if not black men and women, whomever may be compared to (nonhuman) animals (gay men and lesbians, for instance) remains a potential target for, say, the denial of civil liberties. Collins's treatment of nonhuman animals as lacking in intellect, civilization, culture, erotic life, and so on effectively appeals to the logic of domination in that she assumes a clear and obvious division of qualities which apply to human beings, but not to nonhuman animals. The effect of such an unexamined appeal, however, is to reproduce the status of what Adams refers to as the *absent referent* (2005: 16–17). Nonhuman animals are, in other words, absent from Collins's discussion except as "wild" or "promiscuous" or able to be domesticated; that is, they are present only insofar as they illustrate the animalizing of black men and women. Collins might well respond, of course, that to have discussed what such comparisons mean for the ways in which we treat nonhuman animals was simply beyond the scope of her project. This is fair enough, but it is inadequate in light of the fact that animalizing is so crucial an aspect of the justification not only of slavery, but also—consider the Obama sock monkey—continuing bigotry. What Collins fails to see is that it is precisely because we so devalue nonhuman animals that we continue to devalue people signified as "other": devaluing the not-human provides the conditions for dehumanizing the human. Hence, even if her primary aim is to address the politics of race, to ignore its absent but crucially defining referent is to ignore the very logic of domination within which racism continues to be institutionalized (303–07).

Among Collins's key insights, however, is that the animalizing of black persons is simultaneously (hetero)sexualizing: it is the rutting buck (i.e., black man) whose domesticated labor is determined by white men, who in turn are protecting white women. Or, as Adams points out, it's the indiscriminate black woman willing to copulate with apes who must be brought under control. Sexual impulses, moreover, provide the paradigmatic justification for oppressive social institutions in that they appeal to our deepest fears of violation and vulnerability; heterosexuality—especially in this racist context—is rationalized as a matter of public safety. A convenient image for the reproduction of chauvinistic institutions, the wild is tamed in order to be mastered, but also to be used, consumed, and marketed. But to accomplish this latter transformation, the particularity of individual nonhuman animals must itself be as systematically erased as that captured by, for example, references to black men as "boys" or to black women as "breeders." Consider Adams's discussion of the sexual politics of animal consumption in which particular cows become "beef" and particular pigs become "pork":

> In *The Sexual Politics of Meat*, I developed the concept of the absent referent to identify the process by which the animal used for corpse eating disappears both literally and figuratively. Animals in name and body are made absent as animals in order that flesh can exist. If animals are alive, they cannot be meat....Animals are also made absent through language that renames dead bodies before consumers participate in eating them. The absent referent permits us to forget about the animal as an independent entity. (1995: 16–17)

Accomplished neither through anthropomorphizing nor animalizing (at least alone), some forms of commodification require the erasure of the particularity of their referents. The naming of plantation slaves after their masters, the alienation of workers as "labor," the debasement captured by the language of "nigger," "spic," or "faggot," and the renaming of dead bodies as "meat" all have at least one thing in common: the erasure of the particularity, and in some cases even identity, of their casualties.

That we anthropomorphize nonhuman animals and animalize human beings demonstrates the extent to which we recognize how much we have in common even with creatures who are otherwise quite different—especially with respect to the capacity for pain; hence the need for erasure. It is perhaps ironic that we should be reminded of our evolutionary continuity with nonhuman nature via linguistic practices whose aims are all too often the reinforcement of institutions underpinned by racist, heterosexist, and chauvinistic presuppositions. Yet while the concept of the absent referent might seem at odds with anthropomorphizing and animalizing, it is not. Erasure functions as just one more means by which sentient creatures—including human beings—are converted into the commodities of "resource first." Yet without an understanding of the patterns by which this erasure occurs, and in what specific and intersectional ways it incarnates the logic of domination at every level of its institutionalized practice, we will remain ill equipped to confront any of its injustices.

HUMAN BEINGS, NONHUMAN ANIMALS, NONHUMAN NATURE: AN ECOLOGICAL APPROACH TO SOCIAL JUSTICE FOR CONTEMPORARY FEMINISM

It is tempting to think that we ought to draw a clear distinction between nonhuman animals and nonhuman nature in the interest of developing the most useful possible approaches to animal welfare or environmental issues where specific cases call for specific forms of moral consideration. And indeed this is often the case, by virtue of the fact that many species of nonhuman animal have capacities and abilities that trees and oceans and mountains, for example, don't have, such as sentience, the ability to experience pleasure and pain, and for some, the capacity for cognition and/or intellect. As Ronnie Zoe Hawkins points out, "[e]volutionary biology offers abundant evidence of human continuity with other life forms, while ecology and conservation biology recognize the difference in the requirements and capacities of various nonhuman organisms that are distinct from those of human beings" (1998: 159). Among the reasons, then, that we might rightly offer for faulting the resource-first approach is the failure to distinguish between entities for whom such treatment constitutes possible harm and those for whom that harm can also be experienced as suffering or injury.

Making such a distinction has been among the projects—and disputed terrains—of important environmental ethicists such as Peter

Singer, Tom Regan, Aldo Leopold, George Sessions, Christopher Stone, and Holmes Rolston III, who, while often in disagreement about the virtues of particular approaches, nonetheless generally focus on some set of particular characteristics or capacities alleged to confer the right to moral consideration on their subjects.[7] Whether what we're talking about are monkeys, puppies, mountains, or individual trees, these theorists aim to establish some form of claim, standing, or right that is premised on a capacity or quality, perhaps sentience — perhaps simply life, uniqueness, or existence. Hence, it is likely to seem that although animal-welfare activists and environmentalists are engaged in different projects, they are nonetheless "comrades in arms" for nonhuman nature and creatures. As Mark Sagoff (2002) shows, however, this is seldom the case. In an essay suggestively titled "Animal Liberation and Environmental Ethics: Bad Marriage, Quick Divorce," Sagoff argues that it is not obvious that the goals of environmentalists are consistent with the goals of "animal liberationists" (38–41). Considering the work of Leopold, Sagoff remarks,

> The policies environmentalists recommend are informed by the concepts of population biology, not the concepts of animal equality. The SPCA does not set the agenda for the Sierra Club.... These organizations which promote a love and respect for the functioning of natural ecosystems differ ideologically from organizations that make the suffering of animals their primary concern. (40)

Sagoff is likely right here: Leopold's central principle that "[a] thing is right when it tends to preserve the integrity, stability, and beauty of the biotic community [the ecological system, including all of its living and nonliving members]. It is wrong when it tends otherwise" (1949: 224–25) in no way considers individuals as its central value, nor does it cover any right these individuals might have not to suffer. Indeed, Leopold might be rightly accused of the erasure that Adams identifies as a central feature of human chauvinism; after all, according to Leopold, it's not the biotic community's members to whom

---

[7] For an excellent sample of essays by many of the environmental ethicists named here, see Schmidtz and Willott (2002). For a feminist perspective on Singer, see Donovan (1993).

we owe moral consideration, but rather the community as a whole—whose stability might be better preserved through, say, hunting.

Christopher Stone's (2002) claim, however—that we ought to consider nonhuman entities such as individual trees or streams to have legal standing in the same fashion as other entities, for example, comatose or senile human beings whose interests must be represented by others—puts individuals, sentient or otherwise, before biotic communities, and thus may not promote their preservation, integrity, or beauty. "One ought," argues Stone, "to handle the legal problems of natural objects as one does the problems of legal incompetents—human beings who have become vegetable" (48). But as we know from situations like Terry Schiavo's, such cases can actually lead to the erosion of communities.[8] Similarly, Leopold might well argue that it is better to hunt deer than to let them overpopulate where there are few natural predators, or that it is better to let a forest fire burn itself out in the interest of producing the ash that is conducive to new growth (1949: 201–26).

My aim is not to attempt to litigate philosophical disputes over what counts as the central unit of value for an ecologically oriented ethos—individuals? species? ecological systems? the Earth itself? Such are very real and important issues, and how we address species loss among predators (say, via Sarah Palin's advocacy of aerial wolf hunting) or the suffering of "beef" cows comes with consequences for all of us. In fact, that's just the point. What advocates an alternative approach grounded in analyses of the patterns of oppression and exploitation institutionalized via the logic of domination is precisely that it circumvents the need to define such units of value in favor of drawing comparisons between the factors connecting, for example, the "resource first" justification of aerial wolf hunting to other forms

---

[8] See Quill (2005). For an account of the events of the Terri Schiavo case, see "Terri Schiavo Dies, But Battle Continues," <http://www.msnbc.msn.com/id/7293186>. Schiavo "suffered severe brain damage in 1990 after her heart stopped because of a chemical imbalance that was believed to have been brought on by an eating disorder. The case rocketed to national attention when Schiavo's parents sought to wrest legal custody of Schiavo from her husband, Michael Schiavo, who wanted to remove the feeding tube that was keeping Terri alive. Michael, however, "consistently won legal battles by arguing that his wife would not have wanted to live in her condition," namely, a persistent vegetative state, or coma.

of genocide, or the suffering of individual cows to other forms of commodification. Such comparisons demonstrate the profoundly racialized, sexed, and gendered reality of precisely the chauvinism that is responsible for unnecessary human and nonhuman animal suffering *and* environmental deterioration. Regardless of whether the focus of our analysis is the suffering of particular cows on their way to slaughter or the institution of beef production and consumption, we can draw comparisons showing that the same logic is behind both.

This is not to say that such an approach is easier, or that circumvention is its point—far from it. In fact, because it draws our attention to the connection between social injustice, nonhuman animal exploitation, and environmental erosion, it presents us with the more difficult task of demonstrating just what such comparisons consist of and why they matter. As we have seen, empirical evidence is key to such an approach; whether from history, science, or contemporary politics, the specificity of example, case study, policy, legislation, and especially of linguistic practice forms the central axis around which comparative analysis revolves. As Hawkins emphasizes, "[r]ecognition of evolutionary continuity...a most powerful principle to which the vast majority of contemporary biologists subscribe...will enable feminist theory to integrate a great deal of empirical evidence in striving to understand the present situation of women non-dualistically" (1998: 172). Few, even among the most stalwart of Leopold's "land ethic ecologists" or, on the other side, animal liberationists would deny this continuity—even though many, including Fred Bender, take insufficiently seriously the extent to which the race (white), gender (male), and heterosexual identity of human chauvinism characterizes the domination of nonhuman nature.

In *The Culture of Extinction* (2003), Bender offers a compelling account of what he calls, following sustainability theorist William R. Catton, Jr., *Homo colossus*: "a culturally evolved hominid species of unprecedented ecological impact" (23). He then argues that "[t]he first philosophical issue is whether only costs to humans—and not to humans *per se*, but to *Homo colossus*—should count" (39). Echoing Leopold's maxim, Bender answers this question: "the culture of extinction undermines the integrity and stability of the ecosphere in myriad unpredictably synergistic ways. Undoubtedly, *Homo colossus*'s way of life is unsustainable. Anthropogenic [human-made] impact already is affecting the most vulnerable, the poor of the impoverished South" (62). And, of course, he's right. However, although Bender does recognize that neither human beings nor nonhuman animals or ecological systems are affected equally, by depicting *Homo colossus* as if reference to it includes all human beings as the beneficiaries of nonhuman animal and environmental exploitation, he effectively reinforces the very chauvinism (particularly its heteropatriarchal face) that he seeks to undermine. Why? Precisely because "the most vulnerable," and many others, including many of the thinkers we have examined here, are vulnerable in very specific ways that are not adequately captured merely by references to "the impoverished South."

Bender ignores the racialized, sexed, and heterosexualized axes of the logic of domination in largely the same way that Collins ignores the relationship between human beings and nonhuman nature—sentient or otherwise. Bender's solution to the ecocide perpetrated by *Homo colossus*, what he refers to as his "ecosophy," begins in the personal renunciation of the *colossus* inside ourselves and the embrace of an ecocentric worldview in which each of us learns to place the interests of environmental integrity before human interests (2003: 419–25). He suggests, for example, a "mindfulness practice" in which you

[s]tart by identifying with ever larger human groups beyond yourself and your immediate or extended family.... try embracing as part of yourself all of your ancestors, living relations, and unborn descendants; then in turn your neighbors, fellow-citizens, all of humanity.... in time you should find yourself less egocentric and increasingly able to see what formerly you took to be the center of the universe (yourself), as a node in a network of human relationships.... Similarly, try cultivating awareness of the ecospheric context of the place where you live.... extend your mind to recognize your interdependence with other living beings.... Such a practice, over time, should transform your sense of who you are as you discover you are not the separate skin-encapsulated individual you once thought you were, but that you belong to all other living beings.... (423–24)

A form of meditation or contemplation—such a practice sounds good, and it may even encourage some of the sustainable activism we want to endorse. However, the difficulty with this program—and it is a serious difficulty—is that it is simply not available, realistic, or even fair to propose to the vast majority of the world's people, particularly its women. As I have stated,

> By insisting that the only way to escape ecocide is to disavow precisely that which women have been systematically denied for virtually the whole of human history—the opportunity to experience and develop a humanly-centered self—Bender effectively reproduces in ecocentrism the male privilege he otherwise eschews. Who, after all, is in a position to disavow their self-interest but those who have enjoyed the material opportunity to realize it? Who are these if not primarily white, Western men? (Lee 2009: 20)

Moreover, it is simply false that "human beings" as a species are responsible for environmental deterioration; some human beings bear a far greater share of this responsibility than others, and many human beings are casualties of those who are the most likely to be in a position to practice the mindfulness Bender advocates.

The irony of Bender's view is that only the privileged—mostly white, male, Christian, heterosexual men—enjoy the time and leisure necessary to discover their lack of "skin-encapsulation" or recognize their interdependence with nonhuman beings; but they are the least likely to be convinced by this argument, or even to hear it, since they are the undisputed beneficiaries of the logic of domination. The corporate executive who drives a Hummer three blocks to the office is *Homo colossus*, not the woman barely surviving the casualized labor of the "McJobs" subsidized by his off-shore enterprises. The well-off couple who can afford outsourced baby-making via Indian in-vitro–fertilization brokers are *Homo colossus*, not the women who, treated not altogether unlike factory-farm hens, sell their wombs out of economic destitution. The sponsors of terrorism—be they religiously motivated soldiers for God or nation-states—are *Homo colossus*, not the human, nonhuman, and ecological fatalities of their quests for salvation. The well-paid academics solicited to write books about feminism in the twenty-first century are *Homo colossus*, not the illiterate both at home and abroad who wouldn't have time for theory even if they could read.

Hence it is difficult to overemphasize the importance of incorporating practice—if not exactly mindful meditation—into theory. For on this point Marx is right: the point of philosophy is not merely to comprehend the world; it is to change it for the better. The question is how? The foregoing analysis offers a first clue: in becoming more acutely aware of, first, how the logic of domination affects specific patterns of institutionalized oppression, we can begin to get a clearer idea not only about what human chauvinism consists of, but also about what it does *not*. That is, we can begin to distinguish between legitimate human interests—particularly with respect to social justice—and the reinforcement of chauvinistic (racist, heterosexist) preroga-tive. Second, we can begin to appreciate that "human-centered" need not mean either "narrowly self-interested" or "institutionally chau-vinistic." Indeed, "human-centered," at its root, merely describes a spectrum of points of view informed by a specific set of capacities of a particular species of animal: *Homo sapiens sapiens*. Indeed, "[o]ur points of view are human-centered because we are human beings. Indeed, even where we endeavor to disavow our human-centered-ness in favor of a more conscientious other-directed disposition, we remain situated animals whose cognitive, somatic, and perceptual abilities are fixed by our evolutionary history and informed by our epistemic, geographic, and cultural conditions" (Lee 2006: 22).

Human-centeredness is not, in other words, inherently racist or heterosexist; it can, in fact, be a source of precisely the critical self-reflection we need to firmly ground an activism whose strength derives directly from an understanding of (1) how the logic of dom-ination underpins patterns of oppression comparable across many axes of environmental destruction, nonhuman animal exploitation, and social injustice, and (2) a reimagined conception of human inter-est that does not imply entitlement: "Far from a birthright, a sanction to dominate, or a coil to throw off, anthropocentrism [human-cen-teredness] is...a potentially fruitful source of self-reflection and accountability which can ground a theory of value consistent with feminist emancipatory goals" (Lee 2006: 22). But only potentially. The vital ingredient of such an approach is its commitment to eman-cipatory goals broadly conceived to include human and nonhuman animals and the environment itself; its *modus operandi* involves taking responsibility individually and collectively for the consequences of our actions for the environment, nonhuman others, and fellow human beings in ways that actively seek to resolve conflicts over vital

issues such as food production, product manufacture, resource allocation, and so on, democratically—but with a clear eye to the value of
an ecologically sustainable worldview. This is no easy mission.

Conceptual insights—however buried they may be in the language of "meat" or "resource" or "buck," or thinly veiled in images
like the Obama sock monkey—can result in comparisons drawn at
one level of the logic of domination having equally meaningful
implications at another. Comprehending the racist heterosexualism
of both slavery-era and more contemporary images of black men
represented as nonhuman animals sheds light on their oppression—
and on that of black and white women (however they might otherwise be different). But it also sheds light on how we conceive of nonhuman animals in the service of maintaining a logic of exploitation
that is as comprehensive as it is oppressive. Human chauvinism, then,
is better considered not as a term describing some single phenomenon of human self-interest, but as what Ludwig Wittgenstein called
a "family resemblance" term, that is, a term describing a collection of
phenomena, each of which bears a resemblance to the others by
virtue of a common denominator—in this case a logic or way of
ordering the world—that makes sense of specific states of affairs. For
our purposes, these states of affairs could include the Obama sock
monkey, or the heterosexualizing of egg and sperm, or the outsourcing of baby-making to developing nations.

Ultimately, it is in coming to understand these patterns from a
human-centered—i.e., critically self-reflective—point of view where
the potential for a contemporary feminist activism lies. The key component of such an activism is its inclusion of nonhuman animals and
nature in its analyses of social and economic injustice, not in any
merely salutary fashion, but as central to a practice of valuing the
creatures and conditions with which we are all interdependent. Even
an activism whose primary focus is injustice with respect to human
welfare can no longer afford to ignore (or worse, tacitly condone) the
consequences of human chauvinism: global climate change will
affect us all, and it will affect those least able to adapt to it—women,
the citizens of developing nations, children, the poor—in unequal
and devastating ways, and for all of the reasons (and more) that I have
endeavored to lay out here. Hence, a twenty-first-century feminism
must be *eco*feminist in the specific sense that it takes seriously the

institutionalized connections between the commodification of human labor and that of nonhuman nature and animals. After all, if our aim is a more just, more compassionate, and more livable twenty-first century for human beings, it will hardly do to have defeated racism, sexism, and heterosexism only to empower an even greater and more devastating destruction of nonhuman nature.

But to what specific practices should we, as feminists, commit in the interest of working toward this livable and more just future? Does such an approach involve vegetarianism, for example? Yes, I think it clearly does—for those in a position to be vegetarian, or even better, vegan, without sacrifice of health or other comparably important goods. Does it involve diligent effort toward recycling, reusing, restoring, conserving, and all the other measures aimed at slowing deforestation, global climate change, pollution, and desertification? Absolutely. But what such an approach also requires—in the very way we conduct our analyses of who and what bear the effects of environmental deterioration—is that this burden fall far more heavily on some than it does on others. Indeed, it falls on precisely those identified by Jaggar, Mitter, Mahmood, Mohanty, Collins, and many others as the beneficiaries not only of the labor, but also of the ecological systems and nonhuman animals upon which labor depends, in other words, what we in the West/North define as "resource first." A meaningful twenty-first-century ecofeminism must avoid hypocrisy and arrogance as much as it must avoid reluctance with respect to joining other emancipatory movements—including animal-welfare movements. We cannot, for example, advocate vegetarianism without simultaneously addressing the very real need for nutritious food wherever starvation is a reality; we cannot continue to condone an inhumane fur industry just because it provides a source of jobs.

The order is therefore a tall one, but one from which we cannot afford to shrink: the most significant task for feminists is to realize as practice, as the way of life that freely undertaken radical change requires, a distinctly philosophical ambition: justice, compassion, and critical self-reflection. As Donna Haraway puts it in *The Companion Species Manifesto*: "feminist inquiry is about understanding how things work, who is in the action, and how worldly actors might somehow be accountable to and love each other less violently" (2003: 7). In light of the egregious and in many ways irrecoverable damage wrought by *Homo colossus*, we must reimagine in what actions these ambitions consist—a perilous mission that demands that we seriously re-examine the consequences of the "free" market, the institutions we take as "natural," and the very ways in which we conceive of the order of nature. To fail in this mission will not mean simply the continuation of the injustice, bigotry, and exploitation of the past. No—faced with global climate change, the stakes could not be higher. Hence it is imperative that an ecologically inspired, essentially socialist feminism seek to align itself with other emancipatory movements and organizations; however hard this work is, we could not be in a better position—given our history as a movement and its immense success—to rise to this challenge. A central question is whether we aspire to a livable, more equitable, and desirable future. Surely we do, but we no longer have the luxury to believe that this can be appropriated, bought, enslaved, or stolen at the expense of human or nonhuman others; hence, we must actively work with others to realize it.

We must work to create new institutions which have at their foundation the wisdom gleaned from recognizing that a logic of domination is not any part of the order of nature, but is rather a human-made artifact crafted to justify a status quo, indeed a culture industry, so deeply entrenched in our religious, patriarchal, and political history that it has become naturalized. Just as human chauvinism is a creation of human motives, so too is a human-centeredness that seeks a very different vision of a good life, one less alienated from the fact that we belong to a species of evolving and finite creatures. Emancipatory movements are inherently utopian in the sense that they aspire to some vision of an ideally just society. No different, the feminist movement is well positioned to transform this notion into one that includes an equally hopeful vision of a sustainable global environment rooted less in domination and exploitation, and more in contemplating just how close we may have come to ecocide, and therefore suicide—and how we could dramatically change this trajectory. Our knowledge, as Haraway points out, is always situated, always open to revision: "The point is to make situated knowledges possible in order to make consequential claims about the world and on each other" (1997: 267). There is tremendously much for a feminist movement to accomplish, but the hour grows short, the earth ever warmer, war increasingly commonplace, and, as Sojourner Truth, Karl Marx, Martin Luther King, and perhaps even the most faithful among our animal companions remind us, justice will not wait.[9]

---

[9] For an excellent example of this discourse and activism in action, see Mary Batson's "Ecores Forum" at <http://www.ecores.org>. Also see Penn State's Rock Ethics Institute, Climate Change at <http://rockethics.psu.edu/climate/>. See also Haraway (2003). This chapter is devoted to my three Greyhounds, (Jackson, Heather, and Charlotte), one Collie-Rott (Cordy), one Dachsi-Pom (Disney), six cats (Rosie, Tess, Fiona, Denver, Madeleine, and Switch), two Indian Ringneck parrots (Rosie-Pie and Taco Bell), and my four-foot green iguana (Savannah, Queen of the Atlantic).

Chapter VIII

Epilogue: Life as Activism

RESISTING INSTITUTIONALIZED VIOLENCE BEGINS AT HOME

I sometimes tell a story about the day I arrived in Bloomsburg with my kids, my then-partner, and a truck full of our worldly possessions. I was diligently unloading the U-Haul when a neighbor put a newspaper in my hands, the local *Press Enterprise*. She was excited to show me something called Thirty Seconds, a column where folks can submit short remarks about whatever issues they think worthy or important, and so long as they don't contain direct threats or obvious slander, they'd be printed in the paper in a few days' time. At first I thought the whole thing sort of quaint—what with its complaints about dogs barking in the night or people hogging parking spots on the main street. But then I read this: "White people were created by God, and black people evolved from monkeys." Anonymous. That was 1992. Not 1892—1992. I made up the kids' beds, got out some toys, and rifled about until I found my computer. This remark demanded a response. Not tomorrow. Now. That wasn't my first letter to the editor, but it was my introduction into the politics of one small but growing, vocal, well-armed, nationalistic, racist, heterosexist, and profoundly theocratic strand of American life.

It's seventeen years later and much has changed—and much has not. Some of the local hate-mongers have organized as a group called the Patriot's Voice.[1] They protest "democrat-socialists," "communists,"

---

[1] See the group's website at <http://www.the-patriot-s-voice.org>.

and "leftist intellectuals." They run for school board seats, rail against the National Day of Silence, promote groups like the Minutemen (a patently racist "border patrol" group), and advertise for the deceptively self-titled National Center for Constitutional Studies on their website (successor to the John Birch Society). They work tirelessly to get creationism taught as public high-school science, agitate to ban books they deem "dirty" from school libraries, demonize the United Nations as a "one world government" conspiracy, and sponsor "Mad as Hell!" anti-government "tea parties" on Independence Day. It's sorely tempting simply to dismiss them as cranks—except they win local school board elections, and this not only empowers their members, but it offers a barometer of the beliefs and attitudes of at least one local demographic, one whose adherents identify themselves as the "real" Christians. These folks routinely deploy racist terms such as "rag-head" and "camel jockey" to describe persons of Middle Eastern descent, condone the murder of "baby-killer" physicians who perform late-term abortions, and vigorously defend the form of torture known as waterboarding.

To be clear: I am not suggesting (a) that first-amendment rights do not fully protect Patriot's Voice members' and their supporters' freedom of speech, or (b) that there is any easy or obvious way to determine what counts as a hate group. But what I am suggesting—a theme implicit throughout these pages—is that the use of violence, whether in its rawest expression as physical or psychological brutality (including hate speech), or institutionalized as slavery, oppression, entrenched poverty, terrorism, heterosexism, racism, meat-production, militarism, etc., is characteristic of the entitlement that endures as the status quo against which feminists, among many others, struggle. Perhaps we think we can relegate such groups to the backwaters of the American political mainstream, but this, I think, would be as foolish as writing off Rush Limbaugh as the "crazy" of his party, or dismissing Glenn Beck, David Horowitz, Sean Hannity, Ann Coulter, or Bill O'Reilly as no more than mob-baiting talking heads. They *are* mob-baiting talking heads—but they're more than that. Some of the people who listen to Limbaugh live in my neighborhood—and in yours. They vote, run for county seats, hoard guns, become representatives, sponsor Tea Parties; indeed, they exemplify the important truth that "all politics are local." Or perhaps better: every struggle

comes with faces and stories that link it to the struggles of others—
including those we struggle against. In fact, more often than not it is
the struggle itself that lights the ground of our convictions, demanding that we be able to give reasons, illuminating our own vulnerability to ideological rigidity. What Patriot's Voice members know is that
the transformation of the American political landscape is achieved
one school board, one letter to the editor, one removed book, one
defeat for science, one Tea Party, one election at a time—a strategy I
think we must take very seriously, particularly with respect to the
various forms of violence that often typify it.

The insight that all politics are local is what I want to encourage
here—not because feminists haven't been so engaged, but because it
may not always be obvious that issues like banning books or creationism are feminist issues. A Patriot's Voice member very nearly had
the works of Nobel Laureate Toni Morrison removed from a local
high-school library. Were it not for citizens willing to protest this as
censorship in the interest of promoting a racist and sexist agenda for
school curricula, local students might not now have access to works
like *The Bluest Eye* or *Beloved*. Raising such a challenge, however, is
not without its risks. As any day in Thirty Seconds makes clear, the
standard response strategy of the Patriot's Voice is to undermine the
credibility of the challenger via name-calling and ridicule, and there's
nothing more local—or personal—than name-calling in a public
venue. But despite the rhetorical weaponry deployed against them,
these citizens saw the "bigger" issue: banning books isn't just about
the local high school; it's about who and whose ideology will have
what say in public education.[2] Indeed, what issue could be more
important than access to education? (Consider Indian women who

---

[2] My own letter of protest was printed in the Thirty Seconds column of the *Press
Enterprise* in the summer of 2006: "Among the greatest threats to a democratic
society is the censorship of free access to ideas. Yet in the name of protecting our
youngest citizens, this is precisely what Nicole Shultz and Robert Ridall
(Patriot's Voice) would have Benton schools do. Shultz' criteria would eliminate
classics such as *Catcher in the Rye*, *Catch 22*, Shakespeare, *Lord of the Flies*, *Animal
Farm*, *1984*, *Frankenstein*—innumerable magnificent works—including [Toni
Morrison's] *Song of Solomon*, from the Benton library. Who, moreover, should
determine the correct application of Shultz' criteria? People who haven't read
the books, like Ridall? Book choice is NOT the appropriate province of school
board members; it is the province of experts—teachers and librarians.
Censorship protects nothing but the perpetuation of ignorance. This proposal
should horrify us."

become incubators for other people's babies in order to send their own children to school.)

Still, it's not simply the importance of an issue that makes it relevant to us as feminists. Although most people would likely agree that removing books from school libraries and curricula is wrong—and many of these see the connection between censorship and access to education—this does not mean they make the connection between a rural school-board member's campaign to ban books and, say, a suicide bomber's self-implosion at a busy marketplace on the other side of the world. But this (among other things) is what theory is for: to help us see that what makes an issue like sex-reassignment surgery, or the uses of in vitro fertilization, or terrorism, or the uses of animalizing language, an issue for feminist analysis and action are the underlying conceptual, political, economic, social, and—as I have stressed here—technologically mediated connections to sex, ethnicity, sexual identity, and economic and social status. Could the board member and the bomber share elements of a worldview that connects them to the "bigger" politics of religious fanaticism, global capitalism, or the culture industry? Yes: a religious worldview no more requires a shared religion than book banning or marketplace bombing requires its agents to recognize the oppressive implications of their actions. What feminist analysis can show is that such actions are not merely oppressive, but oppressive in a way that is consistent with a logic of domination that can illuminate the roles of their agents as actors and subjects, empowered and disempowered, cheerleaders and casualties of, in this case, a religious worldview committed to very similar configurations of sex, gender, and race.

Hence the purpose of books like this one—to get us to see the possibility of these connections, to see the patterns that emerge as a response to, for example, the vertigo of secularization or the explosion of communication that is the Internet. This is no easy project. Even those of us long engaged with issues that are global by definition (such as climate change) are not always in a position to see the deeper connections (and sometimes we are in the least optimal positions).[3] Moreover, what distinguishes the school board member from

---

[3] This point was brought home to me during the first incarnation of the online EcoRes Forum conference (<http://www.eco-res.org>) when several of the

the suicide bomber from the larger forces legitimated by the logic of domination may be little more than the scale of violence to which each resorts in pursuit of their goals. It is therefore vital to the future of our movements that our activism be informed as a critically self-reflective, non-violent approach to the patterns (the connections and relationships between issues) and their instantiations (this school board, that book) in specific local contexts. In short, being a feminist, or a social-justice activist, or an environmentalist, or an animal-welfare advocate isn't just about what we theorize, what organizations we support, what we believe: it's about how we live.

CHANGE REALLY DOES BEGIN IN MY COMPOST BIN: THE ACTIVISM OF THE ORDINARY

In one sense, then, my closing message is pretty simple: until enduring progressive change comes to countless towns like Bloomsburg, it will not, in fact, endure anywhere, and given communication technologies like the Internet, we no longer have the luxury of ignoring this fact. Consider the spring 2009 elections in Iran. Not only can we know something about potentially fraudulent election results and the protests that followed via online news, but through networking sites like Facebook and Twitter, or via video uploads on YouTube, we can actively participate in being witnesses to these events, we can organize and argue, we can take part in the demand for democratic institutions—and we are offered the opportunity to critically evaluate our own assumptions about the lives of the others whom we meet in cyberspace.

This reality was made clear to me through my exchanges during the 2006 inaugural launch of the global online EcoRes conference (see note 3, above). Social-justice advocates, environmentalists, feminists, union shop-stewards, mothers, geologists, anthropologists, farmers, industrialists, representative of "green" corporations, and a cornucopia of others spanning class, ethnicity, religion, and culture participated in several heady days of discussion, organizing, arguing,

---

participating (and uniformly male) environmental philosophers argued strenuously for highly restrictive policies concerning sexual reproduction. Attentive neither to issues of reproductive rights (whether with respect to conception or contraception) generally, nor to the specific reasons or motives for particular women's reproductive choices (if there are choices), this argument for curbing human overpopulation met with stiff resistance from a number of feminists and social-justice advocates.

and theorizing over climate change. We talked about who was online and who wasn't, who could be and who couldn't. We scrapped over everything from government policy to composting for apartment dwellers. But what was most instructive, what brought home the most significant, often poignant, grounds for a self-reflective activism was the extent to which many of the issues brought to the Internet table were local. From contaminated wells, to lack of access to safe birth control, to the production of fuel-efficient vehicles, to having been beaten "like a fucking animal" for being gay, to access to the Internet itself, much of the discussion epitomized not only the value of solving problems where they emerge, but the extent to which every issue intersects at some level with so many others.

While the specific focus of this online exchange was climate change, what became immediately clear was that no discussion of it, or of desertification, habitat loss, species extinction, or pollution could be had without a simultaneous discussion of the contributions made to these through human action (and inaction); and this in turn led inevitably to dialogue—and debate—over human population, the uses and abuses of reproductive technologies, class inequalities with respect to resource access, the disparate effects of climate change on the most vulnerable, the role of religion, terrorism, and war in environmental deterioration—in short, all of the issues I have dealt with here, and many more. Among the many issues, however, that made this conference instructive was that of the philosophical struggles that some of its participants—especially its more educated ones—had with technology. As they hastened to point out, many technologies have been deployed to ends whose cost in the destruction of humans, nonhuman animals, and ecosystems has been immense. Hence it is understandable that many activists would be wary of any wholesale promotion of the latest technological fad. Yet the conference discourse did reflect something more than the merely wary or skeptical, and this came in two forms: the first and most common response was to advocate a kind of "return to nature" worldview premised variously on the wisdom of indigenous cultural beliefs or Buddhist practices, etc., the central idea being to revive ways of life more attuned to the rhythms of nature, ways that were (at least in theory) less wasteful and less alienated from the ebbs and flows of natural processes and events. The second group held that the environmental destruction perpetuated by *Homo colossus* was irreversible, essentially ecocidal/suicidal, and urged a survivalist's view of the future replete with "low-tech" subsistence alternatives that rely neither on computing technologies nor on things like cars, washers, or cell phones. Both camps argued that since technology got us into environmental trouble, it is technology that we must reject in favor of returning to a simpler, presumably greener, way of life.

As we have seen, however, it's just not that simple—and I think this is important for contemporary feminists and activists generally to think about more than we have so far (with important exceptions like Donna Haraway). There's just no obvious argument to be made that "technology," whatever this entails, by itself is what gets us into trouble. Expansionist capitalism, after all, might well be slowed without the Internet, but many of its most profitable institutions—slavery for instance—grew at virtually exponential rates primarily on the backs of human beings, not fancy robotics. And as the Grameen Bank experiment shows, the survival and flourishing of small-village business ventures can be accomplished via relatively simple technologies that ensure, for example, clean water and suspended fertility. No doubt the use of IVF as opposed to adoption offers little to the advocates of reducing human population growth, but international adoption without the Internet is prohibitively difficult. Clearly, the global marketing of fast food contributes to obesity, but few would dispute the benefits of technologies used in cardiac or gastric bypass. The same speed of communication that contributes to the organizing of terrorist activities also makes available to the entire world the sentiments of Iranians in the wake of a disputed election. Even where radio and television are shut down, there's no stopping Twitter and YouTube.

Not only, then, are all politics local, but so too is "the personal political" in ways unimaginable by our foremothers. Far more than a classic feminist slogan, these words reach well beyond borders constrained by geography, sex, sexuality, ethnicity, class privilege, political party, or religion. The personal, after all, includes the bodies of the anorexic, the surrogate, the transsexual, the "McJob" worker, the jihadist, the terrified animal en route to slaughter; and similarly the political embodies and legitimates the conditions that define beauty, motherhood, sexual identity, labor, God, and food for the global culture industry. The personal is political because what we eat (or don't eat), and how we determine who counts as a parent, a woman, a man, a true-believer, or an edible is up to us more now than ever, by virtue of our capacity to alter, manipulate, and communicate information. This doesn't mean, however, that there is such a thing as "technology," and that this thing is either the savior to be embraced or the monster to be repudiated; what it means is that we're all cyborgs in the sense Donna Haraway suggests when she interrogates the ever-permeable borders of our skins. The personal is political because there is no opting out of the global culture industry; the personal is political because the risks we must be prepared to take for real and substantive change begin at the point of departure that is more local than any other—the experience encapsulated by our stories as mothers, women/men, workers, believers, consumers, and consumables.

The personal becomes political at the moment we see that, especially in light of global climate change and environmental destruction, every action we perform has implications for what the future will be like, and that some of us are far more empowered than others to alter this trajectory. Commentator Rachel Maddow recently interviewed an abortion-rights advocate who expressed some disappointment with what she saw as a lack of feminist outrage at the murder of George Tiller, who had tirelessly risked life and limb to save women's lives by performing late-term abortions. If we don't begin to tell our own stories about abortion, the advocate said, we will continue to allow the domestic terrorists of the pro-life movement to define us as guilty of a crime. Her point was that our silence condones their portrayal of us as guilt-ridden baby-killers. So I consider writing a new letter to the editor: one in which I point out that you can identify with the reproductive-rights objectives of the feminist movement—and regard abortion in your own case as unethical, a letter in which I condemn Tiller's murder as the act of a domestic terrorist whose religious motives put him in league with the jihadists he likely reviles. But this is the easy part. Were I braver, I'd talk about the abortions I have had, one compelled by ill health and one by the decision to take care of the children I'd already borne, and I'd dare the hate-mongers to attack me. Yet there's likely no more risk in this for me than some hate mail and the possibility that I would be made to feel guilty, or that I would be made to remember some of the most wrenching moments of my life. This would be uncomfortable, but that's all. Why? Because I have a house that locks, a job that sustains my ambitions, and an education that empowers me more than anything else could. Calling me a baby-killing bitch isn't much at all when I consider the countless women for whom telling such a story could mean risking the loss of their children, their jobs, their husbands, or their lives.

So while the personal may be political, the responsibility for some of us—the privileged by whatever criteria—to make these words mean what they say is greater than it is for others. I am in a position to undertake the critical self-reflection that fuels an activist life in ways that some of my sisters are not. Does this obligate me? No. Can I be convinced through accounts and stories like the ones on these pages that nothing less than the future of a livable, just, and desirable world hangs on coming to see what connects them, how we're all located in them, and how what happens in my own corner of the world matters? Perhaps. Will being convinced get me out to the next school-board meeting? Will it get me to set up a compost bin, cut down on my use of plastics, curtail my use of herbicides? Talk to my daughter about body image? Maybe. Not every revolution comes with an announcement or a cataclysmic event to set it in motion.

And so it may be with the feminist movement. The forms our activism will likely take throughout this century will be different than those of the previous one. This is not to say we'll see fewer marches, for example. But it is to say that the meaning of non-violent protest, of resistance to oppressive institutions, of progressive change, can now come to be informed in a way impossible until relatively recently, namely, through the lives and experiences of people everywhere—lives that we can recognize in our own, lives that validate and challenge our own practices. Such, I think, is the stuff of a thinking activism of the ordinary. It challenges me to see myself in the place of the transsexual, the surrogate, the anorexic, the jihadist, the woman stoned by the Taliban, the women of Sarah Palin's base, the animalized slave—the animal, a "seeing" that entails the greatest possible risk. For with understanding can come anger—righteous, justified, uncontainable anger at the immeasurable cost in suffering for far too many whose bodies and labor ensure the institutionalized privileges of far too few. The biggest challenge, then, is to channel anger into action—non-violent, but as resistant to being ignored or discredited as the sun's rising. This is a tall order, but one that in the face of climate change, the prospect of nuclear or bio-chemical warfare, or ecosystemic collapse, is one we must rise to meet, each day, fortified by the fact that we can, in fact, keep Toni Morrison on the high-school library shelves, and we can send out a message in a Twitter cyber-bottle to the Iranian protestors. All politics are local. All politics are global.

References

Adams, Carol J. 1995. *Neither Man nor Beast: Feminism and the Defense of Animals*. New York: Continuum.

American Civil Liberties Union (ACLU), Eastern Region Office. 2008. Letter to the Honorable Stewart J. Greenleaf, Chair, Pennsylvania Senate Judiciary Committee. 17 March. p.2.

Atwood, Margaret. 1986. *The Handmaid's Tale*. Toronto: McClelland & Stewart.

Badgett, M.V. Lee. 2004. "Will Providing Marriage Rights to Same-Sex Couples Undermine Heterosexual Marriage: Evidence From Scandinavia and The Netherlands." <http://www.iglss.org/media/files/briefing/pdf>.

Bageant, Joe. 2007. *Deer Hunting with Jesus*. New York: Crown Publishers.

Balsamo, Anne. 1999. "Forms of Technological Embodiment: Reading the Body in Contemporary Culture." In Janet Price and Margrit Shildrick (eds.), *Feminist Theory and the Body: A Reader*. Edinburgh: Edinburgh UP. 278–90.

Barker, Drucilla, K., and Susan F. Feiner. 2004. *Liberating Economics: Feminist Perspectives on Families, Work, and Globalization*. Ann Arbor: U of Michigan P.

Bender, Frederic. 2003. *The Culture of Extinction: Towards a Philosophy of Deep Ecology*. Amherst, NY: Prometheus Books.

Berlin, Isaiah. 1963. *Karl Marx*. New York: Time, Inc., Book Division.

Bhagwati, Jagdish. 2007 [2004]. *In Defense of Globalization*. Oxford: Oxford UP.

Boetzkes, Elisabeth. 1999. "Equality, Autonomy, and Feminist Bioethics." In Anne Donchin and Laura M. Purdy (eds.), *Embodying Bioethics: Recent Feminist Advances*. New York: Rowman and Littlefield. 121–39.

Bordo, Susan. 1995. "Reading the Slender Body." In Nancy Tuana and Rosemarie Tong (eds.), *Feminism and Philosophy: Essential Readings in Theory, Reinterpretation, and Application.* Boulder, CO: Westview Press. 467–88.

Brachear, Manya. 2008. "How Religion Guides Palin." <http://www.chicagotribune.com/news>. September 6.

Brasch, Walter. 2008. "A Turkey By Any Other Name—Is Still the Governor of Alaska." <http://www.opednews.com/articles/A-Turkey-By-Any-Other-Name-by-Brasch-081121-37.html>. November 21.

Brody, David. 2008. "Sarah Palin Signed Christian Heritage Week Proclamation." <http://www.cbn.com/cbnnews>. August 30.

Butler, Judith. 2003. "Performative Acts and Gender Constitution: An Essay in Phenomenology and Feminist Theory." In Carole R. McCann and Seung-Kyung Kim (eds.), *Feminist Theory Reader: Local and Global Perspectives.* New York: Routledge. 415–27.

———. 1993. *Bodies That Matter: On the Discursive Limits of "Sex."* New York: Routledge.

———. 1990. *Gender Trouble.* New York: Routledge.

Cervone, Frank P. 2008. Letter to Members of the Pennsylvania State Senate concerning SB 1250. March 13.

Chesler, Phyllis. 2006. "Intellectual Conservative" (Interview by Bernard Chapin). <http://www.phyllis-chesler.com/482/feminist-at-the-gates-of-reason>..

———. 2005. *The Death of Feminism: What's Next in the Struggle for Women's Freedom.* New York: Palgrave Macmillan.

———. 2004. "A Radical Feminist Comes Out for Bush." <http://www.frontpagemagazine.com>. January 9.

Clark, Danae. 1993. "Commodity Lesbianism." In Henry Ableove, Michele Aina Barale, and David Halperin (eds.), *The Gay and Lesbian Studies Reader.* New York: Routledge. 186–201.

Clough, Sharyn, ed. 2003. *Siblings Under the Skin: Feminism, Social Justice and Analytic Philosophy.* Aurora, CO: The Davies Group.

Collins, Patricia Hill. 2005. *Black Sexual Politics: African Americans, Gender, and the New Racism.* New York: Routledge.

Coulter, Ann. 2001. "This is War." <http://www.nationalreview.com/coulter/coulter.shtml>. September 13.

Cuomo, Chris, Wendy Eisner, and Kenneth Hinkel. 2008. "Environmental Change, Indigenous Knowledge, and Subsistence on Alaska's North Slope."

Scholar and Feminist Online 7(1). Barnard Center for Research on Women. <http://www.barnard.edu/sfonline/ice/cuomo_eisner_hinkel_01.htm>.

Daly, Mary. 1975. "The Qualitative Leap Beyond Patriarchal Religion." *Quest: A Feminist Quarterly* 1(4): 20–40.

Denike, Margaret. 2003. "The Devil's Insatiable Sex: A Genealogy of Evil Incarnate." *Hypatia* 18(1): 10–43.

Diamond, Irene. 1994. *Fertile Ground: Women, Earth, and the Limits of Control.* Boston: Beacon Press.

Diniz, Deborah, and Ana Christina Gonzalez Velez. 2000. "Feminist Bioethics: The Emergence of the Oppressed." In Rosemarie Tong (ed.), *Globalizing Feminist Bioethics: Crosscultural Perspectives.* Boulder, CO: Westview Press. 62–95.

Dolnick, Sam. 2008. "Pregnancy Outsourced to India: Infertile Couples Look Overseas for Surrogacy." *The Press Enterprise* January 3: 5.

Donchin, Anne. 2004. "Integrating Bioethics and Human Rights: Toward a Global Feminist Approach." In Rosemarie Tong, Anne Donchin, and Susan Dodds (eds.), *Linking Visions: Feminist Bioethics, Human Rights, and the Developing World.* New York: Rowman and Littlefield. 31–56.

Donovan, Josephine. 1993. "Animal Rights and Feminist Theory." In Greta Gaard (ed.), *Ecofeminism: Women, Animals, Nature.* Philadelphia: Temple UP. 167–94.

Eagan, Jennifer. 2006. "Unfreedom, Suffering, and the Culture Industry." In Renée J. Heberle (ed.), *Feminist Interpretations of Theodor Adorno.* University Park: Penn State Press. 277–99.

Ehrenreich, Barbara. 2007. "It's Islamo-Fascism Awareness Week!" <http://www.thenation.com/doc/20071105/ehrenreich>. October 22.

———. 1997. "What is Socialist Feminism?" In Rosemary Hennessy and Chrys Ingraham (eds.), *Materialist Feminism: A Reader in Class, Difference and Women's Lives.* New York: Routledge. 65–70.

Eisenstein, Zillah. 1990. "Constructing a Theory of Capitalist Patriarchy and Socialist Feminism." In Karen V. Hansen and Ilene J. Philipson (eds.), *Women, Class, and the Feminist Imagination: A Socialist-Feminist Reader.* Philadelphia: Temple UP. 114–45.

Falwell, Jerry. 2007. "Quotes from Jerry Falwell." <http://newsgroups.derkeiler.com/pdf/Archive/Alt/alt.politics/2007-05/msg02551.pdf>.

Farrell, Warren. 2004. *Why Men Earn More: The Startling Truth Behind the Pay Gap — and What Women Can Do About It.* New York: Amacom (American Management Association).

Glazov, Jamie. 2007. "Academic Feminists and Sharia." <http://www.front-pagemag.com/readArticle.aspx?ARTID=29071>. December 7.

Gruen, Lori. 1993. "Dismantling Oppression: An Analysis of the Connection Between Women and Animals." In Greta Gaard (ed.), *Ecofeminism: Women, Animals, Nature.* Philadelphia: Temple UP. 60–90.

Halberstam, Judith. 1999. "F2M: The Making of Female Masculinity." In Janet Price and Margrit Shildrick (eds.), *Feminist Theory and the Body: A Reader.* Edinburgh: Edinburgh UP. 125–33.

Haraway, Donna. 2003. *The Companion Species Manifesto: Dogs, People, and Significant Otherness.* Chicago: Prickly Paradigm Press.

———. 1997. *Modest_Witness@Second_Millenium. FemaleMan@_Meets Oncomouse: Feminism and Technoscience.* New York: Routledge.

———. 1992. "Human in a Post-Humanist Landscape." In Judith Butler and Joan Scott (eds.), *Feminists Theorize the Political.* New York: Routledge. 86–100.

———. 1990. "A Manifesto for Cyborgs: Science, Technology, and Socialist Feminism in the Last Quarter." In Karen V. Hansen and Ilene J. Philipson (eds.), *Women, Class and the Feminist Imagination: A Socialist Feminist Reader.* Philadelphia: Temple UP. 580–617.

Hartmann, Heidi. 1981. "The Unhappy Marriage of Marxism and Feminism: Towards a More Progressive Union." In Lydia Sargent (ed.), *Women and Revolution: A Discussion of the Unhappy Marriage of Marxism and Feminism.* Boston: South End Press.

———. 1976. "Capitalism, Patriarchy, and Job Segregation." *Signs: Journal of Women and Culture in Society* 1(3 [2]): 137–69.

Hawkins, Ronnie Zoe. 1998. "Ecofeminism and Nonhumans: Continuity, Difference, Dualism, and Domination." *Hypatia* 13(1): 158–97.

Hayles, Katherine. 1990. *Chaos Bound.* Ithaca, NY: Cornell UP.

Hoagland, Sarah Lucia, and Marilyn Frye, eds. 2000. *Feminist Interpretations of Mary Daly.* College Park, MD: Penn State Press.

Hochschild, Arlie Russell. 2000. "Global Care Chains and Emotional Surplus Value." In Anthony Giddons and Will Hutton (eds.), *On the Edge: Living With Global Capitalism.* London: Vintage. 130–46.

Holmes, Helen Bequart. 1999. "Closing the Gaps: An Imperative for Feminist Bioethics." In Anna Donchin and Laura M. Purdy (eds.), *Embodying Bioethics; Recent Feminist Advances.* New York: Rowman and Littlefield. 45–64.

Hopkins, K. 2006. "Little Play." *Anchorage Daily News* August 6.

Horkheimer, Max, and Theodor Adorno. 1972. *Dialectic of Enlightenment.* Trans. John Cummings. New York: Herder and Herder.

Horowitz, David. 2007. "Islamo-Fascism Awareness Week." <http://www.frontpagemag.com/articles/Read.aspx?ARTID=28203>. September 21.

Hunsaker, Brent. 2008. "Utah company causes nationwide uproar over 'Sock Obama.'" <http://www.abc4.com>. June 14.

Hymowitz, Kay. 2005. "The Sisters They Ignore." Manhattan Institute for Policy Research. <http://www.manhattan-institute.org/html/_an-the_sisters.htm>. March 8.

Hypatia 9.4 (Fall, 1994). Special Issue: Feminist Philosophy of Religion.

Irigaray, Luce. 1985. *This Sex Which Is Not One.* Ithaca, NY: Cornell UP.

Jaggar, Alison. 2002. "A Feminist Critique of the Alleged Southern Debt." *Hypatia* 17(4): 119–42.

———. 1983. *Feminist Politics and Human Nature.* Totowa, NJ: Rowman and Littlefield.

Jameson, Fredric. 1991. *Postmodernism, or The Cultural Logic of Late Capitalism.* Durham, NC: Duke UP.

Kirk, Gwyn. 1997. "Standing on Solid Ground: A Materialist Ecological Feminism." In Rosemary Hennessy and Chrys Ingraham (eds.), *Materialist Feminism: A Reader in Class, Difference, and Women's Lives.* New York: Routledge. 345–63.

Kleefeld, Eric. 2009. "GOP Blasting Obama Over Gates Arrest Comments —Limbaugh Warns of Whites Under Assault." < http://tpmdc.talking-pointsmemo.com/2009/07/gop-blasting-obama-over-gates-arrest-comments——limbaugh-warns-of-whites-under-assault.php >. July 23.

Klein, Naomi. 2007. *The Shock Doctrine: The Rise of Disaster Capitalism.* New York: Henry Holt and Company.

Kopelman, Loretta M. 2006. "Female Genital Circumcision and Conventionalist Ethical Relativism." In Patricia Illingsworth and Wendy E. Parmet (eds.), *Ethical Health Care.* Upper Saddle River, NJ: Pearson/Prentice Hall. 484–96.

Lara, Maria Pia. 2003. "In and Out of Terror: The Vertigo of Secularization." *Hypatia* 18(1): 183–96.

Latour, Bruno. 2004. *Politics of Nature: How to Bring the Sciences into Democracy.* Cambridge, MA: Harvard UP.

Lee, Wendy Lynne. 2009. "Restoring Human-Centeredness to Environ-mental Conscience: The Ecocentrist's Dilemma, The Role of Hetero-sexualized Anthropomorphizing, and the Significance of Language to Ecological Feminism." *Ethics and the Environment* 14(1): 29–51.

———. 2008. "Environmental Pragmatism Revisited: Human-Centered-ness, Language, and the Future of Aesthetic Experience." *Environmental Philosophy* 5(1): 9–22.

———. 2007. "Jamie Glazov's Frontpagemag Interview with Professor Daphne Patai." <http://www.freeexchangeoncampus.org/index2.php?option=com_content&do_pdf=1&id=821>. December 5.

———. 2006. "On Ecology and Aesthetic Experience: A Feminist Theory of Value and Praxis." *Ethics and the Environment* 11(1): 21–41.

———. 2005. "The Aesthetic Appreciation of Nature, Scientific Objectivity, and the Standpoint of the Subjugated: Anthropocentrism Reimagined." *Ethics, Place, Environment* 8(2): 235–50.

———. 2003. "But One Man Opens His Seeing Eye: The Epistemic Ubiquity of Anthropomorphizing and its Implications for Conceptions of Gender, Race, and Sexual Identity." In Cressida Hayes (ed.), *The Grammar of Politics*. Ithaca, NY: Cornell UP. 167–85.

———. 2002. *On Marx*. Wadsworth Philosophers Series. Belmont, CA: Wadsworth/Thompson Learning.

———. 1999a. "The Sound of Little Hummingbird Wings: A Wittgen-steinian Investigation of Forms of Life as Forms of Power." *Feminist Studies* 25(2): 409–26.

———. 1999b. "Spilling all Over the Wide Fields of Our Passions: Frye, Wittgenstein, and Butler on the Contexts of Attention, Intention, and Sexual Identity." *Hypatia* 14(3): 1–16.

Leopold, Aldo. 1949. *A Sand County Almanac*. New York: Oxford UP.

Lerner, Gerda. 1986. *The Creation of Patriarchy*. Oxford: Oxford UP.

Lorde, Audre. 1984. *Sister Outsider*. Berkeley, CA: Crossing Press.

Mahmood, Saba. 2005. *Politics of Piety: The Islamic Revival and the Feminist Subject*. Princeton: Princeton UP.

Mandel, Ernest. 1994. *The Place Of Marxism In History*. Atlantic Highlands, NJ: Humanities Press International.

Martin, Emily. 1999. "The Egg and the Sperm: How Science Has Con-structed a Romance based on Stereotypical Male-Female Roles." In Janet Price and Margrit Shildrick (eds.), *Feminist Theory and the Body: A Reader*. Edinburgh: Edinburgh UP. 179–89.

Marx, Karl. 1981. *The German Ideology.* Ed. C.J. Arthur. New York: International Publishers.

———. 1964. *The Economic and Philosophic Manuscripts of 1844.* Trans. Martin Milligan. Ed. Dirk J. Struik. New York: International Publishers.

McClure, Kirstie. 1992. "The Issue of Foundations: Scientized Politics, Politicized Science, and Feminist Critical Practice." In Judith Butler and Joan Scott (eds.), *Feminists Theorize the Political.* New York: Routledge. 341–68.

McLellan, David. 1972. *Karl Marx: Selected Writings.* Oxford: Oxford UP.

Merchant, Carolyn. 1980. *The Death of Nature: Women, Ecology, and the Scientific Revolution.* San Francisco: Harper, Collins.

Mies, Maria. 1982. *The Lacemakers of Narsapur: Indian Housewives Produce for the World Market.* London: Zed Press.

Mitter, Swasti. 1997. "Women Working Worldwide." In Rosemary Hennesy and Chrys Ingraham (eds.), *Materialist Feminism: A Reader in Class, Difference, and Women's Lives.* New York: Routledge. 163–74.

Mohanty, Chandra Talpade. 2003. *Feminism Without Borders: Decolonizing Theory, Practicing Solidarity.* Durham, NC, and London: Duke UP.

Mrozek, Andrea. 2008. "The New Face of Feminism." *National Post* [Toronto]. <http://www.nationalpost.com>. September 3.

Newman, Amy. 1994. "Feminist Social Criticism and Marx's Theory of Religion." *Hypatia* 9(4): 15–37.

Palin, Sarah. 2008. "Polar Bear." Alaska Governor's Office press release. August 4.

———. 2007. "Convince the Rest of the nation to Open ANWR." On the Issues. <http://www.issues2000.org/Governor/Sarah_Palin_Environ ment.htm>.

———. 2006. *New Energy for Alaska.* Campaign booklet. November 3.

Parikh, Rahul K. 2008. "Sarah Palin's Choice." <http://www.salon.com>. September.

Patai. Daphne. 2006. "Letter to a Friend: On Islamic Fundamentalism." <http://www.butterfliesandwheels.com/articleprint.php?num=272>. September 11.

Pennsylvania for Marriage. n.d. <http://www.PA4marriage.org>.

Petchesky, Rosalind. 2002. "Phantom Towers: Feminist Reflections on the Battle between Global Capitalism and Fundamentalist Terrorists." In Betsy Reed and Katha Pollit (eds.), *Nothing Sacred: Women Respond to Religious Fundamentalism and Terror.* New York: Nation Books. 357–72.

Pew Forum. 2008. "Sarah Palin on the Issues." <http://pewforum.org/religion08/profile.php?CandidateID=20>.

Pollitt, Katha. 2007. "'Feckless'? No way!" *The Nation.* <http://www.thenation.com/doc/20070611/pollitt>. May 24.

Quill, Timothy. 2005. "Terry Schiavo: A Tragedy Compounded." *The New England Journal of Medicine* 352: 1630–33. April 21.

Roberts, Dorothy. 1996. "Reconstructing the Patient: Starting with Women of Color." In Susan M. Wolf (ed.), *Feminism and Bioethics: Beyond Reproduction.* New York: Oxford UP. 116–43.

Russell, Kathryn. 1997 [1994]. "A Value-Theoretic Approach to Childbirth and Reproductive Engineering." In Rosemary Hennessy and Chrys Ingraham (eds.), *Materialist Feminism: A Reader in Class, Difference, and Women's Lives.* New York: Routledge. 328–44.

Sagoff, Mark. 2002. "Animal Liberation and Environmental Ethics: Bad Marriage, Quick Divorce." In David Schmidtz and Elizabeth Willott (eds.), *Environmental Ethics: What Really Matters, What Really Works.* New York: Oxford UP. 38–44.

Schmidtz, David, and Elizabeth Willott. 2002. *Environmental Ethics: What Really Matters, What Really Works.* New York: Oxford UP.

Schultz, Vicki. 1992. "Women 'Before' the Law: Judicial Stories about Women, Work, and Sex Segregation on the Job." In Judith Butler and Joan W. Scott (eds.), *Feminists Theorize the Political.* New York: Routledge. 297–338.

Schweitzer, Jeff. 2008. "Sarah Palin, An Environmental Disaster." <http://www.huffingtonpost.com>. October 23.

Seelye, Katherine Q. 2009. "Obama Wades into a Volatile Racial Issue." <http://www.nytimes.com/2009/07/23/us/23race>. July 23.

Seigfried, Charlene Haddock. 1996. *Pragmatism and Feminism: Reweaving the Social Fabric.* Chicago: Chicago UP.

Shanthi, K. 2004. "Feminist Bioethics and Reproductive Rights of Women in India: Myth and Reality." In Rosemarie Tong, Anne Donchin, and Susan Dodds (eds.), *Linking Visions: Feminist Bioethics, Human Rights, and the Developing World.* New York: Rowman and Littlefield. 119–32.

Sherwin, Susan. 2000a. "Feminist Reflections on the Role of Theories in Global Bioethics." In Rosemarie Tong (ed.), *Globalizing Feminist Bioethics: Crosscultural Perspectives.* Boulder, CO: Westview Press. 12–26.

———. 2000b. "Normalizing Reproductive Technologies and the Implications for Autonomy." In Rosemarie Tong (ed.), *Globalizing Feminist*

Bioethics: Crosscultural Perspectives. Boulder, CO: Westview Press. 96–113.

Shiva, Vandana. 1994. "Development, Ecology, and Women." In Carolyn Merchant (ed.), *Key Concepts in Critical Theory: Ecology*. Atlantic Highlands, NJ: Humanities Press International. 272–80.

Small, Meredith F. 2001. "Sigma Chi Chimpy: Forget the Ladies ... For Chimps, Hunting is About Fraternity." *Scientific American* July 26: 25–27.

Sommers, Christina Hoff. 2002. "Case Against Ratifying the United Nations Convention on the Elimination of All Forms of Discrimination Against Women." <http://www.aei.org/publications>. June 13.

Stone, Christopher. 2002. "Should Trees Have Standing? Toward Legal Rights for Natural Objects." In David Schmidtz and Elizabeth Willott (eds.), *Environmental Ethics: What Really Matters, What Really Works*. New York: Oxford UP. 46–50.

Tong, Rosemarie. 1999. "Just Caring About Maternal-Fetal Relations: The Case of Cocaine-Using Pregnant Women." In Anne Donchin and Laura Purdy (eds.), *Embodying Bioethics: Recent Feminist Advances*. Lanham, MD: Rowman and Littlefield. 33–43.

United States. 2009. Environmental Protection Agency. <http://www.epa.gov/climatechange>.

Verbeek, Peter-Paul. 2005. *What Things Do: Philosophical Reflections on Technology, Agency, and Design*. University Park: Penn State Press.

Warren, Karen. 2002 [1990]. "The Power and Promise of Ecological Feminism." In David Schmidtz and Elizabeth Willott (eds.), *Environmental Ethics: What Really Matters, What Really Works*. New York: Oxford UP. 234–37.

Weisbrot, Mark. 2009. "Right Wing Media, Strategists Seize Upon Gates Arrest and Controversy." <http://www.cepr.net/index.php/op-eds-&-columns/op-eds-&-columns/gates-arrest-and-controversy/>. July 30.

Wilchins. Riki Anne. 1997. *Read My Lips: Sexual Subversion and the End of Gender*. Ithaca, New York: Firebrand Books.

Winters, Jonah. "Martyrdom in Jihad." 1997. <http://bahai-library.com/personal/jw/my.papers/jihad.html#3>.

Wolf, Susan M. 1999. "Erasing Difference: Race, Ethnicity, and Gender in Bioethics." In Anne Donchin and Laura M. Purdy (eds.), *Embodying Bioethics: Recent Feminist Advances*. New York: Rowman and Littlefield.

Wolfe, Alan. 2007. "The Stone is Cast." <http://www.salon.com/opinion/feature/2007/05/15/jerryfalwell/>. May 15.

Yardley, William. 2008. "Sarah Heath Palin: An Outsider who Charms." *New York Times* August 29.

Young, Iris Marion. 1997. "Socialist Feminism and the Limits of Dual System's Theory." In Rosemary Hennessy and Chrys Ingraham (eds.), *Materialist Feminism: A Reader in Class, Difference and Women's Lives*. New York: Routledge. 95–106.

Yunus, Muhammad. 2007 [1999, 2003]. *Banker to the Poor: Micro-Lending and the Battle Against World Poverty*. New York: Public Affairs.